PRACTICAL PRODUCTION CONTROL

A Survival Guide for Planners and Schedulers

Kenneth N. McKay
Vincent C.S. Wiers

APICS.
THE EDUCATIONAL SOCIETY
FOR RESOURCE MANAGEMENT

Copyright ©2004 by J. Ross Publishing, Inc.

ISBN 1-932159-30-4

Printed and bound in the U.S.A. Printed on acid-free paper
10 9 8 7 6 5 4 3 2 1

Library of Congress Cataloging-in-Publication Data

McKay, Kenneth N., 1953–
 Practical production control : a survival guide for planners and
schedulers / Kenneth N. McKay, Vincent C.S. Wiers.
   p. cm.
 Includes bibliographical references.
 ISBN 1-932159-30-4 (hardcover : alk. paper)
 1. Production control. 2. Inventory control. I. Wiers, Vincent C.S.
II. Title.
 TS157.M39 2004
 658.5—dc22

                                           2004007060

Microsoft® Excel, Project, Access, and Microsoft Visual Basic® for Applications (VBA) are registered trademarks of the Microsoft Corporation.

Direct all inquiries to J. Ross Publishing, Inc., 6501 Park of Commerce Blvd., Suite 200, Boca Raton, Florida 33487.

Phone: (561) 869-3900
Fax: (561) 892-0700
Web: www.jrosspub.com

TABLE OF CONTENTS

DEDICATION

Dedicated to wives and family

Dedicated to the fallen scheduler —
burned out in the backwaters of a factory from hell.

FOREWORD

This is an exceptional book. It describes the reality of production planning, control, and scheduling, warts and all. Indeed, its strength is that it tells the reader what typical problems are and where planners and schedulers are most likely to fail. While it offers a lot of informed advice on how to overcome and avoid problems, it does not propose any simplistic solutions or use any three-letter buzzwords to magically overcome the problems. Rather, it gives recommendations and ideas that the authors have discovered work. It covers many important issues, such as how to choose and acquire software, how to hire a new planner/scheduler, and how to deal with consultants. But its real impact is its advice about how to cope with the typical problems every planner/scheduler meets, like dealing with uncertainty, finding useful information, and what typical self-inflicted wounds are and how to avoid them. Every scheduler needs to be given a copy to read.

This book is quite different than other books on planning and scheduling. They typically focus on a limited aspect of production control, such as the scheduling of machines or enterprise resource planning systems, or they propose some special approach like total quality management that claims to provide a unique framework for thinking about the design of the production control system. This book takes an overall view of what happens in production control and clearly describes what planners and schedulers really do. It describes their day-to-day challenges and the tools available to help them. Above all else, it is a guide for production controllers. Anybody who works in production can benefit from reading and studying it, and a great deal can be learned from its content.

Both authors obviously have had many years of experience observing planners and schedulers, helping them do their job more effectively, and designing production control tools and systems to aid them in performing their job more effectively. This experience comes through in every chapter. However, they also have an academic background that enables them to ground and support their observations of real-world planners and schedulers and justify their conclusions. They do not lose sight of the complexity of the real world and they do not oversimplify. So enjoy the book and be challenged by it!

John Buzacott, Professor Emeritus
Schulich School of Business
York University, Toronto
Former President,
Production & Operations Management Society

PREFACE

This is not a book about economic order quantities, safety stock, reorder points, plant location, transportation routes, statistical quality control, or scheduling algorithms. There are enough other books that deal with these subjects. It is also not a book for all industries and all situations. The primary focus is on discrete part manufacturing with batches, operations, and routings. However, many of the ideas will be applicable to any production control situation. It is a book that goes behind closed doors, into the factory at 6:00 AM, behind the scheduler's desk, and into the planning meetings. It provides ideas and concepts for identifying limiting factors for improved production control and a number of ideas for taking production control up a notch.

We have spent almost twenty years studying, learning from, and working with schedulers in a variety of firms and industries. Together we have over thirty years of analysis in production control and we have spent a great deal of that time developing, installing, maintaining, and evolving scheduling systems. We have seen awesome scheduling performances and we have also seen pitiful mockeries of production control. We have tried to reflect on what we have seen and what we have learned and package it into a form we can share with others. You will find a lot of opinions. While some of the opinions are admittedly gut-feel and emotional, most of the opinions are supported by studies and projects we have done. All observations and experiences are firsthand unless otherwise noted.

We will talk at length about the problems we have seen and some ideas that may help alleviate the pain. We have tried to show how ideas and solutions can address whatever we describe as problems. We hope we have succeeded in that.

Our goal is to bring many problems and issues to a conscious level, instead of a "business as usual" mode. Recognizing that a problem or an opportunity for improvement exists is the first step toward improvement. Always remember: Do not blindly follow or do anything in this book without thinking first. There are other good ideas out there and we do not have a monopoly on them.

Although there are different audiences for this text, the major audience is the practitioner — the planner or scheduler in a real factory. While most of the writing is directed to these people, there is also material of interest for the production control manager or supervisor. If you are in production control, you probably would want to know what we think about your specific situation. How well are you doing? What could be done differently? Should you give yourself a pat on the back or a kick in the butt? We have tried to help you here. Take some time and look at the downloads (available at www.jrosspub.com) for many of the chapters. We gathered our usual questions about certain topics and our interpretations. You can try to answer the questionnaires and do a self-assessment.

Another targeted audience is the academic researcher or consultant. If you are starting off in your career, you might be interested to know what kinds of questions to ask and what to look for when visiting a factory. You might also want to know what to expect, that is, how factories actually do production control. We hope this book will help you understand the problem domain and provide you with a special set of glasses with which to see and understand production control. It might help you to craft field instruments such as structured interviews and surveys. It might also help you to know where to look for information and insights. Finally, if you are trying to create or enhance models of the production control situation, you might find concepts and ideas to explore. There are many unsolved and unexplored aspects of the real-world production control problem: how to incorporate the issues within existing modeling frameworks, what kinds of new models are needed to capture the essence of the problem, how to model and control the dynamic nature of the problem. Perhaps something will inspire you to address an identified problem or to prove that we are wrong; either way, the field is advanced.

Each chapter begins with a quick list of idea for "the busy person." This is a list of what we consider the key messages to be in the chapter. It is not all of the messages, and what is key for one might not be for another. Suggestions for further reading can be found at the end of the book.

Whether or not you find the book useful, we would enjoy hearing from you, hearing about your thoughts on production control and any stories you might want to share. The publisher's website (www.jrosspub.com) offers a variety of self-assessment surveys, chapter illustrations, and other goodies that can be downloaded.

ABOUT THE AUTHORS

 **Kenneth N. McKay** is a Professor of Management Sciences in the Faculty of Engineering at the University of Waterloo. Dr. McKay's original career focus was software development, and he was a software architect and product designer for NCR in the late 1970s and early 1980s. In the fall of 1984, he returned to the University of Waterloo to pursue graduate studies in management sciences and was Associate Director of the Waterloo Management of Integrated Manufacturing Systems (WATMIMS) research group until 1991. During that time, he won awards for his research and was involved in many factory studies concentrating on the use of simulation methods for analyzing flows in factories and the use of decision support tools for planning and scheduling. His graduate research was interdisciplinary and looked at what planners and schedulers actually did in factories and the contribution of human judgment when the situation was rapidly changing. While at Waterloo, he was co-author of WATPASS (WATerloo Planning And Scheduling System), which was an early finite scheduling tool that was later commercialized. He was also the primary researcher on a factory benchmark and production control software survey conducted for CAM-I that was to become known as *The Factory From Hell*. In 1991 and 1998, Dr. McKay was a Visiting Scholar at the Sloan School of Management at the Massachusetts Institute of Technology and was affiliated with the Leaders For Manufacturing Program.

Since graduating with his doctorate in 1992, Dr. McKay has continued to study the plight of planners and schedulers and has been active in the design and development of planning and scheduling software to help them. Seeing how planning and scheduling software is used over a long duration has been instrumental in understanding the challenges facing the scheduler. In addition to research on planners and schedulers and their decision support systems, his research includes concepts for adaptive control, supply chain issues relating to outsourcing modules or large subsystems, the history of manufacturing, and the impact of information systems on individuals and organizations. Throughout his career, Dr. McKay has been active in industrial research and consulting, and this has been a key factor in guiding his research and in the development of concepts for advanced production control.

Dr. McKay can be contacted at kmckay@uwaterloo.ca or Department of Management Sciences, Carl Pollock Hall, University of Waterloo, 200 University Avenue West, Waterloo, Ontario, Canada N2L 3G1.

Vincent C.S. Wiers is the founder and director of VCS Consulting (http://www.vcs-consulting.com), a small consultancy company focusing on implementing APS systems. He obtained his Master's and Ph.D. degrees from the Eindhoven University of Technology, investigating the question why scheduling techniques from academia were used so little in practice. Since graduation in 1997, he has continued to seek a better understanding of the realities of planning and scheduling. He has been involved in a variety of implementation projects involving APS systems and has worked for various consultancy firms. In 2001, he rejoined the Eindhoven University of Technology part time, in the area of Operations Planning and Control, to continue his research on the human factor in planning and scheduling. While still conducting APS projects in practice, his academic ambition is to apply accepted, rigid methods of research in studying the human factor in planning and scheduling.

Dr. Wiers has published several papers on his work in *Production Planning and Control, International Journal of Production and Operations Management, OMEGA, Journal of Manufacturing Systems, Computers in Industry,* and *Cognition, Technology and Work.* He was also involved in the first comprehensive book on the human factor in planning and scheduling, edited by Dr. Bart MacCarthy and Dr. John Wilson.

ACKNOWLEDGMENTS

For me, **Kenneth McKay**, the first and foremost personal acknowledgment must be to John Buzacott, who asked me in the mid-1980s "What is scheduling?" and "What does scheduling mean in real factories?" These questions started a long journey that is not yet finished. John's wisdom, insights, encouragement, and friendship have helped me constantly through the years. Frank Safayeni was also instrumental in creating my sociotechnological approach to the problem and helping me see my way through the early years. There have been many others who have also encouraged, challenged, debated, and supported my search for a better understanding of production control. Of special recognition are Jim Alderfer, Neil Charness, Dick Conway, Jan Fransoo, Masahiko Fuyuki, Stan Gershwin, Steve Graves, Eldon Gunn, Nigel Henriques, Peter Higgins, Sarah Jackson, Sanjay Jain, Bart MacCarthy, Mike Magazine, Bill Maxwell, John Moore, Tom Morton, Mike Pinedo, Robin Roundy, Steve Smith, Reha Uzsoy, Toni Wäfler, and Scott Webster. Vincent Wiers must also be acknowledged as being the harassing force for getting me to start this book. He started asking in 1996 and did not give up. Special thanks to my mother, Mary McKay, for her love and support through the years and to my wife, Emily, for her infinite patience.

For me, **Vincent C.S. Wiers**, the quest to answer the question "What is scheduling?" only really began when I visited Memorial University of Newfoundland in 1996 and had lengthy discussions with Ken McKay. Ken has been the primary reason I have been motivated to dive into this question ever since. Compared to Ken, I know very little, but I am very grateful that we have been working together as "peers" since. Other people that I need to thank are those who inspired me to do research and projects: Sarah Jackson, Jan Fransoo, Bart MacCarthy, Will Bertrand, Ton de Kok, Paul Bagchus, Hans Wortmann, and

Victor Allis. I dedicate this book to my wife, Alice, and my children, Jip, Sam, and Finn. They are already showing the same persistent curiosity.

There have been many people who have taken the time to read drafts of this book and to provide very valuable insights about the content and style. Many IOUs will need to be repaid, and it was amazing how many things had to be fixed or changed. Everyone provided something of value, and this has been very much appreciated by us. The book is far better because of their efforts. The people we dearly owe are: Rhonda Altman, Gary Black, Mitchell Burman, John Buzacott, Dick Conway, Ron Epp, Jan Fransoo, Stan Gershwin, John Hilborn, Dave Holzschuh, Sanjay Jain, Louise Liu, John Moore, Tom Morton, Jeff Naden, Yasuyuki Nishioka, Eric Scherer, Con Sheahan, Hartmut Stadtler, Patrice Swaager, Reha Uzsoy, Pat Valeriote, Scott Webster, and Judith de Winter.

Last, but not least, are the many schedulers, planners, and managers that we have learned from and worked with over the years. The Ralphs, the Jakes, and the ones in between. For various reasons, we cannot thank each of you individually. Without you and the lessons you have taught us, this book would not have been possible. We hope that we have done justice to the invaluable lessons you have provided and that through this book some of the debt is repaid. Your patience, tolerance, and open sharing of information and insights are especially acknowledged.

ABOUT APICS

APICS — The Educational Society for Resource Management is a not-for-profit international educational organization recognized as the global leader and premier provider of resource management education and information. APICS is respected throughout the world for its education and professional certification programs. With more than 60,000 individual and corporate members in 20,000 companies worldwide, APICS is dedicated to providing education to improve an organization's bottom line. No matter what your title or need, by tapping into the APICS community you will find the education necessary for success.

APICS is recognized globally as:

- The source of knowledge and expertise for manufacturing and service industries across the entire supply chain
- The leading provider of high-quality, cutting-edge educational programs that advance organizational success in a changing, competitive marketplace
- A successful developer of two internationally recognized certification programs, Certified in Production and Inventory Management (CPIM) and Certified in Integrated Resource Management (CIRM)
- A source of solutions, support, and networking for manufacturing and service professionals

For more information about APICS programs, services, or membership, visit www.apics.org or contact APICS Customer Support at (800) 444-2742 or (703) 354-8851.

Web Added Value

*Free value-added materials available from
the Download Resource Center at www.jrosspub.com*

At J. Ross Publishing we are committed to providing today's professional with practical, hands-on tools that enhance the learning experience and give readers an opportunity to apply what they have learned. That is why we offer free ancillary materials available for download on this book and all participating Web Added Value™ publications. These online resources may include interactive versions of material that appears in the book or supplemental templates, worksheets, models, plans, case studies, proposals, spreadsheets and assessment tools, among other things. Whenever you see the WAV™ symbol in any of our publications, it means bonus materials accompany the book and are available from the Web Added Value Download Resource Center at www.jrosspub.com.

Downloads available for *Practical Production Control: A Survival Guide for Planners and Schedulers* consist of supplements to help assess production control operations with tips for making improvements and production control cartoon illustrations that practitioners will enjoy. The illustration below is the cartoon associated with Chapter 12: Scheduling Tool Failures. Other cartoons exist for each chapter

INTRODUCTION
AND REALITY CHECK

PREDIGESTED THOUGHTS FOR THE BUSY PERSON

- Scheduling situations are good, bad, or just plain ugly.

- If you cannot predict it, you will find it damn hard to schedule or plan it.

- If you cannot come close to following and executing a generated sequence, it may be deceptive to use the term "production control."

- To plan, you need information, a lot of it. It has to be timely and accurate and come from the manufacturing system and from the physical world.

- You need firm and consistent goals and objectives. It is difficult to hit targets attached to a bungee cord or when you are working in a fog.

- Scheduling and planning processes need to be flexible and to have flexible options for dealing with risks: minimization and avoidance.

THE GOOD, THE BAD, AND THE UGLY

Production control varies greatly from one firm and one plant to the next. It truly ranges from the good and the bad to the ugly. There are situations where effective production control is possible, the appropriate methods are used, and the smooth production that results is something of beauty to behold. However, there are other cases where the inappropriate methods are used for the situation and production control makes the situation worse; forgive them, for they know not what they do. And, there are situations where the manufacturing challenge is so large that it is almost impossible to generate any kind of feasible plan and all production control can do is react to the immediate crisis. These are the good, the bad, and the ugly.

- **Good** is where the manufacturing system is very healthy, appropriate production control methods are used, and the actual production can follow the schedule.
- **Bad** is where the factory is reasonably healthy, effective production control is feasible, but the production control methods are faulty.
- **Ugly** is where the factory is sick, effective production control is infeasible and impossible, but production control is held accountable anyway.

The purpose of this book is to give planners and schedulers, and their direct supervisors and management, the tools and knowledge for better, more effective production control. There might be others reading this book, but the *you* in the book is directed to the personnel directly involved with the tasks of planning and scheduling, the people trying to craft plans and coordinate resources. You might be starting out as a junior planner learning the trade, a crusty old bugger checking the book out for new ideas, a newly appointed supervisor of production control trying to get a handle on production control, or a seasoned professional in charge of a department wondering if there might be some ideas that you can introduce into the group. You are the audience. Although the book is primarily written for the actual planners and schedulers, there are a few sections that should be of use to supervisors and managers.

If you have a better understanding of your situation and what makes sense for it in terms of production control, you will be in a better position to improve the effectiveness and efficiency of the plant. Hence, we start the book with an overview of the good, the bad, and the ugly. For the good situations, is there room for improvement? For the bad situations, what should be done differently? For the ugly cases, where do you start to address the problems? We have been lucky; we have had experiences with some of the world's best plants and with some of the worst. We have also had experiences with the ones in the middle. We have seen low tech and we have seen high tech. We have learned something from each and have been able to help many. Unfortunately, we are but mere mortals and we have also failed. Such is life. We will share with you some good stories and some sad tales. For obvious reasons, we have disguised **all** firms and factory specifics to ensure that privacy of the innocent and guilty is maintained. We will not tell you what software to buy, what vendor to contact, or what consultants to hire. Instead, we will try to give you ideas and strategies for how you can make your own choices. Each factory is different, the same in many ways, but still different, and there is no one solution or strategy that is appropriate for all factories.

The chapters in the book can be grouped into three main sections:

1. The what — Chapters 2 to 7
2. The tools — Chapters 8 to 14
3. The how — Chapters 15 to 19

In Chapter 1, we will discuss the general role of mathematics and computer support tools in production control and then start the journey towards understanding the production control situation. Most factories are not so perfect and we will introduce you to Jake and his factory. The majority of schedulers and planners exist in factories somewhere between peaceful bliss and Jake's world. After we describe a day in Jake's life, we will discuss what we call scheduling hardness.

CONTACT US!

We want to hear from you. We want to hear about success stories (manual and with software), what happened and why, about tricks or ideas that you have seen or used to improve production control, about challenges and issues that continue to face you. We have a weird sense of humor and also want to hear about wild constraints or issues that mess up simple sequencing. We would also enjoy Factory From Hell tales. If you are deserving of a Jake or Ralph designation, we will send you a personalized note via e-mail!

MATHEMATICS AND SOFTWARE GOODIES

We need to say a few words about mathematics and software systems before getting too far into this book. Production control has a lot of numbers, arithmetic, calculations, ratios, and percentages. Software is a logical place to look for help. Manufacturing types have been inventing and advocating various tools and aids for production control since the early 1900s. Some of these tools have been mathematical concepts for determining economic order sizes, how much safety stock is needed, what the lead time should be for quoting orders, how to forecast, where inventory should be kept in the supply chain, and how to use detailed scheduling algorithms for better sequences. In the best of all worlds, these tools and aids help you run the factory more efficiently and effectively, and also help you do your own job more efficiently and effectively. However, if the tools are not appropriate, are misused, or not installed and maintained correctly, they might not have any effect or they might even have negative effects.

Admittedly, we will be harsh on what we consider snake-oil solutions or solutions that are prescribed for the wrong problem, both mathematical and software. We are not totally negative on mathematics and software though; we do some quantitative and mathematical research and we have built and installed software systems for production control. We just advocate the wise use and deployment of mathematical tools and the associated software.

There are cases where mathematical techniques and sophisticated software tools have made great sense and are being used with outstanding results. Unfortunately, such success is not obtained automatically by simply using the same math and software in every situation. This sounds trivial, but the error is made many times in practice. The proper use depends on many factors that we will discuss later. For example, there are different levels of the problem that might be suitable to model. It is possible to model supply chain level versus plant planning versus department scheduling versus machine dispatching. There are also different areas of a firm that might be better suited to model, repetitive flow lines versus job shop. It is important to know what makes sense for each situation and to use common sense. Our opinions, reflections, and recommendations often look like common sense in hindsight, but if common sense is so common, why is the lack of it so often lamented?

So keeping this perspective in mind, let us visit Jake.

A DAY IN THE LIFE OF JAKE

Hi, how's it going? I'm Jake. They call me a lot of things, some printable, some not; but I am what they call here a Senior Planner. I do a little bit of everything; dispatching, scheduling, and planning.

Hey, let's duck into the cafeteria for a minute and hide out for a bit. I've actually been running since I got here. I need a break. I want to tell you what my day's been like so far. Have a seat...Coffee?

Came to work this morning about 5:30 AM. Still dark out. Looked like it was a nice night and would be another beautiful day. Was nice to hear the birds singing before dawn. Peaceful. Soothing.

As I arrived, I noticed Guaranteed-Freight's truck at the loading dock. Ouch! It should have been at the customer's dock by then and not ours.

Passed by Carl in the hallway on the way in, didn't say hi to me, just nodded, kept mumbling to himself. Not a good sign; knew then I would need to put on an extra pot of coffee.

Started to get production reports from the night shift as soon as I got to my desk. Instead of making fifteen thousand type A parts in cell six, they made ten thousand type Bs in cell five. @#@(*@#&*(@#@. I do not need Bs till next month and they used the material I needed for Cs due tomorrow. As, not Bs. Where did they get this? Do they just make it up? Now, where I am supposed to find replacement material? Where? Up my sleeves? In my hat? That's a good one. And, what happened to the Es????? They were supposed to be run in cell five and on that Guaranteed-Freight truck by 3 AM and at the customer by 6 AM!!!!! Sun was not even up yet. Started on my second cup of java then.

So much for cells five and six. They were pooched. What else is new? There goes a few hours to fix this mess. Good thing I have a sense of humor.

Betty then stopped by. Gave me the night shift update for cells one through four. Started with the good news from cell one. Made what they were supposed to — nice change — even the right quantity — bonus! Not a priority part, but no point looking a gift horse in the mouth.

Joe came by looking for Fs. Know that we made them just two days ago. The stock chasers have not found them yet. I saw them with my own eyes when we made them. Verified the production count too. Where did they go? Where could they be hiding? Joe needs them in an hour, else forty workers will be counting holes in the ceiling tiles. First Easter Egg hunt of the day. If we cannot find them, will have to do a priority setup and start cranking them out. Perhaps it was a good thing they did not make the As last night — can use that material for the Fs now. Will need some help on this one. Sometimes we get fouled up by the wrong counts and adjustments going into the system and we think we have more or less of something and then get a surprise, but I am really sure that the Fs are out there — somewhere. Perhaps Buddy put the weight of the production run into the computer as the count? Has done that before.

Luck is fickle. Cell two? Glad you asked. More coffee?

The setup took an extra hour and then the first part verification took three hours instead of twenty minutes. Couldn't find the inspector, then the inspector couldn't find the gauges, then the inspector could not find the process sheets she misplaced while hunting for the gauges, then it was time for the lunch break. @#@&*(^#@@#* At least they got something made. More bad news though. Sam is on the day shift today. Odds are that he will bugger something up by the end of shift. Will try to find something idiot-proof for Sam today.

Hang on a minute, let me get the radio. Cannot get any peace and quiet with these handsets, even in the restroom.

Bloody HELL! The @#@*(#&(@ idiots! Tooling was not set up right in cell four. Jenna wasn't sure what was wrong, but she thought she heard a crunching sound as the first machine closed. They moved the tools to cell three and tried the tooling there. Ha, the crunching sound was part of the tooling and when they moved the tooling to cell three and closed the first machine, there was a louder crunch. Great! Just @#@*@#& GREAT!!!! Cells three and four are down now — the first machine in cell four had indeed gone berserk and damaged the tooling which in turn damaged cell three. Three for three — takes talent. Do they practice this stuff? There goes the whole day now. This is going to cost. Big time.

Can't concentrate, can't think. Caffeine slow to kick in this morning. Supervisors hovering like buzzards over a rotting corpse. "What do I do next? What do I do with my crew? Where is the material? Where are the tools? I do not have enough material. I do not have a brain!" What do I look like, their Mother? They want to know where to put it? I'll tell them where to put it. OK, OK...I know, calm down. Gimme the decaf. Gotta get a grip.

You know, its all the scheduler's fault. It is always my fault. The plan is terrible. The biggest problem is always bad planning. Worker leaves a hammer in the machine and it is poor planning. Oh, the litany — I hear it every day. The plan cannot be executed in a month of Sundays. The setup is not given enough time. The estimated processing time is too optimistic. I scheduled a part on a machine that could not do it. We started changing the cell over before the material arrived. We started changing the cell over while tooling was being worked on. The sequences did not use the resources efficiently. The resources are left idle. The plan wastes material. The plan does not allow enough time for maintenance. There is too much overtime scheduled. There is not enough work planned. There is too much work planned. There was too much inventory on Monday. There is not enough safety stock today. What kind of cheese do you want with your whine? Yes, I make mistakes, but who wouldn't in this zoo? Just got to keep some of them happy, can't make everyone happy all of the time. Morning is turning into a bore. Cannot wait till I go home.

There's the radio again. Sorry. Yes...yes...no...fifteen hundred...by noon.

Where was I? Right. As if I was supposed to know that the workers would damage both cells. I was supposed to know that the engineering prototype left the machine slightly altered and incapable of running a standard part. If only — if only I knew. Of course I was supposed to know in advance that Jason mistakes Bs for As and that he would make the wrong parts. Why not? Of course I should have known. I can see through walls and jump buildings in a single bound and stop a speeding train. Who can't? Was that really decaf?

Am I a scheduler or a ferret? Have to dig to get the information I need. Every morning, check with shipping, check with receiving, check with the supplier, check with the customer, check with tooling, check with supervisors, check the weather, check with other planners, check with engineering, check with quality, check with maintenance, check with management, check with the plant gossip, check, check, check. Got to get information, got to verify it, got to cross-check it. Got to keep on top of it. Gotta lotta java. Get it, I make joke. Did get some good info today though. Larry in purchasing told me that one of the vendors is scheduled next month to make physical plant changes and do a major upgrade. Will have to think about what this means and what I have to do about it.

Blasted walkie-talkie, worse thing ever invented. Darn thing squawks at me every few minutes…Hello?…You want what?…I'll see what I can do…

Listen, want to know what really irks me? What's good today was not good yesterday and might not be good tomorrow. Metrics and objectives always changing or seem to be part of a secret club. Some managers play games — say one thing, mean another. Wink wink nod nod. Give that job priority and get it out the door — ya, right. They know that I know that they just got off the phone to the customer who just yelled at them and that they promised to tell me to focus on their order. Allows them to sleep at night. I wonder which of the five number one priorities I should expedite? Which one will hurt me the least? Any career limiting options there?

They change the rules and don't tell me. They change the goals, don't tell me. They say that the job is a high priority, don't really mean it. They say trust the data, they don't keep them up to date or accurate. They say use the industrial engineering standards, standards have not been met in years. They say trust the system, they do not have the right system for the problem at hand. They say to use historical performance data, the system has not been reliable or predictable for years. If I cannot predict it, how can I plan it? Monday morning they say that we cannot have overtime this month, change their minds by Monday afternoon. They say to keep inventory down, change their mind when there is not enough work on the automated flexible assembly line. They tell me that the plan is no good, do not tell me what is bad, and do not suggest any ideas that could improve it. Just tell me what you want the schedule to be and I will issue it. Am I supposed to make decisions? They change everything I create. Did they replace the decaf with extreme caffeine? Anyone for triple espresso?

Oh? Just ignore it. I'll turn the volume down. If it is important, they will send someone to find me. If I answered every call, I would never get anything done.

Speaking of which, how do they expect me to create better plans when I have no time for thinking? Multiple plans? What-ifs? Comparing options? Optimizing? Good joke. I would be happy to get one plan done before they change the rules. They do not want to hear excuses or reasons why the plan is not feasible, they just want it to happen. They want the plan to say what they want to hear. Emperor's clothes are a bit tattered.

They always use the most optimistic numbers and estimates I give them. For example, I tell them that I want six hours to run a batch. They might not like that and ask for a better number. If I say that we once did it in four hours, but that it has also taken eight, and we have not seen five in six months, they converge on the four like politicians around a baby. They say to use four hours as the standard and put it into the plan. It will happen this time I am told. No proof, no hard evidence to support the four hours except faith and hubris. Put a few of these decisions together in a plan and you have a really great situation to chew on. But that again is my fault. No one ever seems to remember when, where, or who made the decision about four hours. Selective memory is a real talent. Can someone just tell me what I am supposed to do? Need a refill?

SCHEDULING HARDNESS

Does Jake's situation sound like your factory? Do you think that we are describing you? There are factories that are considered healthy and top performers, and others that are on life support. No real factory actually matches Jake's. The description is a composite of dozens of factories and dozens of situations.

In the best-of-the-best factories, the production control department almost looks as if it is doing nothing because its personnel are not running around and screaming directives and muttering profanities. The planners and schedulers might actually put their feet up and have time for thinking and reflecting about the future. They have lower blood pressure, less stress, and are a tad less edgy and cranky. In Jake's world, the days before retirement are tracked daily and a state of siege exists with the planners and schedulers hunkered down and they are all defensive. They are not having fun.

In the better factories, the scheduling problem is not that hard because the physical system is healthy and a proactive stance is used to view the future. The production control personnel and their management actively make the problem easier. If the planners just reacted instead of thinking about the future, their day-to-day life would be drastically different because all of the little things would start to add up quickly and create chaos. The better factories are a reasonable balance of problem and solution, and the physical and logical systems work in harmony. These high-performing factories can consider using mathematics and advanced control ideas to tune and tweak inventory levels, flow times, and responsiveness. They are excellent candidates for software tools such as advanced planning systems and operations management models.

Jake's world is an unhealthy factory and unhealthy management practices. This is indeed the **Factory From Hell**. Jake has a very hard scheduling problem to deal with. Everything is against him and the aura in the factory could have come from a horror movie. Jake is far from being able to use mathematics and advanced ideas. The basics need to get fixed, many things improved, and then, and only then, can advanced concepts be considered.

Before reading the rest of this book or looking at various chapters, you should reflect on your situation or those that you have seen. Do you have a hard production control problem or are you blessed? Throughout the book, we will be discussing production control in terms of the good, the bad, and the ugly, and it will be useful for you to have your perspective sorted out in advance. If you want, you can use the download to this chapter (available at www.jrosspub.com) to do a self-assessment of hardness. The questionnaire, assessment material, and interpretation guides are on the publisher's website (www.jrosspub.com). When we first visit a factory, we implicitly and explicitly try to get a handle on these questions so that we can focus on the right problems and potential solutions. The illustrations for each chapter are also available for download.

PUTTING SCHEDULING AND PLANNING IN PERSPECTIVE

Although there might be a few situations that look like Jake's day in, day out, year in, year out, most schedulers or planners might have a bad day like this once or twice a week, or once a month, but sometimes there are whole weeks and months that read like this. Situations like Jake's can be seen periodically in what would be considered top plants running JIT (just in time), where you would not predict Jake to be found. You can also find Jake in plants known to be in the throes of death. Of course, all of this reflection begs a few questions:

- How much can production control help or hurt situations that are evolving towards Jake's world?
- What is the value of better planning and scheduling to a firm when coupled with other good manufacturing practices?
- Are planning and/or scheduling being done "good enough" for the situation or could they be done better?
- What is the benefit to the firm if production control can be improved?
- What are the damages caused by poor planning? Is Jake contributing to his own problems?
- What tools and organizational infrastructure can schedulers have to do their jobs better?
- What things hurt planning and scheduling and reduce the quality of decision making?

- Who would make a good scheduler and why would someone want to be one?
- What characteristics of the overall manufacturing system encourage and support good production control or hinder it?

To begin answering these questions, we need to first understand why we have planning and scheduling in the first place, what planners and schedulers do, when they do it, how they do it, and why they do it. Although every plant and situation is different, there are a number of common themes, common challenges, and similarities in the way they are different. In understanding the context and the dynamics of the situation, we can provide a better overall situation for the firm through better decision making and also create a better situation for the planners and schedulers. These topics will be addressed in the next few chapters.

Some of the ideas we will share are ones that we have observed. Other ideas are ones that we have thought of and developed. Many ideas for better production control originated close to one hundred years ago — 1900 to 1930 — focused factories, JIT, continuous improvement, pulling work through manufacturing, and many more. The originators of these ideas also talked about production control and what planners and schedulers were expected to do. We will introduce examples and ideas from our forefathers at various points in the book. Many ideas were common sense when first stated and they are common sense now. It is important to understand the origins of production control and what ideas exist to leverage and learn from. If you know or understand the various tools and ideas that can be used, you will be in a better position to adapt to the changing requirements of production control. We hope that you will enjoy the historical tidbits.

It is very important to choose the right type of production control for your situation. Production control is quite different if you are in discrete manufacturing with a job shop profile and have functional groupings of machines, if you have flow lines for discrete parts, if you have one big behemoth of a machine that takes in raw material and spits out a finished product, if you are processing chemicals prepared in batches, chemicals prepared in flows or pipeline fashion, etc. The list goes on. The methods are different, expectations are different, possible analytical aids are different, and even the production control skills are different.

Not only are the situations different, but they imply different requirements for the personnel. Do you need a high school diploma, an undergraduate degree, or a graduate degree to be a planner or scheduler? It depends. To complicate matters, a discrete parts firm may evolve from a simple flow process of a few machines in a small setting, to a functional job shop with many specialized machines, to dedicated flow lines for the high-volume production as the product becomes a commodity, to cellular manufacturing as variety increases and flow lines become unwieldy.

This variety in the manufacturing profile makes it impossible to have one best practice for any and all, and it is impossible to simply use the same best practice forever. You need to understand what you are and what methods make sense. We cannot tell you and we cannot create a simple table to pick from. There are simply too many factors and issues that prevent such simple tables and prescriptions to be made. You need to think it through, not be dogmatic, adapt ideas as necessary, and be ready to evolve and change. You need to sit back periodically and reflect on your current manufacturing situation and determine if your current practices make sense. Times change and so should your production control practices. First assess what type of manufacturing situation it is and then think about solutions. Never start with a solution.

SUMMARY

The description of Jake is an extreme version of what a scheduler's and planner's life is all about. A scheduler or planner simply does not create sequences of demand-supply marriages. Production control is not 100 percent sequencing. The people and systems used for production control seek out information about the past, present, and future that might be useful for decision making; they disseminate information, they try to satisfy many official and unofficial objectives and constraints, they do dynamic real-time problem solving, and they try to anticipate future difficulties. Some factories make these tasks easy for the person and system to do, some do not.

You probably cannot avoid mathematics and software tools in production control. They are necessary and useful things to understand and to use. Like any set of tools, there are many types and many possible degrees of quality. The appropriate suite of tools will depend on how difficult your scheduling situation is and what is reasonable and feasible. You should first understand your problem, address any manual or basic issues, and then contemplate more sophisticated or complex solutions.

The following chapter gives a brief introduction to a variety of production control concepts used in the book.

2

PRODUCTION CONTROL CONCEPTS AND ASSOCIATED SYSTEMS

PREDIGESTED THOUGHTS FOR THE BUSY PERSON

■ Supply chain management is easiest when there are few choices to make. One plant makes something, one plant uses it in an assembly.

■ Supply chain management is hard when there are many possible places to obtain the material or component and many places that can assemble the final product.

■ Hierarchical production control reduces complexity by having each layer guide the next. For example, planning for the whole problem is done and then the master plan is given to the scheduling level for sequencing.

■ Focused factory control models reduce the complexity by having fewer products, parts, and resources for each person or decision processes to deal with.

■ Lean and agile manufacturing strategies require excellent basic manufacturing to be in place first. First comes quality, then comes repeatability, then comes speed and efficiency. Not the other way around. You do it backwards and you get the stuff that is usually associated with the back end of a process.

- There are many information systems used for production control (MRP/MRP-II/ERP), but the core philosophy and approach are the same.

- A good manufacturing execution system is an essential element of a solution strategy if the manufacturing process is complex.

INTRODUCTION

In Chapter 1, we introduced a view of production control that centered around Jake and the concept of scheduling hardness. Jake and other schedulers do not exist in a vacuum and production control is a concept-heavy activity.

There are many concepts and theories associated with production control. Terms like supply chain management (SCM), advanced planning and scheduling (APS), material requirements planning (MRP), just in time (JIT), shop floor control (SFC), and many more abound. It can be confusing. Some of these terms refer to paradigms for structuring production control decisions while others relate to the design of the primary production process. To make the confusion worse, there are also techniques that are associated with each concept.

There are many textbooks on production control theories, frameworks, techniques, paradigms, and systems. At the back of this book, you can find a listing of some of the excellent ones that are available. These books provide the depth and detail that we do not. However, to ensure that a common foundation exists, we will provide a short overview of the basic production control concepts and the usual information systems involved with production control.

CONCEPTS

Supply Chain Management

In many ways, today's supply chain management is not much more than the way production control was practiced by firms such as Ford in the early twentieth century. Then, as now, there were firms that looked beyond the factory, to consider upstream and downstream flow, and firms that did not. To those practicing system-wide production control, it was nothing special. They were just making sure that their end-to-end supply processes were efficient and that they would have material where and when they needed it. They analyzed what was in route, what was at various locations, and what operations should be done where.

Today, there are many factories working together, or attempting to work together, in the same firm or across firm boundaries. The cooperation or collaboration between manufacturing entities can range from simple arrangements to complicated agreements including intellectual property rights.

In a very simple supply chain, there might be one location that builds a certain part and one plant that uses it. The plants can build and use multiple parts, but there is only one building a part and one consuming the part. These are simple chains and can be modeled readily in many tools and systems. The software tools have a relatively straightforward task of determining when a part is built, how much should be built, and how much should be kept in inventory.

Most supply chains are not that simple. You might have multiple plants that can make the necessary part and multiple plants that can perform the assembly. The plants might be in different parts of the world with all kinds of issues that affect cost, material movement, and inventory levels. In these more complicated situations, the software systems try to determine which plant should be supplying the part to which assembly point throughout the supply chain, and it quickly becomes very messy and very complex.

Another aspect is the sharing and coordination of forecast and shipping knowledge. In these cases, the various players in the chain share information and attempt to make better choices for the whole chain, possibly at the expense of some individual players. This is commonly called collaborative planning.

We will revisit supply chain management concepts when we discuss advanced planning tools later in the book.

Production Control Paradigms: Hierarchical and Focused

If you stand back from a factory, way back, there are two common ways that the factory decision processes and resources are structured. One is a hierarchical structure with layered, centralized decision making, common support services, and shared resources. The other is a focused factory model where the factory is split into smaller self-contained factories with their own decision structures, supporting infrastructures, and dedicated resources. Just like other things in life, it is not possible to say that one paradigm is always better than the other. It depends on your situation: what type of product you are making, the mix, and the volumes. The type of suitable control paradigm is also likely to change over time.

The production control problems in most large companies are probably too complicated to be solved by a single decision-making process. In a large plant, one person cannot make a plan that satisfies both the long-term horizon and the short-term scheduling decisions on the shop floor. Think about it, they would have possibly hundreds or thousands of products and possibly hundreds and thousands of resources. Because the production control problem in most plants is large and complex, it needs to be decomposed for it to be solvable. The

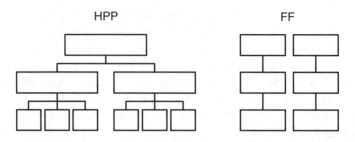

HPP   FF

Figure 2-1.   Hierarchical and Focused Factory Paradigms.

production control paradigm or model basically tells you *how* the production control problem is decomposed.

The hierarchical production planning (HPP) paradigm prescribes a hierarchical decomposition of the production control problem: aggregated planning functions on a high level and more detailed planning and sequencing functions on a lower level. The focused factory takes a different approach. It creates mini-factories within a factory where each mini-factory does its own planning, scheduling, and dispatching. The two paradigms are visualized in Figure 2-1.

The HPP paradigm has been the most common approach for the past century. The paradigm fits the hierarchical organization structure and management levels of many companies. The most important aspects of the HPP paradigm are:

- Layers of decision making; aggregated decision levels proceeding to detailed decision levels
- Coordination of sales and production via a master production schedule
- Factory-wide coordination versus production unit coordination

In some ways, the distinction between planning and scheduling can be explained partially by looking at the HPP production control structure. Planning is done on a higher level, with longer decision-making horizons, and takes both material and general capacity into account. Planning often deals with product groups. In the short term, scheduling and dispatching have a more or less fixed capacity and deal with individual products or components. During the last fifty years, there have been many mathematical models, algorithms, and software tools constructed for the hierarchical situation. The tools are often specialized for each level of the hierarchy. There are tools for dealing with forecasts and orders, tools for planning, tools for scheduling, and tools for dispatching. One tool does all of the planning for all of the factory. Another does all of the scheduling for all of the factory or for major parts of the factory. Yet another tool is perhaps used for all dispatching decisions. This decomposition and hand off of plans reduces the overall complexity of having one big system try to plan, schedule, and dispatch all at once. This decomposition approach is good when the product mix and volumes are balanced reasonably and no single product or group of products has sufficient demand to warrant dedicated resources.

The focused factory paradigm takes a different approach to the problem. The factory is realigned to high-volume products, product families, or processes. This decomposes the problem along a different axis. You can think of a vertical decomposition instead of a hierarchical horizontal decomposition. In the focused factory, the complexity and size is reduced via a reduction in products and associated resources. There are less products and resources to plan, schedule, and dispatch. If the mix is relatively low and the focused factory flows the product through the dedicated resources, the overall problem is quite manageable for an individual or small team. It is also possible to think about having the same tool used for the various planning tasks instead of having a separate one for each layer.

Lean and Agile Manufacturing

Lean and agile manufacturing have been added to the suite of production control concepts. While not always, they are often built on well-run JIT implementations. The JIT philosophy of manufacturing control included kanban cards, containers, designated inventory locations, and consumption-based production. When a factory is suitable for kanban-triggered production, dispatching is not performed, neither is scheduling, but there is planning and a lot of it. The planning with kanbans involves determining the quantity of bins, quantity per bin, resource balance issues, and making sure that an empty bin is refilled before the consuming resource starves.

The lean manufacturing initiatives are aimed at further reductions in response times, flow times, resource inefficiencies, material waste, and scrap. Strategies such as strategic placement of inventory, delaying customization until the last moment, and other similar ideas are used to extract any fat in the system. The agile angle comes into how well the system can respond to minor or major changes in demand, product evolution, improvement in processes, and realignment of resources.

Lean manufacturing requires excellent basic manufacturing. The first step is quality. You need to know how to make the quality parts or products you need. You know the targets, can you do it? Can you do it almost every time? You have to be able to build the suitable quality consistently. Almost going hand-in-hand with consistency in quality is consistency in execution. The system has to have low variability in processing times, setups, and yield. If you expect a hundred pieces in two hours, it better be close to that every time. Not eighty pieces in four hours this time and 120 pieces in three hours next time. Once you are consistent on both quality and execution, you can start the next phase of lean: organized elimination of waste and the improvement in efficiency and effectiveness. Reduce the setup time, reduce material handling, flow the work from operation to operation, look for the material just as it is unloaded; all good things. But do so after you know how to make the product, can make it well, and can do so repeatedly.

INFORMATION SYSTEMS

MRP/MRP-II/ERP

Information systems are very well equipped to support the massive amount of data that is involved in production control decisions. Information about products, customers, orders, production history, maintenance, quality, and inventory levels abounds. The common terms for information systems to be found are material requirements planning (MRP), manufacturing resource planning (MRP-II), and enterprise resource planning (ERP). MRP-II does MRP and more. ERP does MRP-II and more.

In terms of production control, MRP and its modern versions are bookkeepers and calculators. They keep track of what orders exist, the current inventory levels, what materials and parts are consumed to make the finished or shipped goods, and how long it takes for each of the major operations along the way. With this, the basic MRP logic tells you that for two hundred bicycles you will need four hundred tires, and if the bicycles are to be assembled on Tuesday, you need to start making the tires by the previous Friday. This is the explosion of the bill of material, scheduled receipts, and the determination of lead times. The MRP logic usually matches the hierarchical production control paradigm with the planning and scheduling levels.

MRP-II extends the basic MRP capability with functions such as finance and ties in other resources directly related to the production process. The MRP-II implementations gain benefits from sharing master data and seeing how one decision affects other parts of manufacturing and finance. Typical MRP-II implementations also have tools for capacity requirements planning. Capacity analysis is described more fully in Chapter 8.

When the MRP-II systems are expanded with more modules like human resource management, the name changes to ERP. An ERP system may have started life as an MRP-II system and was extended, or it might have been written from scratch. Either way, it contains the basic MRP-II types of functions for production control. Although there are over one hundred ERP vendors, the market is now dominated by only a few ERP vendors, with SAP AG by far being the largest. The benefits of implementing an ERP solution are often debated.

Tools for planning and scheduling are often attached to MRP, MRP-II, and ERP systems. Many of the ERP and MRP-II vendors either have their own planning tools or are associated with a specific tool vendor. There are also over one hundred planning tools to choose from. With such a variety, it is difficult for any firm to know what ERP/MRP-II and planning tool to choose. Planning and scheduling tools are explained in greater detail in subsequent chapters.

Manufacturing Execution Systems

Manufacturing execution systems (MES) are also known as shop floor control (SFC) systems. These systems operate the actual production processes and capture machine data and are linked to the equipment's controls with PLCs (programmable logistical controllers), DCSs (distributed control systems), and other interesting devices.

Most MES are linked to an ERP system for coordinating what is done where and what remains to be done. The ERP system may transmit order numbers, part numbers, and quantities down to the MES for verification and tracking purposes, or it might be a simpler interface with the ERP just receiving production counts from the shop floor: so many of a certain part made at a certain work center since the last update. The MES may also be attached to a planning and scheduling tool.

A good MES, one that is matched to the ERP and possibly a scheduling tool, is essential if you want to achieve the potential benefits of the information systems. The MES must also be matched to the manual practices and methods in the factory. Between the humans, physical systems, and computers, it is important to know what you have done, what you are doing, what inventory you have, and where the inventory is located. If the factory workforce does not understand the MES or does not have the discipline to keep the inventory and production records up to date and accurate, then garbage will be fed into the MRP logic and the planning subsystems. The ERP systems and other manufacturing systems need information that is timely and accurate. A very high degree of compliance is necessary. There are no shortcuts.

In some factories, the MES is considered a poor cousin and does not get the attention it deserves. It might be added as an afterthought, it might be implemented in a hurry, or it might be done on the cheap. The manual systems might be in a similar state. In either case, the ERP and other systems will be disadvantaged. You should pay as much attention to the MES systems and processes as you do other parts of the system.

JOB SHOPS AND FLOW SHOPS

The organization of the physical production system determines how production control should operate and its basic challenges. A job shop is a production unit with medium material and resource complexity, where the machines are not very specialized, and where a large variety of products/components are being manufactured. The specific challenges of a job shop lie in its unpredictable processing and setup times. It can be compared with one thousand families going to a large theme park and each family member having its preferences on what attractions to visit. Now try to predict when each family will have processed its complete "route." Figure 2-2 shows the difference between flow shops and job shops.

A flow shop is much more specialized in terms of the product that is being produced. Machines are organized according to the sequence of the routing steps necessary to produce the product. A flow shop is much easier to plan and control, but is only economical when a certain volume can be realized with limited product variety.

Another distinction is that production flows can be discrete or continuous. What is made can either be counted or the production can be measured in volumes or rates. Process industries usually produce nondiscrete products at large, expensive installations. In these cases, setup times, start-up times, and cleaning times are the issues to determine better sequences and schedules.

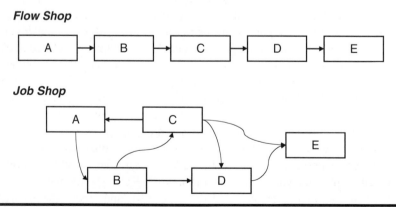

Figure 2-2. Flow Shops and Job Shops.

Process industries processes are usually more predictable and better suited for implementing decision support tools than job shop situations.

GANTT AND GANTT CHARTS

Do you have a wallboard, piece of paper, or a computer screen showing time horizontally, machines or resources shown vertically, and magnets, bars, or lines for work assigned? Does it look like what is commonly called a Gantt chart as shown in Figure 2-3?

It is hard to think of a plant that does not use something like this to help plan or describe the plan. It is probably the most common tool in production control for creating and showing a schedule. The bars in the chart usually represent jobs on machines. The Gantt chart may display setup times and nonproductive periods (e.g., weekends, holidays). The length of the bars represents the time needed to process the job. An alternative view might show a contract or job down the left on the vertical axis and the bars represent the operations associated with the job. One view or graph focuses on who is doing what, the other on what is being done by who; two charts, both are considered Gantt charts. These charts will also be the most common displays you will find in scheduling tools.

Since there is a lot of confusion about the history of the Gantt chart, we want to share a little bit of history with you. Gantt developed a large number of graphical tools in the early 1900s for tracking and planning work. He was not alone and there were many others developing charts at the same time (e.g., Knoeppel's articles in *The Engineering Magazine*). The closest to what we now commonly call a Gantt chart were two of four charts he formally introduced

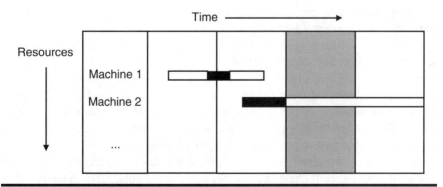

Figure 2-3. Gantt Chart.

in his book *Organizing for Work* (1919). He called them the *progress* and *order* charts. As Gantt described them, they had been used during WW-I by various government agencies and dated from just before the United States entered WW-I. They were used for laying out expected activities and tracking progress, providing visibility to the plan or schedule. The progress chart had articles, the work, on the vertical and the order chart had contractors, the who, on the vertical. The charts had horizontal lines showing targets, the percentage of orders or performance actually received, and figures for cumulative quantities desired and actually received. They were very good for tracking shipments and basic activities that had quantities and due dates. Gantt noted that these charts had been used for tracking suppliers, articles within contracts, and were also used to schedule and track the building of ships, shipyards, and flying boats. He said that they were being used for the manufacture of many kinds of machinery. These two charts were very similar and he claimed that the charts were suitable for any activity having a common measure of time. On page 82 of the book, Gantt claimed "The great advantage of this type of chart, known as the straight line chart, is that it enables us to make a large number of comparisons at once."

Why go into this history? It is important for you to think about what information you want to see on the screen or report while planning, and while thinking about decisions to make. Do you want to easily see the original targets, the remaining amounts, the names of parts, descriptions of parts, or the percentage remaining? What is useful to you? Gantt had a number of pieces of information on his chart; how much does a vendor supply and what are the options? Gantt seemed to emphasize percentages and relative progress. Is this important for your situation? You could see instantly if something was 10, 25, or 75 percent complete and use this in decision making. In today's systems, the charts are usually updated daily and it is not clear if any tools allow you to go back in time and show history and the current percentages of completion. As tool features and screens are enhanced constantly, it is wise to check out what is available versus what you might need.

There is something interesting about Gantt's charts. Gantt did not talk about how the progress and order charts could improve efficiency or whatever was being managed. The main claim was visualization and comparisons. Great for that purpose, but what were the other two charts about? We think you should know about them and think seriously about using them! They fit well with many ideas talked about in this book. If you currently have a software tool or are thinking about a tool, see if you can do something like them.

In the next two chapters of his book, Gantt discussed the two remaining charts: the *man record* chart and the *machine record* chart. The chapters where these are introduced are 100 percent focused on improving efficiency and effectiveness. These charts have straight lines and have columns for dates, but they have additional features that we have not seen on modern Gantt charts. They were also used differently than how we use Gantt charts today. He introduced them on page 86 by describing how the world was just becoming aware of how inefficient things really were. "Other peoples have realized that the real asset of a nation is its human power, and undoubtedly will soon begin to adopt means of measuring this power to the end that they may use it more effectively. Some of us have made a start in this work by keeping individual records of operatives, showing as nearly as possible what they have done in comparison with what they might have done, with the reasons for their failing to accomplish the full amount. By systematically attempting to remove the obstacles which stood in the way of complete accomplishment we have secured a remarkable degree of co-operation, and developed in workmen possibilities which had been unsuspected." On page 87, Gantt went on to say that "it is a foreman's function to remove the obstacles confronting the workmen…" The man record chart was the tool to be used by the operators and foremen. The machine record chart was targeted to foremen and higher management. These charts were clearly more interesting and more important to Gantt than his progress and order charts.

The man record chart indicated the amount of work that the man should have done in a day, time taken to do the work, estimated time for work done, time on the job, and the cumulative time. The chart provided codes and reasons for not achieving the goals: absent, defective work, green or new operator, lack of instruction, lack of or defective material, tool troubles, lack of tools, or holiday. The foremen were responsible for fixing or responding to these problems. The sheets also helped the individual workers. In describing the benefits of the man record chart on page 89: "That the methods which I have here inadequately described are of broad applicability, has been proven by the fact that they have received enthusiastic support of the workmen wherever they have been tried. As previously said, it is undoubtedly true that the 'efficiency' methods which have been so much in vogue for the past twenty years in this country, have failed to produce what was expected of them. The reason seems to be that we have to a large extent ignored the human factor and failed to take advantage of the ability and desire of the ordinary man to learn and to improve his position. Moreover, these 'efficiency' methods have been applied in a manner that was highly autocratic. This alone would be sufficient to condemn them, even if they had been highly effective, which they have not." Although this was written in 1919, parts could have been written recently. Do you or your factory ignore the human factor? How successful have your plant's various improvement activities been?

The machine record chart had major resources listed and looked at reasons for inefficiency: lack of help, lack of or defective material, lack of power, repairs, lack of tools or tool troubles, and lack of work. This was the interface between the foremen and the higher-level managers. The high levels were responsible for creating a situation in which the foremen could succeed. Page 92: "The problem of the manager is much wider than that of the superintendent or the foreman, for he must see that there is work to be done, materials to work with and men to do the work, besides numerous other things which are not within the sphere of the foreman."

Do you have a systemized way to track performance, attributing causal relationships at the levels suggested by Gantt? Few do. It is not clear why the world gravitated to his progress and order charts and why the record charts faded from view. Perhaps it is the way that Gantt held foremen and managers accountable. It was lamented by the late 1920s that management had a habit of picking certain recommendations from consultants and the scientific management crowd and ignoring bits they did not like. If you can do it, try to create reports and tracking similar to the man and machine record charts and use them in the spirit of their creation. They are active, helping tools to improve efficiency and effectiveness. You will need management understanding and backing for them to work. Initially, there might be some finger pointing and defensive posturing. Try to work that through, take the higher ground, and try to solve the issues together. This is not easy, but it is clearly one approach for how to identify barriers to improvement. The charts also give you a way to track improvements as the frequency of problems decreases. It will be hard to get people to stand up and accept responsibility. Why these two charts were not widely adopted and embraced by management is not clear, but we have our suspicions.

SUMMARY

There are numerous production control concepts used in running factories and there are many different information systems. It is impossible to avoid talking about concepts such as supply chain management, different styles of production control (e.g., hierarchical and focused factory), flow shops, and job shops. There are also the various information systems used by the production control department. For each of these topics, there are many things we have left unsaid and you are directed to many of the fine books available. While this has been a very brief overview, we hope that sufficient information has been provided so that you know what we are talking about.

The following five chapters focus on the *what* aspect of production control:

- What are the roles and objectives anchoring production control?
- What are the functions of production control?
- What are the tasks associated with production control?
- What are the traits and characteristics that planners and schedulers should have?
- What are the types of information used in production control?

3

OBJECTIVES
AND ROLES

PREDIGESTED THOUGHTS FOR THE BUSY PERSON

- Describe the job of production control in one sentence without using the word "and"? *Make appropriate decisions to discount troubles foreseen in the future.*

- Challenges or issues for production control to focus on are **any undesirable results** — direct, indirect, immediate, or delayed.

- The best scheduler is likely to be the lazy scheduler whose laziness is rewarded when things are going smoothly and the factory is calm.

- The best organizational structure recognizes, institutionalizes, and supports the concepts of anticipation and forward control.

- Not all schedulers and planners are good schedulers and planners. Production control is a cognitive skill and exhibits varying degrees of skill and expertise.

- Factors outside of the scheduler's control affect some of the measures used to assess the performance of schedulers.

- World-class production control is boring. Sorry.

INTRODUCTION

What is production control really about? Chapter 2 talked about control structures and the information systems that you will find in production control, but they are not what production control is about. Here is one definition of production control:

> Well-organized and carefully executed work routing, scheduling, and dispatching are necessary to bring production through in the required quantity, of the required quality, at the required time, and at the most reasonable cost.

This quote is from Younger's 1930 book on production control. It is perhaps the first book dedicated to the production control problem. It clearly targets the required quantity, quality, time, and cost as key factors. In this chapter, we will discuss the origins of production control and the objectives and intent that production control should embrace.

HISTORIC PERSPECTIVE

In practice, the production control department has been charged from the beginning of organized manufacturing systems with initiating production orders and scheduling the sequence of tasks, in addition to follow-up tracking and recordkeeping. Diemer produced one of the first textbooks on production management in 1910 and noted this purpose.

By the 1950s, production control's scope was expanded somewhat to include materials, machines, and men; still with a time focus. In 1952, O'Donnell described the scope as: "It is necessary for the production department to have the raw materials delivered at the proper time, to have the machines available to produce the material at the proper time, and to have the men available to work on the machines." In 1967, Plossl and Wight continued the theme to include maximum customer service, minimum inventory investment, and efficient plant operation: "Production control determines what items and quantities should be made and when they should be made, taking into the account the three basic objectives."

If we combine these views, we get:

> The orchestration of materials, machines, and personnel through the sequencing, scheduling, initiation and tracking of production orders in order that the required quantities, quality, and customer service are efficiently achieved in a reliable fashion with minimal costs.

In fact, Reinfeld, who was instrumental in the creation of APICS (American Production and Inventory Control Society), had a comprehensive definition in 1959:

Production control is the task of predicting, planning and scheduling work, taking into account manpower, materials availability and other capacity restrictions, and cost so as to achieve proper quality and quantity at the time it is needed and then following up the schedule to see that the plan is carried out, using whatever systems have proven satisfactory for the purpose.

Reinfeld's definition is similar to our richer composite definition and describes a discipline that is very broad, from the predicting to the follow-up, from costs to manpower, and from quality to quantity expectations. Production control is not simply sequencing work, it is also the involvement to see that the plan is indeed carried out. This is the definition and view that guided the APICS formulation. However, neither our composite view nor Reinfeld's has a clearly stated objective and intent. Both of them try to include many aspects and many specific goals.

The composite definition and Reinfeld's share the usual view — right amount of the right quality of the right part at the right time with the lowest costs — but is this sufficient as a statement of objectives? Are they too limiting? Do they really capture the essence of day-to-day production control? The next section discusses the possible limitations and how the above descriptions may restrict the view of what production control is often defined to be.

PRODUCTION CONTROL IN PRACTICE

Do schedulers actually think about and focus on what Reinfeld defined? Probably not. Do they do less or more? Probably more. Does the traditional objective capture the essence of the job? No. Is the traditional objective ingrained in job descriptions, task definitions, and job assessment structures? Probably. If you are a planner or scheduler, how do you feel about the description?

If the traditional definition is rooted deeply in the task, does this restrict or limit what you could or should do? In well-run plants, good schedulers can be seen to look beyond the definition. They focus on future troubles and *discount* them. By discounting, we mean what Coburn meant in 1918: reducing the impact associated with the future problem. Consider Coburn's description of a desirable scheduler: *"He must have imaginative powers to...foresee trouble...he will get the reasons underlying conditions which point to future difficulties...see to it that future troubles are discounted."* The scheduler at a top-performing plant fits Coburn's description perfectly and was also the laziest scheduler we have known. He was also the best scheduler we have seen. However, plain laziness combined with poor job ethics does not result in good scheduling behavior. Laziness works only if real problems cause real pain for the lazy scheduler. Thus, laziness should be combined with realism and ownership. The scheduler knows that he or she is responsible for a smooth flow and tries to realize this with as little effort as possible. If the flow is not smooth, their own little world is upset and this creates personal discomfort. Schedulers should not enjoy pain.

Not only was our great scheduler lazy, he relished the laziness, was proud of it, and did everything possible to have the maximum amount of time to enjoy it. What did this translate into? A very smooth production environment where troubles were anticipated in advance, impacts were avoided or minimized, and production was allowed to do what it was good at: producing parts. He tried to keep out of the way of production and tried to create situations in which the factory could produce what they were supposed to produce when they were supposed to produce it. Anything else turned into a headache.

Coburn would have loved him. This scheduler was anticipating production issues two to three months in advance and orchestrating the environment (resources, demand, and inventory) in order to avoid being called into meetings or being beeped on his pager at 2 AM. He hated meetings and hated getting beeped. He truly enjoyed doing nothing and getting paid for it. His cognitive objective function was **maximum nothingness** and his operational objective was **minimal trouble**. Not bad for someone with a high school education and only six months in the scheduling job. To be fair, he had spent about fifteen years in the plant doing almost everything before taking on the scheduling job. This was one of his secret weapons; he knew almost everyone and knew how the factory worked or could work. We will call this grand master of a scheduler **Ralph** and discuss more of Ralph's scheduling gems occasionally in the book.

There is another interesting perspective from Knoeppel, an efficiency engineer in 1911, that also captures the spirit exhibited by Ralph:

> Did you ever see a bird, in its search for twigs, straw and the like? Hunting these things for fun? Hardly. It is simply planning ahead against the time when a warm comfortable nest will be wanted for the little ones to come. It does not wait until they have arrived – the bird sees to it that the nest is ready before it will be needed, and, as a result, we call it a wise bird.

The wise bird is obviously avoiding trouble. This intent and objective discussion sounds like general problem solving. There could be a whole lot of trouble if things do not get executed in a certain way. You have to be able to sense or perceive the trouble in a mass of environmental noise. You need to understand what the trouble really means, understand or be aware of ways to deal with the trouble, and have the means available to actually deal with it in a very real sense. You also need to know if the trouble is indeed being avoided, minimized, or otherwise dealt with. You need to know if the trouble has been put to bed, is smoldering, or will flare up elsewhere in disguise.

There are some manufacturing situations where there are few production control troubles. If there is sufficient spare capacity, many troubles can simply be absorbed. One factory had no production control problem. Yes, that is right, no production control problem, or at least they should not have had one.

They had a perceived production control problem that was not rooted in reality. They were making low-volume, low-mix, high-value luxury items, each in the hundreds of thousands of dollars range. They worked one shift per day. They made twenty per day, two thousand per year. Do the math, how many shifts of actual production were done per year? One hundred shifts of production per year. Capacity was not a problem. They also had firm customer orders for a horizon of two to three years. Demand uncertainty was not a problem. Of course, there were machine-level uncertainties, bottlenecks, and flow problems, but obviously there were many options available for the manufacturing concern whenever something did go wrong. They had the time and they had the capacity to deal with the troubles. Considering that almost all of the items were also prepaid, very exclusive, and in a market where delays were expected, they had the best of both worlds. There was no penalty for a late order. And yes, the firm is still in business. They had trouble with fixtures and palettes. They had trouble with prototype parts. But they certainly did not have a scheduling problem.

Unfortunately, not all firms are so lucky. They are working without great excesses of spare capacity, orders are not prepaid, there are late penalties, and there is often little room for error. Too many factories can still be described by Emerson's commentary:

> ...but most of the industrial plants of the world are still in the stage of civilization of which as to transportation the old freight wagons and prairie schooners across the plains were types. They started when they got ready, they arrived some time, and nobody knew where they were nor what route they were taking in between.

Emerson wrote this in 1913 and if this description captures what your factory feels like, you have big troubles. A factory in the late 1980s had over five thousand work orders active on the floor, all of which were late and behind schedule. Emerson's description for this plant was 100 percent accurate. There were areas of the plant that work went into and eventually reappeared — no one knew when or why. Parts would go in and out of specification on the factory floor with so much as a two degree ambient temperature change. They had many expediters working the floor. A few years later, they had no late work orders. None. Sounds like amazing progress had been made in the manufacturing process and system. Imagine, going from over five thousand late orders to zero. What was their secret? Had they improved basic manufacturing or installed state-of-the-art production control? Hardly. They had such poor performance that they lost half of their business. Talk about doing it the hard way! A factory from the 1980s. OK, that was then and this is now. Do you think that things have changed? Recently, a factory reported a delivery reliability of 6 percent; 94 percent of the orders were late. Déjà vu.

If chaos describes even one department in your factory, you have significant troubles since it only takes one such area to destabilize and mess up production throughout the system. The self-assessment associated with Chapter 1 will give you some clue to your situation. A situation rated as hard or ugly is likely to match Emerson's description quite closely. In factories or departments that can be described as being ugly, phrases like Six Sigma, continuous improvement, Toyota production system, and lean manufacturing are oxymorons. Emphasis on the moron.

You must first systemize and stabilize the foundation, ensure that quality can be achieved, and ensure that you have repeatability before you are even close to considering these advanced concepts for improving efficiency and effectiveness. You must have basic manufacturing down pat before you can think about the advanced stuff.

We will repeat this message a few times. This is not a new message and we did not invent it, but it is a message that does not seem to have been often heard, remembered, or understood. Take a look at the following twelve symptoms of a factory in chaos as reported by Knoeppel in a consultant's study circa 1918:

1. We did not find an analysis of parts from the standpoint of importance to sub-assembly and final erection. Lacking this it is impossible to work up sequence and flow of parts and subassemblies.
2. Little has been done in the matter of standardizing operations or supplying records with sequence of operations on parts. Without this knowledge it is impossible to route parts through the shops.
3. There are no estimated times for operations on file. This is necessary in planning, in order to estimate the length of time to allow for work at the different points of travel.
4. While you have part orders, there are no regular manufacturing orders for building a definite number of certain models, making it a difficult matter to know what to control.

5. You have orders in the plant for too long a time. This not only holds up your records but increases the chance of errors creeping in, or having the orders lost or sidetracked.

6. You do not have your stock situation under the kind of control that would enable the planning department to depend upon these records, which would mean constant changes and corrections in schedules.

7. Your time reports are loose and unreliable, as the men keep their own time or your clerks enter what the men tell them. Correct times and correct counts are essential in watching and controlling progress, from day-to-day, or work which has been planned.

8. You have too many changes and errors during process of manufacturing, to schedule intelligently the work of assembly and testing. These departments, not knowing what is coming to them from serving departments, cannot get things in readiness in advance. Very often they have to do extra work because of a failure to complete work on a preceding operation.

9. Due to the present congestion in the shops it would be exceedingly difficult to control production efficiency without a full knowledge of what is in the shop and the conditions with reference to completion.

10. Because of the lack of advance information, departments do not know in all cases what is coming to them, until material arrives on the floors. Under these conditions no scheduling is at all possible.

11. Weaknesses in both tool room and inspection departments would interfere at present with attempts to schedule work properly through the plant.

12. As was repeatedly pointed out, there is an almost entire absence of shop procedure, the unforeseen and the unexpected largely governing the department heads.

Does this list sound all too familiar? It is the same message. If you do not have the basics down, you cannot be effective or efficient. You cannot plan or coordinate your resources. Unfortunately, there are plants today that can be described by Knoeppel's summary. It is true that not all of these symptoms or factors are relevant for today's factories. For example, everyone uses bills of material and has shop floor tracking processes. The other factors may apply, but you are using the principles of MRP. However, are the data in your system up to date? Accurate? Representative? Do you really have an accurate picture of your inventory position: quantities, quality, and location? Are you in a factory from the new millennium or from the early 1900s?

The intent and objective of production control must match the firm's situation. If your firm is crisis driven, your production control must focus on the basics and not try to evolve too quickly. There are certain techniques that you can use in chaotic manufacturing to reduce the troubles initially and these must be the focus. As the manufacturing process improves, then the higher-order objectives, or other kinds of troubles, can be addressed. It is similar to the situation with statistical process control. You cannot use statistical process control until you are actually in control. You cannot use best-of-class production control methods or have world-class control objectives until you are close to world class in the first place. Unfortunately, not everyone understands this and there will be corporate mandates and other directives issued that just do not make sense. For example, some firms mandate JIT levels of inventory for job shops. This is just plain wrong as job shops have dynamic routes, resource conflicts, and queues that will build up. However, this does not prevent people from stating that as an objective, charting it, or rating performance by it.

The scope of production control needs to be stated clearly within the organization. The scope needs to address the types of troubles production control is expected to mitigate and the authority it has to implement countermeasures. Sounds like a military campaign? Sounds like war? It is. It must be made clear to the production control department and others that there are risks and troubles in the future that are reasonable to perceive and anticipate. Of course, not everything can be perceived or anticipated, but it is also not necessary to pretend that everything falls out of the sky as a total surprise either. We speak more about this later.

Once the scope and intent has been formalized, then performance measures and tracking mechanisms can be instituted. For example, it is possible to track the special decisions relating to perceived trouble and determine if production control is improving or not in its perception and countermeasures. If the production control personnel have the same personal desires as Ralph had, then the formal mechanisms are not necessary. His personal desires matched, in a weird and perverse way, what was good for the plant. He wanted smooth production and trouble-free shifts. However, if the production control personnel are not so motivated personally, then formal organizational processes of setting metrics, measuring against them, and associating them with performance reviews will need to be implemented. A major mistake is made in many organizations by stating objectives and goals, but not actually making them *measurable* goals and *measuring* the individuals against them. If there is no incentive, it is doubtful that the goal will remain in the fore. It might not be possible to set good, measurable goals for all tasks at the individual level. It really is hard to measure scheduler performance. However, it is possible to set some measurable goals at the aggregate level and see how production control is performing as a single entity.

REALISTIC PRODUCTION CONTROL

Perhaps the realistic and practical objective of production control can be stated rather more succinctly:

> The objective is to ensure that future troubles are discounted.

This is shorter than the composite or Reinfeld definition and it avoids repeating all of those terms: time, quality, and quantity. But what are these future troubles? Is it too vague?

It is the trouble caused by a late shipment to a customer. It is the trouble caused when the wrong material is used to manufacture a part. It is the trouble caused when the work is started too early and the parts rust on the factory floor. It is all of this and much more. It is as general as it implies.

It is **any** trouble caused by **anything** that is:

- Contrary to production requirements
- Wasteful
- Inefficient
- Ineffective
- Damaging

While we would love to lay claim to this view, we cannot. Here is the full version of Coburn's 1918 definition for the coordination effort in production control:

> The schedule man must necessarily be thorough, because inaccurate and misleading information is much worse than useless. It seems trite to make that statement but experience makes it seem wise to restate it. He must have imaginative powers to enable him to interpret his charts and foresee trouble. He must have aggressiveness and initiative and perseverance, so that he will get the reasons underlying conditions which point to future difficulties and bring the matter to the attention of the Department Head or Heads involved and keep after them until they take the necessary action. He is in effect required to see to it that future troubles are discounted.

If you cannot avoid or correct the trouble in its entirety, then you have to think about trade-offs and compromises. This is where you start to minimize the total number of late jobs if you have to have any late jobs. Of course, the goal is to have no late jobs. If you will be penalized financially by late jobs, then you want to minimize this financial trouble. Get the picture? When we talk about improving a schedule, we are actually minimizing the trouble we are in. But there are many forms of trouble and the production control department cannot be myopic or close-minded about this. Troubles can arise from union agreements where a person with seniority, but no skills, will be chosen over a junior worker with skills. You have to anticipate and deal with this. Troubles can arise from the weather and road conditions. Again, you have to deal with this. When factory workers mumble under their breath "Here comes trouble!" as you approach, they do not realize how true that statement really is.

PLANNING, SCHEDULING, AND DISPATCHING

In many organizations and situations, there are people called planners, schedulers, and dispatchers and/or activities called planning, scheduling, and dispatching. These are not all one and the same, there are differences. The essentials are summarized in Table 3-1.

For example, a planner usually has multiple horizons and variable units of time and work to play with, has reasonable data for making plans with, does not need to deal too much with the daily details of the actual production, and the time pressure is not as severe as the dispatcher's. The dispatcher works with the immediate reality and thinks about what to do next. The dispatcher often works with partial, ambiguous information as decisions are made on the run and the demand for an immediate answer is enormous. Schedulers have a little bit of both worlds and need many of the same skills as both. Both the planner and scheduler have expectations of the future and both scheduler and dispatcher work with orders, assignments, or specific work units.

Table 3-1. Planners, Schedulers, Dispatchers

	Decision Inputs	Decision Outputs
Planner	Expectations of the future, tactical challenges	Volumes, rates, tactical realignment of resources, assignment of product flow, inventory targets
Scheduler		Orders, assignments, or jobs/real-time, inventory use, operational realignment of resources
Dispatcher	Current situation on the factory floor, operational control	

Each of the roles and tasks carries with it implications about what information is needed, when the information is needed, how accurate the information must be, how the information should be displayed, what reports and analysis tools are required, and what kinds of what-if or decision aids are suitable. A tool for planning is not likely to be useful for detailed sequencing and dispatching. The tasks are also dependent on the type of industry and organizational form that the plant has. For example, if the plant is a focused factory or a small facility, one individual may be the planner, scheduler, dispatcher, and occasionally the order taker, receiver, and shipper. By way of contrast, in a larger plant with a hierarchical structure, there might be separate and well-defined planners, schedulers, and dispatchers. You usually need special software tools for each of the planner, scheduler, and dispatcher tasks, and have unique tools for any combined tasks. The same software does not always work for all cases. The planner, scheduler, and dispatcher system in a focused flow shop is substantially different than the dispatcher and scheduling tools in a large job shop. There are also differences between dispatcher and scheduling tools when there are two people in the roles and a merged system for when one person needs to do both.

Look at each production control role and task separately to understand the needs and issues regardless of who is doing it, and how the roles will be combined. Once you know the larger set of requirements and issues, then you can decide on appropriate solutions. It would be a mistake to get a system for planning and then assume it can be used for scheduling or dispatching and vice versa. Do not assume that planning, scheduling, and dispatching are the same problem or that the same person can do any or all of the roles. There are different sets of factory knowledge, different conditions under which decisions are made, and different types of creative problem solving.

Unfortunately, almost every factory uses a different variant or definition for what a planner or scheduler is and what a planner or scheduler does. In this book, it has not been possible to use these terms, planner and scheduler, consistently in a pure way. We could be trying to describe a planner issue and someone called a scheduler might yell out "I do that!". Please use considerable freedom to interpret any sentence with *you*, *planner*, or *scheduler* in it. If the basic message or content of the sentence makes sense in your situation, then use it.

INTRA– AND INTERPLANT

Intra- and inter-. Sounds almost like a mantra. Intraproduction control is what happens within the four walls of the facility once material arrives at the receiving dock and before finished goods depart from the shipping dock. Interproduction control is what happens between you and suppliers and you and customers. In a supply chain, you might also interact with plants further upstream or downstream in the chain. There are times when you have to deal with outsourcing that is related to your plant and the outsourcing is not really part of the linear flow of goods through the chain.

In various chapters in the book, we touch on supply chain issues and will share with you what we know and do not know. It is probably more of the latter since few well-designed studies have been done and much is made of speculated cause and effect relationships without supporting evidence. However, we do have some ideas on the general supply chain topic suitable for this chapter. Production control throughout a supply chain is easiest when the product mix is low, volumes relatively high, each element in the chain is supplying one main customer and plant, customization is delayed until assembly, and everyone is running a focused factory with flow lines. If you visualize a chain, each link looks the same and the capacities are matched. In these types of chains, the goods can flow through the system with low inventories, predictable times, and quick response.

We call these types of ideal chains homogeneous. Everyone acts and looks like each other in terms of material flow, control logic, and manufacturing tactics. In these cases, a plant can be pulled easily by the downstream customer and the objective of production control is to have the least amount of centralized control possible. Indeed, the system should almost run as if there was mechanical scheduling without human intervention. The planners at each link in the chain would not need much knowledge or visibility of upstream or downstream details, and would need minimum communication.

A heterogeneous supply chain is a different kettle of fish. Very different. In a hetero chain, you will find job shops and flow shops intermixed, some plants high volume and low mix, and others relatively low volume and high mix. You will find plants supplying multiple plants, possibly competing customers, and at least one link in the chain looks and feels substantially different than the rest. Hetero chains are harder to manage, will have greater difficulties trying to achieve lower inventory, and will have greater resources tied up in production control. Hetero chains might also have large or lengthy distribution components where it is not a simple matter of pulling production processes, and inventory control requires centralized analysis. In hetero chains, production control will need to have greater visibility of upstream and downstream conditions, greater flexibility in dealing with shifts in demand and supply, and take extra precautions around any critical build times.

Comparing homogeneous and heterogeneous chains is like comparing a flow shop to a job shop and expecting the same levels of inventory and predictable flow times. It is also like trying to substitute a cat, dog, rat, pig, or horse for a cow on a dairy farm: four legs, ears, tail, some kind of hairy coat, and all feed their young — what's the problem?

In some firms, production control has decomposed the problem and some-one may be responsible for outsourcing and the supply chain, while someone else deals with the issues within the plant. This is not always the case though. Regardless of organizational design, it will be important that the suitable tools, communication channels, authority, and information flows exist for either in-house or out-of-house production. Management must recognize that additional resources will be needed as complexity increases on the receiving, shipping, or outsourcing dimensions. It will be harder for production control to meet its expectations for flow times, inventory levels, and for forecasting future prob-lems. It is possible, but it will require greater recognition and support by upper management. If the support is not forthcoming, production control is in a boxing ring with a blindfold on and the gloves tied together. There is no ability to anticipate or react effectively.

PERFORMANCE MEASUREMENT

In operations management theory, the performance of a scheduling or sequenc-ing technique is regarded as very important. The usefulness of various tech-niques is often evaluated by a set of specified performance criteria or key performance indicators, such as delivery reliability, delivery speed, flow time, number of late jobs, degree of lateness, and resource efficiency.

In practice, the theoretical performance measures of scheduling are not perceived as being as important as they are in theory. A small set of formal performance criteria probably does not match the actual criteria used by you, and a compromise has to be made between multiple performance criteria. You are not likely to be told "Yesterday's plan only had three late jobs, good work," but will be asked "Three jobs were late, why?" At this time, it would not be smart to point out that three late jobs is better than the four late jobs on a previous revision of the schedule. Furthermore, the performance of a production unit fluctuates over time and it is not easy to relate a decrease or increase in performance causally to specific scheduling actions or specific disturbances.

To complicate matters, the performance of a production unit in a specific time period might have been achieved at the cost of its performance in subse-quent time periods or at the cost of the performance of other production units in the same production chain. There might be games being played for the fiscal quarter, the fiscal year end, and the end of the month reports to the corporate office. If a supply chain planner is truly trying to make good decisions for the whole chain and not do myopic decisions for each element in the chain, it is likely that various elements of the chain will have fluctuating performance month to month. The whole chain might be improving, but one or more factories in the chain might have lower results occasionally. Therefore, the performance of production units can only be judged to a limited extent by comparing the realized performance to past performance; a larger view is needed.

The current situation is that most schedulers are hardly interested in feedback about their performance as it relates to scheduling metrics such as percentage of late jobs. The fact that scheduling performance is very difficult to assess is only one possible explanation. Another possible explanation is that performance goals are very difficult to relate to scheduling actions. Performance feedback in a complex task might even be counterproductive. This is because outcome feedback might cue a focus on evaluating one's competence on one metric rather than on increasing the overall performance. This is unfortunate, because performance feedback might have been intended to be a measure to improve the motivation of schedulers to use scheduling techniques.

One technique to improve feedback and performance is to perform periodic tracking of execution performance to plan. Once or twice a year, for several weeks at a time, you can explore the interface between production control and production. Each day you take another half hour or so at the morning meeting and discuss what was supposed to happen yesterday according to the plan and what really happened. You can create a matrix of common causes, reasons, or excuses and track how much went according to plan. If something executed better than plan, why? If something did not happen as planned, why? Look at the quantities, qualities, elapsed time, and resources consumed. You also reflect on the plan for today. Yesterday you had a plan or expectation for today. What have you already changed? Why? You also had a plan for tomorrow and the next day. What has changed in the plan for the next two days? Out of all possible jobs and operations being scheduled, what went as planned and what did not? You can then look at the categories of reasons and determine the causes of variation. While not a precise science, you can identify major groupings of causal relationships such as problems caused by material, maintenance, scheduler's decisions, management interference, and tooling. You can track percentages for each category and the percentage of aggregate change. Did 80 percent of yesterday's plan execute as planned? 20 percent? How much of today's plan survives unchanged? Jobs moving to different resources? Different start times? Preemptions? Different job quantities? If you do this periodically, you can determine if each area, including production control, is improving or not. It is not a fun exercise, but it can generate many insights if you take it seriously. A major benefit of this type of tracking exercise is focusing the management and workers on variability and stability. The plans and actual production must be reasonably steady and predictable if costs are to be contained and efficiencies improved. It is impossible to coordinate resources when hardly anything is as it is supposed to be. It would be ideal to do this type of tracking and reflective thinking all of the time, but this is probably too idealistic. If you look at the basic concept and process, it is similar to the goals of Gantt's man and machine record charts described in Chapter 2.

PRODUCTION CONTROL SUPERVISION

Planners and schedulers usually do not report to the president or plant manager. They report to lower or middle management: the production control supervisor or manager, the production area manager, or perhaps the operations manager. What should a production control manager know and do? Of course, there are the usual management type skills: an affinity for meetings, the ability to sleep with the eyes open, imaginative budgeting and sorcery skills for foreseeing and controlling the future, and knowing when to avoid a career-limiting or terminating move. These are skills all managers can find uses for, not just in production control.

Our ideal supervisor knows almost everything the planner or scheduler does about the system being controlled. They need to know what can be made where, when, and by whom. They need to know what cannot be done as much as what can be. The manager does not always need this information and does not use it daily unless the factory is challenged, but when the push is on, the supervisory level must be able to pitch in and help the schedulers and planners, must be able to notice any glaring oversight on the part of the schedulers and planners, and must be able to explain and justify any decision made by the actual decision maker. Supervisory personnel with this knowledge would be preferred any day. This is similar to the argument where the best engineers or software programmers should be in quality control. How do you expect a lower-skilled individual to see, understand, detect, and prevent something, with less time to think about it, that was overlooked by the dedicated, originating engineer? If a supervisor is being parachuted in or is being placed in production control for training, a key aspect has to be process and system training to understand what the workers are making decisions about. Without the knowledge, the supervisor may override a lower decision mistakenly or make a rash judgment.

The supervisor needs to know what the planners and schedulers are doing, how they plan, and how they schedule. Some of you supervisory types might be reading this and with a smile mutter that you do know, you taught them everything they know. Or, if you are a planner or scheduler, you might think that you taught the manager everything he or she knows. Well, some will and some will not. When was the last time the manager spent a whole day, from the crack of dawn to the inevitable sunset, with the scheduler? When did the manager sit with the planner for two to three days while a plan was crafted? Supervisory personnel who have *lived* with the planners and schedulers for a day or two are more likely to know what is actually going on. Those who know by faith and hubris are not wise. Managers should take some time out and spend a day or two with their workers to really understand. Most do not do this, a small number do. Perhaps it is thought to be a sign of weakness or will be perceived to be fraternizing with the hired help, but many managers do not want to show any lack of knowledge or understanding and will not take the steps necessary to fill in the holes that do exist. When a manager takes the steps to understand the problem, the manager will gain credibility. The planners and schedulers have more confidence that the manager knows what is going on and what should happen. There is nothing wrong with admitting that knowledge needs to be gained or that time must be spent learning.

What other knowledge is needed? Well, in most firms the production control supervisor also needs an excellent knowledge of the ERP system in terms of material flow: purchasing, receiving, production flow, and shipping. They need to know what current options are set and what options are not used. It is not necessary to know on what screen the option can be found or what codes are used for a field; it is necessary to know that such an option exists or does not exist and that such a transaction exists or does not exist. The supervisor needs to know the basic transactions that are performed dock to dock that affect inventory accuracy and production tracking. They also need to know where and how demand or forecast information is obtained and any oddities associated with it.

The first thing the supervisor needs to do daily is to develop a snapshot, perhaps at an aggregate level, of the area being controlled. This can be done on an exception basis. For example, what did not get done as planned and what is the recovery plan? Are there any changes to today's plan that need management input or awareness? Are there any changes in the demand, or forecast, that warrant supervisory attention? Are there any changes to the status quo that need to be planned for? Did any hot or expedited jobs stall? These are the types of questions and focus that a supervisor should have. If the issues or problems are small and routine, the planner or scheduler should be able to deal with them in conjunction with their counterparts in materials and production without supervisory intervention. Supervisors and managers should not micromanage; this is obvious and is often said, but it continues in many situations nonetheless. Only those issues that require additional resource allocation or special actions should be raised. Only those problems that will ricochet or ripple throughout the plant should be escalated. The manager should be helping where additional focus or capacity is needed, assisting with decisions that require multiple departments and negotiation, and where policies need to be relaxed or extraordinary steps taken.

At some point during the day, the scheduler or planner may stand back and say "This is the plan for tomorrow, or the next week, or the next month, or the next year." The plan or schedule should be bought into by the production department, materials, key support groups, and production control supervision. Either electronically or physically, the plan should be distributed for review and if problems with the plan are not noted, the plan is considered accepted. It is the responsibility of those using the plan to look at it, vet it for feasibility, and bless it. Too often, the plan is generated, issued, and then in hindsight obvious problems noted. Production should not accept a schedule unless it agrees that the schedule is achievable. "You gave us a bad schedule." "You know that this machine cannot do that job, why did you schedule it that way?" If it was bad or infeasible, then why did no one in production raise this objection when the schedule was issued? People should actually look at and review plans before accepting them or before blindly distributing them for execution. This will ensure that better plans and sequences are generated and also helps in the education of the production control department. Production control supervision is a key part of the vetting and sequence review.

Production control supervision is responsible for creating a satisfactory environment for planning and scheduling. Every effort should be made to provide a working situation that encourages good thinking and good problem solving. This includes workstation design, minimal noise levels, interruption reduction, and information processing tools. While all workers should have adequate environments, the planning and scheduling workspace is vital. Few other positions and tasks in a firm affect so many others. If someone makes a mistake in shipping or receiving, some damage results, but usually the whole plant is not in chaos as a result. Missing a new demand, not noting a change in existing demand, not setting the right resource levels, not scheduling a changeover at the right time — these can be very costly mistakes for the firm.

Production control supervisors should take an active role in the education and awareness of the production control staff. Lead by doing. The supervisor should take responsibility for the creation of risk management practices and the operational execution of them. The manager can host and chair the weekly risk management session: what is coming down the train tracks, who needs to know, what should be done before, during, and after the collision.

Finally, the supervisors must evaluate and track the planner's or scheduler's performance. It is necessary to set realistic measures, identify and isolate planning mistakes, and take corrective action. Errors and mistakes are a natural part of learning and they are not always bad things. The bad errors and mistakes are the ones that have been made before and nothing was learned from the experience. Organizational learning is important and unless people can make mistakes in a healthy environment, the learning will be stifled or nonexistent. It is one thing to promise not to rip the scheduler's head off for making a mistake and another to look at it as a learning opportunity and great for the organization's knowledge base. As long as the organization benefits and can avoid similar pitfalls in the future, the mistake must be looked on as a good thing. Knowing what not to do is often more important than knowing what to do. However, if there is no evidence of learning, or sincere attempts at avoidance, head ripping may be required.

MINIMAL PRODUCTION CONTROL

It is also possible that a firm finds itself without a real need for explicit, elegant, or sophisticated production control. For example, what planning and scheduling do you need in a high-volume, low-mix, long-term contract base, stable-forecast, pulled plant with relatively few suppliers and few customers? All you need is some planning and mechanical scheduling. The planning is more tactical and the scheduling can be mechanical in the form of kanbans. You do not need dispatchers, Gantt scheduling tools, high-tech software technology, or weekly schedules and sequences. You match your firm to the customer's production or consumption profile, keep inventory flowing, and production control becomes a different type of problem.

You can think of controlled work-in-process and kanban strategies as a virtual conveyor system throughout the plant. This is a concept where only so much stuff can be on the conveyors. If there is nothing to take off or put on the conveyor at a point, nothing is done, you are gated or pulled by the downstream need. Firms actually did this with physical conveyor systems in the 1920s and they got the same benefits that today's firms get with kanbans and controlled flow. One is very physical, the other is more method based, but both end up in same place. In the 1920s, this was called mechanical scheduling and there was no need for daily scheduling or dispatching. It is sometimes possible to create focused factories out of a larger mess where each focused factory can run without complicated production control. However, there are many assumptions necessary for this: sufficient demand, ability to group and organize by product, physical plant space, enough money in the bank, and enough time to restructure. If you can, go for it. Henry Ford is widely known for his assembly lines at Detroit. At the Highland Park factory complex, he also had about five hundred factories within the factory, each a focused activity creating something in its entirety for the assembly line. He also had work cells in the mini-factories where an operator would run several different types of machines. He had the space, resources, and product demand to justify the methods.

You can also have minimal production control if you have a factory that resembles one large machine. One of the best known was the A.O. Smith factory for making automotive frames. It was built in the 1920s and lasted into the early 1960s. It operated as one big, automated machine. It could produce ten thousand automotive frames per day, each with hundreds of operations involved, with only two hundred workers. The same two hundred workers could change the plant over to another model in about one shift. They had flexible, high-speed mass production lines and in the 1930s even made pipes for pipelines. No scheduling. No dispatching. Very little production control.

There are few large, single-machine factories like A.O. Smith's. There are few factories 100 percent wired together with conveyors. These types of plants can have minimal production control, but there are few of them. There are many small, single-purpose factories with specialized lines and equipment arrangements. For example, some automotive parts suppliers specialize in creating many small factories, each dedicated to a single part or a small number of similar parts. The facility is small and there is little overhead. There is minimal production control in these small, specialized factories. There are other factories with multiple, dedicated lines in the middle of a supply chain, and the work is pulled from the customer and the necessary components and materials pulled in turn. These too require minimal production control. The rest are not so lucky.

SUMMARY

In this chapter, we briefly summarized what we view the intent and objective of effective production control should be: *the foreseeing and discounting of troubles*. We also talked about production control supervision. Later chapters will revisit the theme of discounting troubles and will discuss specific methods for perceiving troubles, techniques for discounting troubles, and concepts for decision support systems that support trouble perception and discounting. Mind you, we should first admit a little thing. This foreseeing and discounting is what we call a cognitive skill, like chess, bridge, or playing music. Not everyone can do it and those who attempt it have varying degrees of success at it. For every great scheduler or planner, there are probably one hundred lesser souls ranging from the novice to journeyman level. There are mental skills involved and it takes a certain mind and personality to be one of our master-class performers. Chapter 6 delves into this murky water and discusses hiring, training, and evaluating schedulers and planners. Do not expect master-class exhibitions from the novice and do not expect a master to appear without training and a conscious effort at learning.

The next chapter takes the basic role of a scheduler and planner and looks closely at what planners and schedulers are expected to do; the functions as expected by the organization.

4

THE FUNCTIONS
OF PRODUCTION
CONTROL

PREDIGESTED THOUGHTS FOR THE BUSY PERSON

- Most schedulers and planners spend very little time actually scheduling and planning.
- Production control is expected to work miracles, moderate the playground activities, orchestrate special events, and in general know everything for everyone.
- The extended functions of production control rarely are officially recognized, rewarded, or taken into account for hiring, budgeting, staffing, or training purposes.

INTRODUCTION

In Chapter 3, we discussed the roles and objectives associated with production control. Simply put, the objective is to foresee future troubles and discount them. This is the primary objective of production control, but does not describe adequately what its complete role or customary function is. What do schedulers and planners do and why do they do it? The answer to these two questions is obvious to some: the function is to create schedules for others to follow.

If you agree with this assessment *create schedules*, please visit a factory and observe the production control department. You are probably not a planner or scheduler. And no, we do not mean at 9 AM, or whenever you usually start work, but when the schedulers and planners actually start work at 5 AM, 6 AM, or whenever it is. Their day and work are basically over by the time other folks normally start. To observe production control and understand its function requires you to be there when the action is happening. If they say that they start at 6 AM, be there at 5:45 AM since it is likely that the schedulers actually start before they say they do.

What does production control do? What is its function? There is no single definition. This chapter discusses some of the functions schedulers and planners do.

THE FUNCTIONS THAT ARE DONE

To determine your functions as a planner or scheduler, there are multiple dimensions to consider. In a small plant, one person can be observed to do almost everything on the following list. In a large plant, there may be dedicated people doing each item and perhaps multiple people assigned to an item. A large plant may even have the list broken into two main areas: materials and production control. Rarely will the same splitting or partitioning be seen in two factories. Each factory takes a slightly different view of the production control function and expectations.

Consider some of the many informal and formal functions that can be observed in a production control department:

1. Buying material, dealing with suppliers
2. Conducting inventory counts
3. Searching for and finding lost inventory
4. Verifying and correcting inventory and production counts
5. Verifying and correcting engineering and material data
6. Communicating and coordinating activities with support departments
7. Researching and explaining curious numbers in the ERP system
8. Tracking engineering changes and controlling the change
9. Balancing out material and inventory as production changes
10. Receiving and shipping goods, issuing paperwork, contacting carriers
11. Monitoring subcontractors and outsourcing
12. Taking orders, contacting customers, verifying orders
13. Planning special periods such as preventative maintenance, line upgrades, vacations

14. Planning work at the day, week, month, year, multiyear levels
15. Crafting work sequences
16. Releasing work
17. Dispatching work

In addition, you will have to answer questions from management and everyone else about what is happening, what happened, what did not happen, what is planned to happen, and what is not happening that was planned to happen.

This is a partial list and contains what we consider to be the routine functions that planners and schedulers end up performing. The list does not include creative problem solving or firefighting. It does not include participation in continuous improvement teams or other support activities that may be asked of you.

It is fair and reasonable to ask why you usually end up doing most of these functions in the list. We are not saying these are functions you should do; these are functions that we see done by planners and schedulers. The functions might not be done every day, but the planners and schedulers are asked to do them occasionally and are expected to know how to do them; on the weekends, after hours, or in the early morning hours. Only the last five functions in the list really relate to actual decision making about what to make when and why.

Should you be the corporate babysitter? After all, that is what the list implies. Others do not know what to do next. Others need to be told what machine to use. Others need someone to check their counts and hunt for things that they misplace. The shipper is out sick and someone has to call the trucking firm. The purchasing department personnel are not in on Saturday and someone has to call the vendor about a late shipment. Ad nauseam. Some of the functions are valid backup or emergency skills, activated on demand. Other functions can be grouped together under one title, babysitting.

Babysitting consumes much of the scheduler's time. If one job has to be stopped prematurely, surely the operator can look at a schedule or list of possible jobs and make an educated decision about what to do next. Theoretically, a department supervisor who knows from the schedule that a certain part is to be made later in the shift should do a start-of-shift check to determine if everything was in order for the shift, thus avoiding surprises. In the same vein, the production department should be accountable for accurately reporting what was made and the forklift operators held accountable for knowing where the inventory was put. People actually receiving and shipping goods should be the ones accountable for accuracy of shipments, paperwork, and timeliness of activity. Shipping should also be accountable for ensuring that distribution is adequate for the planned production (e.g., trucks have been ordered). How much of your time is spent doing things that should not have been done if the proper methods and procedures had been followed by others? Why do you end up thinking for others?

Alas, life is not so simple. Thinking is hard. Thinking hurts. Easier if someone else thinks. And safer. If a worker thinks and makes a decision, he or she then becomes accountable for the outcome of the decision. It is easier and less career threatening to palm it off on someone else. It is easier to just say that something exists, that someone else is wrong, that the production count is accurate, and implicitly force someone else to prove them wrong than to actually do the job right or sort it out. It is also easier to ask someone else to look up something and provide an answer than to look it up. Hence, you are asked what to do next. You are asked to locate and prove that certain inventory exists or does not exist. You have the information about what is going on, so why should people not ask you? As a result, production control is often asked to think for everyone else.

In some respects, this is not bad in and of itself. You usually do have the information. Production control is the information hub of the factory. You should know what has been done, what is being done, and what is expected to be done. By searching for inventory and doing the other tasks on a regular basis, you develop skills that individual production department personnel would never acquire. After all, you are searching for parts or thinking about what should be done all of the time and not sporadically. Compared to a floor supervisor, you probably know your away around the ERP system far better and can look things up in seconds compared to their painful stumbling. In terms of efficiency and effectiveness at the systems level, the people in the production control department are the professionals at information acquisition and production tracking, and can do it well. Be sure, though, that these functions are truly valid and needed. You should not be covering up other people's mistakes and perpetuating bad practices. Also, these functions are often not planned for, budgeted for, staffed for, or formally recognized. This is the problem. How often do you get recognized or rewarded for doing a good job at finding lost parts? For answering questions? Is this reflected in your bonus or mentioned on the yearly review? How many minutes a day are you allocated for answering questions that you really did not need to be involved with?

All of these functions beyond sequence generation are time eaters and time fragmenters. These various nonplanning functions preempt and disrupt the normal processes of generating a plan. When have you been left alone long enough, without interruption, to actually complete a plan or schedule? Even when you come into the plant on the weekend to work on the plan, you are besieged.

Who thinks when you are not there? In one plant, planning was done on a single shift with plans made for the two other shifts and instructions left for the afternoon and evening personnel. The two shifts without a scheduler usually managed to make their parts without the constant help of a scheduler. At one point, they decided that more planning was required and they went to a split scheduler shift with the detailed planning and dispatching done on the day shift and more longer-term planning performed on the later afternoon shift. This seemed logical. It was assumed that the afternoon scheduler would have more time for planning and have good quality time as well. This scheme worked for a short time. The afternoon shifts quickly discovered that they could not function without the constant help of the scheduler. The afternoon supervisors and foremen suddenly did not know what to do. They did not want to make any decisions. The scheduler ended up with very little time to perform long-term planning. Miraculously enough, when the second scheduler shift was cancelled, the afternoon supervisors rediscovered their cranial cavity and were able to think again.

INFORMATION PROCESSOR

The information processing function of the scheduler is extremely important. You need to know where things are, the amounts, the quality, what materials exist, what the state of each major resource is, what the operator skill and capability is, when repairs are needed, and when repairs will be made. This is a partial list. You gather, you vet, you disseminate, and you translate. Personnel in the production control department regularly talk to over a dozen parts of the organization each day. A main activity is gathering data from sources and sharing knowledge that is possessed.

The information is processed actively and is not viewed as passive numbers on a screen or piece of paper. You may amplify information when the information is sparse by guessing and filling in the blanks based on prior experience and knowledge. If an operator does not volunteer a certain piece of information that is conveyed regularly, you might suspect something is not right. You may vet the information for accuracy and correct the data as required. The industrial engineering data might not be trusted and you might have to verify the drawings and calculations. You may also attenuate or reduce the information flow and rid it of irrelevant or redundant data. You might not care about what is going right and is on target. The information about problems and potential problems is more important to track and gather.

As a result of the broad and deep knowledge held by planners and schedulers, everyone that needs a particular piece of information phones, calls on the radio, or worse, steps into the office. Some calls go beyond simply asking for information. When something has gone wrong, when someone needs to be blamed, you are usually involved, as the plaintiff or as a witness.

SPECIAL EVENT COORDINATOR

Special events and their coordination are a second major function. The production control department is often expected to perform all synchronization tasks related to new product introduction, production trials, material changeover, and resource upgrades. Some special events involve almost as much effort as a royal or head-of-state visit. Visits by the board of directors, the division and corporate presidents, potential customers, current customers, or community groups all take planning. The number of groups involved and the number of items to keep track of can be mind boggling. You have the anxiety associated with the time just before the event is to take place and the nerve-wracking period as the event begins. Special events cause a few problems.

First, it is hard to do this planning when you are not told about the event until after it has started. Because the information role is not formalized in many firms, there are often miscues. Second, although many are involved, precise accountabilities and deliverables are sometimes hard to pin down. Stirring choruses of "Not my job" and "I thought you were doing that" can be heard. Third, these special events are rarely budgeted for, staffed for, or formally recognized as part of anyone's job. Everyone tries to take care of the everyday and the special with the same number of hours in the day.

A special event in any single department may be a relatively rare event and only happens a few times during the year. However, with all of the departments converging on production control, you can have a special event almost every month and sometimes more than once a week. Other managers do not give the production control manager much support or sympathy in dealing with special events because they see only a small part of the big picture and do not see what all of the fuss is about.

If possible, keep track of the special events and note the amount of time and effort that is expended. Ensure that supervisors and managers understand the accumulated impact.

ARBITRATOR, MODERATOR, AND BOOSTER

A third major function is similar to the conductor of an orchestra, a traffic officer at a busy intersection, or recess moderator at the children's playground.

This includes the obligatory waving of hands and excessive body language. The members of the orchestra are cajoled, enticed, and encouraged to play their utmost by the conductor. The enthusiastic beckoning for a quieter note or a resounding bellow is similar to you working with the supervisors and foremen. Sensitive egos are stroked and flattery provided, along with words of encouragement "Give us a little more, you can do it!" Caught in the middle of a big spider's web, you have to arbitrate conflicts while boosting and encouraging the efforts.

As a conductor cannot make all musicians happy, you definitely will not make all supervisors and foremen happy. Such is life. Each department or manufacturing area will want to be the first violin, get the sweetest parts for highlighting their talent, and be brought into the piece at the most opportune time. You are responsible for the complete system's performance, but have to do this given the individualistic nature of supporting teams and competing departments. More like the traffic officer and less like a conductor, a scheduler's performance is rarely looked at positively in the past tense. How often do you hear a driver complement a traffic director with a pleasantry or a manager say to you "That was a great schedule you gave us yesterday. It really kicked butt." Conductors will often get praised, but schedulers will usually get criticized with negative overtures. "Why was this done? Why did you not see that? Why did you do this before that?" Unfortunately, in production control the negative is normally dwelled on and not the positive. You have to be driven by internal desires, your own knowledge about how well the job is done, and your own view of what today would have been like if you did not make those special decisions yesterday. There can be a great deal of pleasure and joy in planning and scheduling, but do not wait to hear it from others.

The role of arbitrator, moderator, and booster is another informal function and rarely is it acknowledged officially or defined explicitly. The number of players in the sandbox, frequency of decisions, and interaction per player will all dramatically affect what you do and how well you can do the expected job. Are all of these interfaces and interconnections documented in the ISO 9000 processes? Doubt it. Is there a standard process for getting an extra 10 percent out of the workers on a Friday afternoon? Are all of these phone calls and interactions taken into account when estimating work load, establishing yearly personal performance expectations, or considering the quality of task output? If the number of interactions and symphony movements increase throughout the year, is your work load analyzed and adjusted? The one suggestion we can make is to document the various types of interactions that occur, what departments are interacted with, how often the interactions take place, and why the interaction was important. Try to identify when the interaction takes place and if there are any patterns. Some of the interactions are very valuable and should be encouraged and, if possible, supported. Other interactions are time wasters and should be identified as such.

MIRACLE WORKER

Perhaps the fourth and last major function is that of being a worker of miracles. Every day, often several times a day, you are expected to pull a rabbit out of the hat. And make that a very specific rabbit if you please. And quickly done, like yesterday. In dynamic job shop environments like Jake's, minor issues arise every five to ten minutes and these are often resolved through the clarification of information or simple decision making. Every half hour or so, a minor miracle is expected. This is where some actual action is needed by someone to make something happen. This might include searching and finding material or parts considered to be nonexistent or contacting a vendor and expediting a shipment. Once a day, it is not unusual for a major panic to occur and you might be expected to walk on water or leap over a building in a single bound. This major miracle may involve contacting customers, product engineering, manu-facturing engineering, or production supervisors, and crafting a new process or new order out of thin air that solves the immediate problem.

How much time does this miracle working consume? Miracles take time and it is not just a thirty-second diversion. What is the impact of miracle working on other tasks? Is this time and effort taken into account when estimating scheduler requirements, training, and staffing? Is it taken into account when designing the work station, layout, or noise barriers? This miracle worker func-tion will be considered a normal part of your day and what you are being paid for. It will be difficult to get sympathy for the time consumed or the interrupted decisions. If the miracle is needed later in the morning, or mid afternoon, the interruption might not be that bad. A miracle needed at 7 AM in the morning is very disruptive.

You can track the number of miracles when they occur and what other activities get disrupted. You can also try to track the reasons for the miracle requests. If you can gather enough evidence, you might be able to get help or at least explain why other activities are not being done, or not being done to the level expected.

SUMMARY

In reviewing these various functions of miracle worker, playground moderator, special event coordinator, and information system, one common thread stands out. These are all informal and are rarely documented or acknowledged. They are not measured or tracked. Neither is recognition given for a good job in these matters. The amount of effort required to perform these functions is not understood and the impact on the planner's or scheduler's process is usually denied.

Do people think that the schedule is not up to snuff? Perhaps they should look and see what you are doing. Where are you spending your time? Schedulers can be seen to spend 90 percent of their time on these other four functions and only 10 percent on actual scheduling or taking care of the daily work assignment. Is it little wonder then that mistakes happen and troubles are not foreseen? If these functions are not managed, it is unlikely that a smooth production plan can be orchestrated.

The next chapter takes a closer look at what schedulers and planners do when they actually get to plan and schedule.

5

THE TASKS OF PRODUCTION CONTROL

PREDIGESTED THOUGHTS FOR THE BUSY PERSON

■ Clues, their acquisition and interpretation, are important for decision making.

■ It takes time to build the historical base for interpretation and understanding of the clues.

■ The initial focus of production control is on what did not happen as expected or what can be expected not to occur as previously planned.

■ Production control is an iterative process where partial problems are solved with partial information. Not everything is known at the same time and not all of the problem has to be solved at the same time.

■ Important, tightly constrained or restricted decisions are made first, decomposing the problem; the remainder of the schedule flows around these anchored decisions.

INTRODUCTION

In Chapters 3 and 4, the objectives, roles, and functions of planners and schedulers were discussed. In this chapter, the focus shifts a bit and looks at part of the work day, the part of the day when planning and scheduling is done. Hopefully there are methods and policies for the actual task of planning and it does not sound like:

> ...but the spirit of things is usually impulsive rather than methodical. 'Get the thing done,' is the order and the procedure becomes one of a rush, hustle, tear-things-to-pieces kind, in a mad effort to obey orders, regardless of whether or not these orders could have been obeyed to better advantage some other way.

Knoeppel made this observation in 1911. He could have been describing Jake's situation and how Jake did his job. Instead of focusing on schedulers like Jake, we are going to direct our attentions to Ralph and other schedulers like Ralph. What do these types of schedulers do? How does it compare to your situation? What might you be doing? We will try to shed some light on the process of how planning and scheduling might be done.

THE SEVEN TASKS

Good schedulers and planners have been observed to proceed through a number of steps each day:

1. Situation assessment — what is where
2. Crisis identification — what needs immediate attention
3. Immediate resequencing and task reallocation — reactive decisions
4. Complete scenario update — remapping the future
5. Future problem identification — what problems can be foreseen
6. Constraint relaxation and future problem resolution — discounting future problems
7. Scheduling by rote — dealing with the rest of the problem

The seven steps are depicted in Figure 5-1 and are the seven categories that relate to the specific role of deciding what to do when. There are slight differences in the steps between planning, scheduling, and dispatching. The descriptions in this chapter use scheduling and dispatching as the base, but it should be easy to figure out the planning equivalent. What is looked at, and what the actions are, will change. For example, a planner will not worry too much about what was done at which machine last night, but will be interested in hearing about any shipping problems. Although the planner might keep an eye towards the physical factory, the focus will be any changes in forecast, changes in mix,

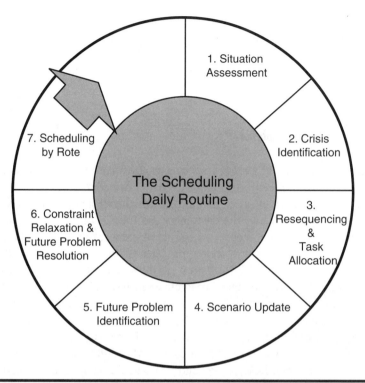

Figure 5-1.   Seven Subtasks for Planning and Scheduling.

changes in policies for overtime, or extra manpower requirements. The types and phases of analysis will be the same, but the details and actual issues are different.

Not all planners, schedulers, and dispatchers actually do these steps in any recognizable way, but many of the good ones do. They organize their time and focus, and have a daily routine of what to look at in what order. They intuitively decompose the work and most just do it subconsciously. Some may even consciously think through the best way to get their job done. On the other hand, there are the spastic planners and schedulers whose processes defy any logic. In some cases, these spastic planners and schedulers never get beyond step 3. They are only reacting to problems.

If you do not have a conscious and reflective approach to how you plan or schedule, it might be time that you thought about having one. It is important to start thinking about each of the tasks consciously, documenting them, getting your manager or peers to understand the tasks, and thinking about how to improve your processes or tools for each task. Conscious reflection and thinking is needed to improve production control processes. This involves where information comes from, what kinds of tools are needed, and how quality and accuracy can be improved. It is also important for training your backup and for protecting the knowledge that you have acquired. What happens if you retire or quit?

SITUATION ASSESSMENT

The situation assessment starts as soon as you awake. The news and weather are the first sources of key information. What is considered key? Anything that might impact the acquisition of material, performance by a subcontractor, the factory itself, distribution to the customer, and the customer. Surely, sales and purchasing should be the ones to worry about some of this information? That is true, but they do not start work until later in the day and the production control process needs this information at the crack of dawn or before. An accident on a highway, announced road closures associated with weather, status of union and management talks at the customer or vendor, or news about financial difficulty will all be clues about the future.

Further assessment occurs as you arrive at the factory. What cars are in the parking lot, what trucks are in the yard, and what lights are on are also clues about the day to come. Discussions and chats while walking to the office also provide key information about the state of the manufacturing process. The walk through the plant may be a bit circuitous or straightforward. Suspected hot spots might be visited or inspected. The way work is piled, the state of machines, and the body language of workers are all clues. Even the smell of production can provide insights, as can the temperature of parts stacked along the wall. Phone calls will be placed and friends contacted to find out what is happening, or has happened, or is expected to happen in different parts of the plant.

There are many possible sources of information. For example, depending on the firm, e-mail will also yield clues: the number and frequency of e-mails about a specific subject may imply an impending crisis if the number and frequency is increasing. For example, Ralph was observed to move a particular job from Tuesday to Monday. When asked why, Ralph said that he noticed e-mails increasing in the last week about a perceived problem in production. *So? What has this to do with moving work from Tuesday to Monday?* Usually, when the e-mail traffic about any production topic started to get fast and furious, there would be a special meeting held. *So?* The meetings usually took place on Tuesdays. *So?* All of the key supervisors and production experts will be at the meeting. *So?* Without the usual amount of supervision and production support on the floor, there is a chance that the production quantity and quality might be at risk. *Ah! The job moved from Tuesday to Monday was a high-profile job that needed to be done correctly; quantity and quality.* The components on the part were relatively rare and Ralph did not want to take a chance of a production error. It did not have a high priority in the normal scheme of things, but if a problem occurred during its production, it would suddenly have a very high priority. It all started with the e-mail traffic. And yes, there was a meeting on the Tuesday as he predicted would happen; production was also not smooth.

These types of clues are all early indicators of problems and are all beyond the scope and ability of computerized data collection tools such as MES. For example, the gossip about someone's partying on the weekend can provide insight about operator performance way before the measurement gauges indicate the parts are being made out of specification. It is far better to avoid the problem in the first place than detect it after the parts have been made, or the shipment is delayed, or when the material runs out.

There is another set of information also being gathered. Yesterday, there was a plan and sequence for expected production activity. What was really done though? You will likely want to do a quick look-see to determine what was really made according to plan and what went awry. Yes, yes, yes. Of course you could wait until you get into the office, turn on the computer, and then access the inventory and production records, look at all of the ERP screens, and then compare against the plan. However, this is a slow process and your capability to scan and assess, in general aggregate terms, is tremendous compared to the time and effort it would take to acquire the same factory information using a bunch of computer screens. Furthermore, answers to "What do we do now?" are likely to be expected as soon as the office is reached and time does not exist to browse the manufacturing status leisurely. Not all schedulers will do the extended look-see, but many do it. The truth is out there — on the floor, what you can see and touch, not always in the computer.

CRISIS IDENTIFICATION

Not all information has the same decision-making value. Some of the information will be next to useless, while other information will be very special and valuable. You really should not care too much about what went as expected. You should care about what did not and what will not. Any information that pertains to the exceptions will be of the most value and the most interest.

The interpretation of the information becomes key. However, information cannot be interpreted in a vacuum or out of context. The interpretation requires a basis for comparison and for pattern recognition. For example, *the last time it was hot and humid in the summer, this particular molded part had trouble with the sand castings.* This type of interpretation requires knowledge of what has gone on in the past: the exceptions, the causes, the effects, and the recovery options. At one foundry, this was a real issue as certain castings produced in the humid weather required six times the number of attempts to get a good part compared to producing the same casting in the winter. Six times is not a simple 10 percent difference in yield and this was a significant hit on capacity at the foundry. Either you will have to have a very good memory or you must rely on recordkeeping to help you out. Some schedulers keep little black books tracking anything odd that happens and they can use this information in the future to refresh their memories. One scheduler kept track of what line made a part last, anything special about the crew and process, and anything special about a production run; if it went well or not. Does it sound like work and a pain in the butt to keep track of all of this stuff? Well, no one said it would be easy, now did they? This particular chap was also that lazy guy we keep talking about; our champion scheduler, Ralph. He had to make an investment and do some work to reap the future rewards.

Just as information has varying degrees of utility, the crises or problems also have variation. Not all crises have the same impact and importance. Hence, it is important for you to know what crisis is more important than another. It will be impossible for you to deal with all problems all of the time and the final solution will be a compromise. The immediate crises with far-reaching or high monetary impact need to be identified from the mundane. This can create some interesting dynamics as every supervisor or product manager sincerely believes that their problem is of the utmost priority and should be addressed before all others.

By now, you have now gathered information from a myriad of sources and have interpreted it. The interpretation has created a set of either real or perceived crises. This whole process can take a few minutes or substantially longer depending on the size of the plant, number of activities within the plant, and access to information. It is hampered when there are multiple people doing the planning and scheduling, or when replacement schedulers are used to cover for you.

IMMEDIATE RESEQUENCING AND TASK REALLOCATION

At the crack of dawn, there are usually very few options available to you. It might be too early for the manufacturing engineers to be on duty, the subcontractor's offices to be open, customers to be at their desks, key managers in the plant, ad infinitum. About the only thing you can do is to choose other work already in the queue to work on. You might be able to play with quantities, where the work is assigned, when to do it, and who does it. Work can be preempted if there are setup crews available and if the tooling and fixtures are ready for the next job. It might also be possible to reassign work to alternate resources or to pick an alternate material. This is all under the resequencing and reallocation set of options. Later in the day, there will be more options to investigate and it is possible that some of the earlier decisions will be reopened and adjusted.

Unfortunately, any resequencing and reallocation of resources will create other problems as the schedule is adjusted. Adjusting one job may require the adjustment of several jobs, or dozens of jobs, as the impact ripples and ricochets around. Hence, solving one crisis yields many little baby problems that also need to be dealt with. You should have the skills and ability to recognize the impacts and minimize them. Again, not all have the skill and not all can learn it. In addition to having the time to do the resequencing, it requires skill and good thinking to make good resequencing decisions. And as we all know, thinking hurts. It is easier to ignore the future and assume that the future will look after itself. However, if the thinking is not done, the pain just gets worse, and the little problems become tomorrow's big problems.

The challenge in the resequencing and reallocation decision is rapid and accurate assessment of the ripple and ricochet effect. If the situation can be comprehended, it is possible for you to minimize the damage downstream. It is important to do this checklist consciously until it is an automatic process:

- What is affected?
- What is arbitrary?
- What can be delayed without problem?
- Is a different quantity or substitute product possible?
- What can be brought ahead in the schedule without problem?
- Is it possible to use another resource?
- Can you do it in another way? Is there a different process or method?
- Can you use a different material?

This list needs to be done for the immediate crisis and for anything affected by resequencing and reallocation. Failing to think it through will result in another "Oh, crap!" later in the day.

It is important to recognize that at this point, you are changing things that you have direct authority or influence over and that do not need managerial meetings or major negotiations. You will be doing minor shifts in demand movement, small schedule changes in shipping, varying the finished goods inventory levels a bit, and requesting the lowering or raising of any short-term capacity options to pull back or push on production. The players, options, tactics, information, and strategies in your realm will be different if you are a scheduler or a planner. The planner will be looking at options in the next week, month, fiscal quarter, or year. There are different people involved, different policies, and options to consider. A scheduler or dispatcher is working on today or this week; it is a different game. In a production control department with multiple planners and schedulers, a scheduler cannot be assumed to be plug-compatible with a planner immediately unless training and skills are addressed. It takes time and training to learn the players, the rules of the game, and how the rules can be bent, folded, stapled, and otherwise mutilated. This is in addition to knowing and learning about the manufacturing specifics; the parts, routings, and manufacturing issues that need to be understood.

The end of this task can often represent the first chance you can take a deep breath. This might be the first time to stretch and think about things calmly. Prior to this, everyone is involved and all departments are focused until the immediate dispatching decisions are squared away. There are usually people hovering, waiting for the return phone call, and verifying or clarifying instructions. It is usually impossible to do anything except get another coffee. For someone to entertain thoughts of having you take the time to explain anything to them is dangerous to their health. You do not have the time then to help someone understand what they should understand already. At this point in the day, you might have little patience and you can get grumpy very quickly. Maybe you do not, maybe you do.

This is one of the stress phases and it is our speculation that if decision support tools like scheduling systems do not address this phase adequately and fail to actually *help* you, it is unlikely that any more than lip service will be given the tool. As soon as the manager, consultant, or information technology person turns their back, the systems will not be used or used in the spirit in which they were purchased because they simply do not help you. It sounds obvious, but it is amazing how many systems exist and get purchased without asking the simple question of whether or not the system will actually help the planner or scheduler in their stress tasks or if the system will make things worse.

COMPLETE SCENARIO UPDATE

Up to this point, the focus has been on partial decision making with partial information. At the first opportunity, you should access and update your complete view of the current situation. Perhaps this is reviewing key production statistics for the past day or looking at a stock-out report for part shortages. It is possible that production reporting needs to be checked and verified to ensure that errors do not propagate. For example, was the date entered wrong? Was the weight entered for the part count? Was the wrong work center credited with rework activity?

This step would include the review of any new demand or forecasts and possible comparison with prior data. Is the demand moving in or out? Is the demand going up or down? Are there any stupid numbers in the demand stream?

The complete scenario should not be built up blindly in a mechanical fashion. Things should be checked and thought about as the scenario is updated. If you are a planner, you will want to know what the capacity side of the profile is and what the demand side is. These are the major characteristics that the planner has to take into account. However, if you are a scheduler, you will be building up a profile of expected changes in the future; things like line changes, material changes, engineering changes, and personnel changes. Any future change to the system is part of the scenario update.

You and the production plan did not just drop out of the sky last night. There were expectations and plans about all kinds of things, such as maintenance, product, marketplace, human resources, purchasing, shipping, receiving, and facilities. This is one of the problems with some academic studies of scheduling skill and scheduling system usage. In a lab or in a controlled environment, a schedule or a demand is presented and the person asked or expected to craft a schedule. This is equivalent to waking up from a coma in your real factory and being asked to make a schedule in the next few minutes. In the real world, this does not happen and does not make sense. There is no big bang and a sudden appearance of machines, materials, crews, and orders out of thin air. You bring to the daily scheduling and planning tasks knowledge of the past, expectations of the future, and suspicions about what might be going on without your explicit knowledge. This is why some lab experiments on scheduling yield questionable and often uninsightful results. The researchers are not studying the real process in which a planner or scheduler functions and where their skill comes into play.

FUTURE PROBLEM IDENTIFICATION

Good schedulers periodically do a complete scenario of what the future looks like for one major reason: they want to see if there is any crap heading their way. Crap is not good. Crap implies meetings and good schedulers sincerely hate meetings. Crap implies panicking and stress-generating activities. Good schedulers hate crap. Novice schedulers, or the challenged ones, do not do the full scenario update described above or fail to pick up the clues to impending crap. For some reason, crap does not bother everyone to the same degree, and either people get used to it or they enjoy the adrenaline rush.

Remember Ralph? Ralph did a lot of future problem identification. He would track and monitor his world consciously for about three months into the future. Anything in the next twelve-week zone was of interest to him. The tiniest bit of gossip would be of interest. About anything and anyone. Why? Anything to him that affected the status quo was a problem to deal with. A planned improvement to the production process was initially a problem to him. He had to deal with the period of time before the improvement, the instability during the improvement's introduction, and the learning curve immediately after. The improvement might make his life easier in the long term, but it was a problem and a pain he had to deal with until the situation stabilized. Ralph could either orchestrate the situation to minimize the pain or he could take it square between the eyes with full force. Since he was not a masochist, he preferred the path of least pain. Each week, he would consciously review a number of topics and see if there was anything different two, four, six, eight, ten, and twelve weeks in the future. The topics were wide ranging. Was a tour planned? Were the seasons changing from spring to summer? Was a key vendor or customer doing anything unusual during the time period, such as line upgrades or a new product introduction?

Ralph would have a plan in his head that was feasible if everything held the course. He would then actively search the future for anything that would mess up his plan. Of course, he would not do this every day. About once a week, he would do his checklist. He would also reflect on the significance of gossip and news about the future as it arrived at his desk.

Why was he so good at this? We suspect there were a few key traits, one of which was his background. He had only been scheduling for about six months when we started to work with him. However, he had been working in the plant for about fifteen years and had worked in almost all departments. He had done things like driving the forklift trucks, being a line technician, and working in shipping and receiving. He had many jobs over the years and knew the manufacturing system from top to bottom. He knew the good and bad patterns in almost every area, knew what the status quo should look like, and knew the clues that would indicate the potential for future doom and gloom. Not only had he worked in the various departments, he had learned and internalized the knowledge he gained. Ralph was a thinker. He was also very sociable, enjoyed chatting, and was obviously liked by the other workers. He was a good communicator.

It is a good idea to copy some of Ralph's behavior if you can. Once a week, perform a 2-4-6-8-10 check. Think about what might be coming down the tracks. Some of the topics to consider are:

- New products being introduced or prototypes being built
- Product changes
- Products phasing out
- New materials — different types, different specs
- New methods being introduced
- Machine upgrades or installations
- Major training exercises — who, when, attitude, results
- Changes at the key vendors — facilities, organization, products, processes
- Changes at the key customers — facilities, organization, products, processes
- Changes in the marketplace — marketing efforts, sales
- Fiscal or corporate milestones or events
- Preventative maintenance activities
- Social events — plant, firm, community
- Weather events — storms, heat, humidity, start of winter, start of hunting season
- Something being made on a different resource than normal
- Something being made that has not been made for a long time
- Something being made that has not been made since the machine was upgraded

All of these types of events, and many more, can signal a potential drop in capacity, productivity, or a change in demand. Anything that changes the normal is a potential source of risk. Ask yourself "What is different?" and then think about it. If you think it will be a problem or a potential problem, then you should do some planning in advance. Can you avoid or minimize the problem? This is the focus of the next section: how you can discount the problem!

CONSTRAINT RELAXATION AND FUTURE PROBLEM RESOLUTION

A constraint is something that forces you to do something or not to do something. For example, an industrial engineering request or mandate to use a specific machine for a specific part is a constraint. This is a constraint that forces you into a limited set of options. A management policy about allowing overtime except during the last weekend of the month is another type of constraint. This constraint allows you more options by forcing you away from a set of possible options. To complicate matters, some constraints (like sizes, weights, and temperatures) might be considered hard constraints and impossible to alter. Other constraints (like the recommended batch size or the policy about which operator to choose) may be soft and can be manipulated. Often a schedule or plan cannot be made unless something bends or someone relaxes a policy, and that is what this section is about.

Once the future has been reviewed and thought about, you need to make decisions about anything special. Specifically, does anything special have to be done in the immediate or near-term future to avoid or minimize problems perceived in the future? If not, you can proceed with just doing simple assignments: using setup information, processing time, machine requirements, and due dates to make sequencing decisions. This is the scheduling by rote described in the next section.

If there are special issues to deal with, you have a number of options to play with. Since the issues are in the future, you can consider the various constraints that restrict decisions and perhaps alter them. For example, you can request that certain machines be upgraded or tweaked in advance of certain work arriving. You can think about certain work that can be subcontracted. You can request that any new work, methods, or processes only be introduced for day shift, Tuesday through Thursday, and avoid evenings and weekends. You can request that an alternative process be qualified and you can think about splitting batches. How about possibly negotiating different quantities or delivery patterns? There are many options. Some will be harder to do than others. A plan can be crafted with any of these assumptions and raised up the flag pole to see if anyone salutes it, or shoots it down. All of these types of options cost money or require other people to actually craft the solutions, so you can only recommend and manipulate.

OK, we can hear your muttering. This stuff is easy for us to say. This section is indeed easier to write than to actually practice. Think about it. To do this well, you need to know how the products are made, alternatives, things to ask for, what options have been used in the past, and what options could work in the future. You need to know what it takes to get the show on the road and you need to know who to talk to about doing the show. Of course, you do not need to know all of the precise details of what size wrench to use, but you need to know that something can be done that probably could use a wrench. You need to understand how support groups like maintenance, quality, manufacturing engineering, industrial engineering, traffic, and purchasing can help you.

Do not rely on others to identify the problems in advance and have everything in place. It should be assumed that they will address their own future problems actively, but do not assume that everything that you know, they know.

It is you who really knows and hears about all of the problems with the last industrial engineering solution or the last trucking bandage. It is you who sets the expectations and knows the results. You are the one who knows what the necessary level of capacity is and are also probably the only one in the room to know what the future mix of job requirements will look like. There is another angle to consider. Some of the supporting departments are very fluid with promotions and job movement. It is possible that you and some floor supervisors are the only ones to remember or have been part of prior solutions. You and others with a similar past are the plant's living history repository. There might be other long-term memory banks in other departments as well, but their focus will be on their own problems and topic areas.

Why is planning and scheduling a wealth of long-term information? When was the last time you heard of a career path for the scheduler, or a scheduler getting promoted, or being transferred to another factory in the area of production control? The production control department may be a temporary position for a management trainee, but scheduling is not a mobile career in most firms. Once you become a planner or scheduler, that might be it. You might become the production control supervisor if you are lucky and they do not fill that position with management trainees. How often are schedulers head-hunted by an outside firm? If the firm perhaps paid you what you are worth, you might be. You are probably going to be a lifer and will be retiring with your favorite pencil. In short, the long-term schedulers and planners need to have a key role in the problem-solving discussions as they are likely to have seen more and have more pieces of the puzzle than the others.

There is an interesting dynamic with constraints and how constraints are enforced. Some constraints are very firm, backed by policies, and documented in standards. There might be firm guidelines specified for batch sizes, overtime during the week, levels of inventory, or specific machines to use. These are the types of constraints that are usually enforced until the crap hits the fan. Once the crap gets closer, it is interesting to watch formerly firm edicts turn to jelly-like consistencies. A former edict to only use one specific machine for an operation turns into "any machine that can get close to the specifications." A former edict not to do overtime, or to subcontract, turns into a mad hunt for people willing to work, or for firms to take on the work. These are the types of constraint relaxation that constantly occur.

SCHEDULING BY ROTE

Finally, the last step of your morning routine. The fires have been put out and some others started indirectly. The immediate dispatching decisions have been made, the future has been reviewed, and appropriate countermeasures initiated. However, the plan and schedule are not yet finished. All of the remaining work, not yet started, has to be sequenced and assigned to resources. This is the stuff that computers are good at. All of the hard, context-sensitive decisions have been made and cast in concrete. The remaining decisions are simple and routine. They do not require much human judgment and they can be sequenced easily using many of the traditional methods. The decisions and sequencing at this stage are also done well by combining some minor human tuning with automated systems.

This step is pure sequencing. As a vice president once said, you have setup and processing times, quantities, due dates, and a list of required machines per operation; what else do you need to know? At this step in the decision process, and for many factories, nothing else. This information is sufficient to take the list of work and generate a sequence. Of course, if there are strange or extreme relationships between setups and queue times, there will have to be more complicated logic. Outside of these strange types of relationships, the information used for scheduling in this phase is relatively black and white, and is quantitative. You do not have to worry that Rick is working the night shift or that the solder machine will be unstable for the next shift. You have already taken those aspects into account and dealt with them. The rest of the work is mechanical scheduling and requires little or no human judgment.

This is the fast part. You are flying. The hurting is gone and you develop a bit of a glazed look. The hands are a blur as work is assigned and the remaining part of the schedule is filled up. It might not be sequenced optimally, but the majority of it may be different in twenty-four hours anyway.

CHANGES TO TASKS

Care must be taken when changing your routine. Are you affecting the timing or frequency of one of the tasks? Is it going to make a task harder or easier? What can you do within each of these tasks to make it easier for yourself? These are important questions. Changes to the status quo are important to think about for the actual production process. The same applies to the planning and scheduling tasks.

A change to the planning and scheduling routine during a peak or stress time might not be a good idea. If it is decided to include more work centers for detailed scheduling, what will this impact? What preparatory work will be needed? What additional information will be needed as a base and what information needs to be accessed or acquired each day? New duties and activities must be analyzed with respect to the seven steps. What will take more time and what will take less? Any impact on training?

The impact on the planning and scheduling task can be linked directly to increasing the scope of the job: more machines and more work. Each additional machine, job, or part has a potential impact. Impact can also arise from changes to how planning and scheduling is actually done. One factory had a tool introduced that moved certain tasks from 9 AM to 7 AM, increased the time horizon for planning consideration, and changed the level of detail from shifts to hours. Additional reports and expectations were also added. The initial introduction of the tool was a failure, pilot project stopped, and the project failure analyzed. The tool was changed to address the tasks and the impacts on the tasks. The tool was then usable.

SUMMARY

We have identified and discussed seven key tasks that schedulers and planners do each day:

1. Situation assessment
2. Crisis identification
3. Immediate resequencing and task reallocation
4. Complete scenario update
5. Future problem identification
6. Constraint relaxation and future problem resolution
7. Scheduling by rote

The amount of time and effort spent on each task will differ with the factory and situation in which you find yourself. Some of the task details can be formalized and practiced by you. For example, you might have a conscious check weekly on the future changes or you can keep a little black book on past decisions and results.

We find it interesting that the vast majority of scheduling research and solutions have been focused on the last and seventh task, and have largely ignored the first six. The consultants and researchers normally are helping you where you do not need the real help. You need real help with the first six, the six done under pressure, and with tight time constraints. Really neat models and methods are presented for the easy tasks in step seven and the focus is on the stuff that is done under relaxed conditions; and the presenters wonder why you are less than thrilled. Some of the scheduling tools, mostly custom, some commercial, do assist with other tasks. For example, systems can help you by drawing your attention to problem areas or they can provide exception reports that highlight significant deviations. Almost all scheduling systems will show work that is late or behind schedule, but none will help you by telling you that an unwanted part was made instead of a desired part on a machine that you did not want to make it, using material targeted for yet a third part. Even custom or unique systems cannot do that.

The following chapter gets personal and explores what planners and schedulers are really like and how this relates to their hiring and training.

6

THE HIRING AND TRAINING OF SCHEDULERS AND PLANNERS

PREDIGESTED THOUGHTS FOR THE BUSY PERSON

■ Planning, scheduling, and dispatching are **problem-solving** cognitive skills and not everyone can do them.

■ Cognitive skills need to be developed consciously if they are to be improved and if the thinking is to go beyond the superficial aspects.

■ The hiring and training of good production control personnel may be one of the most important decisions in the plant, but is rarely thought about that way.

■ The planners and schedulers need to manage their knowledge. They need to be given the tools to acquire, manage, and disseminate their knowledge and the results of their decisions.

INTRODUCTION

The first five chapters have not really addressed the planner or scheduler as an individual or a person. We talked about objectives of the department, various roles, functions, and activities that may be done as part of production control, but who is this person — the scheduler? In this chapter, we will get into the individual characteristics of a planner or scheduler.

There are a number of possible questions when we start thinking about the individual. Who should you hire as a planner or scheduler? What skills should they have? What should they know? What makes a good scheduler versus a bad one? How does one proceed from a novice scheduler to an expert one? How do you know how good the scheduler is? If you are a planner or scheduler, how do you know how good you are?

In this chapter, we will attempt to address these questions. We do not have all of the answers. It is possibly the hardest position to fill within a plant. The following sections discuss the type of knowledge that a scheduler needs to function and the skills and attributes that a scheduler should exhibit. This chapter is mainly written from the perspective of a production control supervisor or manager. If you are a planner or scheduler, you can read this chapter in a self-assessment kind of way and contemplate how close you are to our descriptions. What are your strengths and weaknesses? How can you improve yourself?

KNOWLEDGE

It is one of our key assumptions that scheduling is primarily a cognitive skill. What does this mean? Cognitive skill is associated with the mind and relates to the person's ability to do mental reasoning and thinking. Activities such as bridge and chess require cognitive skill. This is in contrast with activities that are primarily physical, such as hammering a nail, or activities that require both mental and physical skill, such as the ability to play music well. Consider chess for a moment. What does it take to be a master chess player? Obviously, you need to know the basic rules of chess, but you also need to know strategies that work for a given situation and you have to be able to look at the board and see what could happen in the future. Not only do you have to deal with what you want to do, you have to analyze and think about what your opponent is going to do. To become a grand master chess player, it takes approximately ten years of constant practice. During those ten years, players develop the cognitive skills necessary to respond to their opponent's actions and to visualize moves into the future. They have many experiences to learn from and many opportunities to fine tune their game. Similarly, a scheduler must understand:

- Basic concepts of manufacturing — production, inventory, MRP logic
- Unique or situational aspects of the firm itself — anything nonstandard

- Products and processes of the firm
- Demand, production requirements
- Production capability — where, how, who
- Where things come from, where things go to
- Expected results of any production activity — durations, yield, side effects
- Relationships and interdependencies between the factors

...and how all of these can be orchestrated in order that demand can be met. Schedulers need to also have an understanding of:

- The present state of all of these variables — capability, availability, quantities, yield, location, quality
- The relationships between these variables, e.g., the conflicting relation between efficiency and service level
- The degrees of freedom or amount of elasticity in each variable
- The future or anticipated state of the variables

SKILLS AND ATTRIBUTES

This knowledge base is crucial for a scheduler. For any reasonably sized shop, the required knowledge is immense. The vast majority of schedulers probably have had a decade or more of experience in their factory, or similar factory, and have worked in many parts of the plant. You do not find too many, spanking new, eighteen-year-olds in planning and scheduling. It is through experience that the bulk of the necessary background knowledge is acquired. The best schedulers have the ability to keep the majority of the information about the present and immediate future in their heads. The result can be considered a mental map or schema of their world. The ability to create and maintain the mental map is critical. A good memory and attention to detail are two skills that a good scheduler will need. If the scheduler cannot create or maintain an accurate mental model of the factory and what is going on where, it is doubtful that the scheduler will be able to be effective.

- Excellent memory
- Attention to detail

These two required skills are not sufficient though. They provide the data and the picture, but really do not capture the total package of what makes a good scheduler. The good scheduler also needs to be inquisitive, creative, and have a love of puzzle or problem solving. With approximately 10 percent of a scheduler's decisions requiring human judgment and problem resolution, the ability to gather loosely coupled data and make use of them to fix a crisis is important. This 10 percent probably makes up the key set of decisions for the scheduler. The only way a scheduler can create options is to be curious, ask questions, know what questions to ask, and be able to use the information later when needed. The best schedulers get excited by being faced with a seemingly impossible mess and love the challenge of sorting it out. They must love neat and orderly situations. That is the goal of sorting out the mess, things happening when they should.

- Inquisitive nature
- Creativity
- Love of puzzle solving
- Personal need for neatness and orderliness

They also need to have the ability to develop and use strategies. This is what separates a reactive scheduler from a proactive one. The proactive ones will use strategies that incorporate more of the future, the anticipating and manipulating. These strategies are relatively sophisticated heuristics, rules of thumb, that help the scheduler anticipate future difficulties and attempt avoidance or minimization. After all, what good is the knowledge or information if you cannot use it?

- Ability to develop and use planning strategies

A plan gathering dust on a scheduler's desk is not a good plan. The plan and schedule must be communicated to others. A scheduler who lacks personal communication skills will be largely ineffective. He or she must be approachable, sincerely interested in every bit of gossip or insider information being shared, and love talking with others. While it may look like the scheduler is not doing anything and is having a prolonged coffee break, the scheduler may in fact be working and working hard. It is not easy being an information sponge all of the time. Along with basic communication ability, the scheduler must be a salesperson and negotiator. A plan will never make everyone happy about everything. It is a compromise and everyone will be dissatisfied to a point. The scheduler must be able to persuade, sell, and get cooperation from people he or she is making unhappy. Often plans call for extra effort or work that is beyond the call of duty and the scheduler must be able to cajole, sometimes with bribes such as pastry or coffee. Remember, the scheduler does not actually build anything and really has no authority; the production and support departments must be manipulated.

- Communication
- Negotiation
- Sales and marketing

All of this activity is done under stress, noise, confusion, and harassment. The results must be perceived as being fair and just. No single department or area can be perceived as getting special treatment on a regular basis. Your scheduler must be level headed and while some occasional temper tantrums and flare ups are unavoidable, the scheduler must be able to concentrate, work coolly, and do it all without taking criticism personally. Almost everything is the scheduler's fault. Absolutely nothing that the scheduler decides is right.

- Fairness
- Level headed, cool thinker
- Thick skinned

What do these traits mean? You have an even-tempered soul who usually is a saint, knows everything, enjoys the thrill of converting messes into successes, and can sell snow to Eskimos. That is our scheduler. Well, almost.

We have noted before that one attribute of a good scheduler is laziness. Laziness is important because it helps drive the objective function and encourages the scheduler to have a smoothly running shop. However, you can be lazy and still be a very poor scheduler. Laziness does not mean that the person is actually inactive or is slacking off; it merely means that the person wants to be doing less and wants to be slacking off. Whether or not the scheduler ever actually gets to relax is a different question.

- Laziness

Bad schedulers rarely last a long time in a factory and most of the schedulers are pretty good at most of the tasks associated with scheduling and planning. Few are like Ralph, but most do a good job.

HIRING

If you interview or hire a scheduler, you should ask questions that probe these fourteen skills and characteristics:

1. Excellent memory
2. Attention to detail
3. Fairness
4. Level headed, cool thinker
5. Thick skinned
6. Communication
7. Negotiation
8. Sales and marketing
9. Ability to develop and use planning strategies
10. Inquisitive nature
11. Creativity
12. Love of puzzle solving
13. Personal need for neatness and orderliness
14. Laziness

You should want to know where the prospective scheduler is in each of these. If an expert scheduler is being sought, you should expect to find strong evidence of many of these traits. Perhaps one in a hundred schedulers would have a complete set of strong skills: the grand master. We suspect that grand master schedulers are rare. In discussing expertise and cognitive skills, it is common to describe five levels of expertise.

The top level is your grand master, the person who is truly world class, or is the best-of-class performer. A grand master has great breadth, depth, and has internalized the clue collection and processing. It is automatic and they will make few errors in assessment. They will know almost all of the constraints and issues that will affect the total production process from the suppliers to the customers. The fourth level is the expert scheduler who can beat the pants off most people. They will know the history, the reasons, the issues, and possible options. They usually will be proactive and anticipate many of the future problems. While they may know many system-wide issues, the decision making is more of a conscious process and is not as automatic as it is for the grand master. The third level is journeyman and is a nice career level. This is the typical level for experienced schedulers. A journeyman should be expected to detect many of the future problems and be able to make decisions from receiving through shipping. The journeyman will know the routings, processes, setups, part specifications, and any special or unusual manufacturing quirks. He/she will know what is supposed to be where for most of production, without looking it up, and what is supposed to happen in the next day or two. The first level is novice and the second is intermediate. The planners and schedulers at levels one and two will rely on lookup sheets, will miss many problems, create situations that are not feasible, and will not have an effective information system. The schedules generated by level one and two schedulers should be reviewed, and the review used as a learning experience. How would you know a level one from a level two? Hard question. Here is possibly one way to think about that question. A level-two scheduler should be good enough that they can be left alone on the weekend without much worry and without much management review of decisions. If the weekend production supervisor has to discuss and review almost all of the decisions with the scheduler, the scheduler is still at level one.

We have just described a five-level view of scheduler and planner performance. This is a problem. Many firms have just two levels for the job title, junior and senior. This two-level job scheme is insufficient to segment and clarify scheduler performance and improvement. A two-level scheme does not create a great structure for career advancement. The senior title covers the journeyman, expert, and grand master. The junior covers novice and intermediate. The two-level view does not provide sufficient separation in remuneration or other forms of recognition.

It is critical to know what level of scheduler you are looking for and what you can afford. While schedulers and planners are rarely paid what they are worth, there are differences between the novices and experts. That is step one. Step two is being able to assess applicants and know what they are and where they are in their development. If you already have a senior scheduler who is close to retirement, it would be wise to hire a novice or intermediate scheduler to work alongside the senior person. Succession planning is very important in production control.

If you are interviewing someone who is currently scheduling, ask them:

- How they currently schedule — the morning routine, sequence of tasks, and decisions
- What information they use
- How they get this information
- What kinds of problems they encounter and how they solve them
- What kinds of things they anticipate and look for in the future
- How they anticipate the future problems, what information is used
- What their idea is of a good schedule or plan
- How others react to their plans
- Are their plans followed, and if not, why
- What strategies they use to smooth production, avoid problems
- How they repair a plan if they pull a job short, or if a job overshoots its targets
- How they think that they could do their job better
- What tools or aids they think would have helped them

Hiring a novice is a different problem. They have never scheduled before. They might be a fresh graduate out of college or someone coming from the shop floor. In this case, you can try to get a read on temperament, attitude, and general approach to problem solving.

In both cases, experienced and inexperienced, you can assess their general knowledge about manufacturing systems, inventory theory, and operations management. You can probe their understanding of the basic processes. If you are in a chemical plant, what do they know about chemical plants dock to dock; if you are in a metal stamping plant, what do they know about presses, forming metal, steel characteristics, and dies?

Someone totally lacking in one of our fourteen skills and attributes is likely to be a problem. You can improve someone's communication, but they need some starting point. If someone cannot handle the pressure — short of a nervous breakdown, recovery, and medication — it is unlikely they will ever be able to deal with the pressures associated with production control. You do not need the problem, neither do they. If someone can handle details, they can handle your details. If someone can manage, coach, and negotiate, it is likely they will be able to do so for you. However, if someone cannot get along with others and is not a team-oriented person, it is doubtful that you can transform the proverbial sow's ear into a silk purse.

In union situations, various people will be able to post into a position with a minimum of requirements. This is independent of the skills and attributes we have listed. Often unions use simple seniority and equivalent job classification schemes. In these situations, several candidates may have to be given a fair chance at scheduling before the person deemed more suitable is given the opportunity. This can extend the period without effective scheduling by many months. It also makes life interesting since the individuals have to be evaluated based on scheduling skill and aptitude. If the scheduling and planning tasks are unaffiliated with the union, these problems can be reduced. If they are affiliated, or if they have to be, you have to live with it. If you have a choice, avoid affiliating the planning and scheduling tasks with the union.

EVALUATION AND PROBATIONARY PERIODS

It is commonplace to have probationary periods and evaluations; with or without a union. How do you evaluate a scheduler?

This is not easy and is perhaps one of the hardest topics in the book to write about. In the various books on production control, this is one topic that is usually absent. We have approached the problem of scheduler evaluation as follows:

- Typical task performance — speed trials
- Basic knowledge — plant, products, parts, process, machines, routings
- Error tracking — things overlooked and mistakes made

The expanded descriptions for the three types of evaluation are:

- First, there are the typical tasks that a scheduler should do in a given day, or on a specific day. Can they get these done on time? This is the simplest and most straightforward test. A new scheduler cannot be expected to produce the same output in the same time as an existing expert. The goal should be adjusted using reasonable expectations, agreed to by all parties in advance, and then measured. If the candidate cannot deliver the basic quantity of goods, then there is no point talking about other aspects. It might be politically correct to suggest that the quality of the schedule matters more than a complete schedule and all of the reports and other outputs, but it does not really. If there is no schedule for part of the plant, that is worse than a schedule that is somewhat right that the supervisor can vet and reinterpret. With no input, the floor supervisor would be totally lost, not merely in a fog.

- Second, it is possible to create a quiz or interview guideline that tests the candidate's basic knowledge of the shop processes. A target can be set in advance for passing the test. After a reasonable time on the job, the scheduler should be held accountable for creating a decent mental model of the shop and acquiring some fluency in the terminology, concepts, and situation. This knowledge should include what is relevant for your factory. This can include things such as setup information, typical batch sizes, what machines or resources are used, if there are special operator requirements, capability of machines, sequence-dependent issues of running A then B versus B then A, what materials are used in multiple products, what products and processes are low risk to run, and what products and processes are high risk.

- Third, it is possible to measure scheduler performance during the evaluation period. A good scheduler has to be capable of quick learning and avoid mistakes previously made. In this case, errors and problems attributed to the scheduler can be tracked and monitored. The same mistakes should decrease during the training period and similar mistakes should not be repeated. This can cover errors such as those associated with misreading or misusing manufacturing status information and overlooking hot jobs. It would be nice to suggest that hard and fast rules could be given, that an expert scheduler should only miss a hot job once in a four-week period. No such luck. We have no idea how to get to that place using generalities. You can sit down in a specific factory, discuss errors, frequency, and set targets. In general, you can discuss mistakes as they occur, their causes, and how to avoid them. If the individual learns and improves, then they are going in the right direction. If there is little or no evidence of improvement and learning, the individual might not belong in production control.

Some people try to measure scheduler performance based on the inventory levels, utilization, and other such metrics. This would be fine and acceptable if the shop floor executed according to the plan and did not deviate. Usually the shop floor is not that obedient and subservient. Furthermore, it is rare for any shop to be so reliable and predictable. But if it was, then you could set targets on manufacturing performance and relate that to scheduler performance. This is similar to the problem people have attributing improved manufacturing performance to the introduction of a scheduling tool. After the initial cleanup and introduction phase, it is hard to know if a certain schedule was better than another unless the shop floor actually follows the plan blindly and accurately. You might be able to set some aggregate levels for performance and evaluation, but care must be taken to ensure that the scheduler can actually affect them. Can the scheduler maintain the finished goods inventory level? In some factories, this will be a reasonable and feasible criterion. In Jake's factory, no. If the situation can be controlled, then you can look at measures such as inventory levels, flow times, numbers of setups, number of late jobs, amount of lateness, number of jobs that are preempted, number of jobs waiting for parts, and numbers of machines set and ready to go, but waiting for material.

TRAINING

Scheduler and planner training is another challenge. There are several factors. First, schedulers and planners usually do not have time for any formal courses and are not allowed too much time away from their hot seat. If you have ever tried to have a scheduler attend a workshop or training session off-site, you will know what we are talking about. As one put it "Not bloody likely!" Second, it is hard for them to concentrate on training while worrying about the shop and production. Since they are almost always at fault, it is not easy for them to tune out the background noise of special jobs, pending work, things to do. Third, what to actually train them in?

With many schedulers coming from the floor, it is likely that a scheduler could benefit from a solid MRP, inventory, and production control education.

This should be in the context of the firm, systems, and terminology. A general-purpose operations management course will be of marginal benefit. There is little benefit of a flow shop lecture to the scheduler who is knee deep in a job shop. They do not have the time, interest, or patience. They will want to know about the MRP options in the software system they are using that are relevant to their factory. They will be interested in examples and concepts that apply to their products and processes.

This training must include applied lessons on the dynamics of MRP and production, in the context of their MRP-II or ERP system:

- They need to know what happens if certain fences are used, orders are locked in, and requirements are regenerated.
- They need to know the relationships between the key data functions dock to dock.
- They need to be able to see and detect odd phenomena such as someone entering the weight of a batch instead of the number of pieces and what this means when the bill of material is exploded. They need to know how to fix this.
- They need to know what happens to the firm and planned orders, stock-out projections, if something is made earlier or later than planned, or when more or less is made.
- They need to know what to do to tune and adjust the loading: the number of jobs and quantities to use to resynchronize inventory levels and cycles.
- They need to know how to identify, track, reconcile, and fix errors in reporting throughout the system; from receiving to shipping.

We want to stress this point. Some schedulers do not understand the dynamics and logic behind MRP in their system. They interact with it daily and with valid naivete do not make the right adjustments in the planning horizon to avoid widespread rippling of problems. For example, some have not understood what a balanced inventory pool looks like in repetitive situations and how to recover it. They do not know how to smooth the patterns of setups and reorder points to avoid gluts and starvation. They also do not know how to interpret and manipulate the MRP settings to affect different control policies.

The schedulers and planners should be trained in basic analytical skills. They should be able to look at demand patterns, usage figures, and do simple analyses. They need to know about percentiles, averages, and variability. Most people can do averages and percentiles well enough, but rarely will a scheduler know what a standard deviation is, what it implies, how to calculate it, and how to use it.

Training is also required in formal or systemized risk management. Rather than do production control in an ad hoc fashion, it is possible to consider the future, anticipate problems, and have a set of processes in place to minimize or avoid problems consciously and consistently. We deal with this topic more in Chapter 15 when we discuss uncertainty. Often junior schedulers and planners are not aware of the clues, what they imply, and how to exploit them. Even with time, some schedulers do not learn these types of things because their heads are too close to the grinding wheel. Until things are pointed out, the view is that the future is one black hole and can only be reacted to. With a focused discussion and dialog, it is often possible to drag out and make visible the patterns, relationships, and techniques that can be used. This risk sensitivity training must also be performed for the management and support staff. The scheduler and planner will require understanding and support when they perform special sequencing that on the surface looks suboptimal, but is being done for good reasons.

It would probably be nice to think about training in communication, negotiation, and the soft skills, but a scheduler better have these necessary skills in place before becoming a scheduler. If they start without the skill, they will not last long enough to take the class.

Do they need to know scheduling theory? Yes, to a point. A scheduler should be aware of the basic principles of bottleneck manipulation, how to group similar work, use of home or preferred equipment, how to read and use capacity tools to smooth the load, where to put slack into the schedule, how to use flexible resources, when to hold resources free waiting for a job not yet in queue, when to batch split, how to analyze inventory requirements, how to calculate efficiencies and utilization, and many other things. Does a scheduler need to know the differences between the fancy algorithms in advanced tools? Probably not.

The scheduler is likely to have a number of good ideas of their own about how production control should operate and how schedules should be generated and followed, but they may be unaware of a number of other tricks and ideas to use that are in the various trade publications, texts, or are in practice at other plants. They may be focusing on one area without being aware that their destiny is really controlled by an upstream department. If they scheduled the upstream area better, any downstream areas might improve automatically. One factory was trying hard to get more efficiency out of a group of machines in a flexible manufacturing cell, a bottleneck resource. The engineers were looking at hardware changes, new floor arrangements, different palette concepts, and special work flows within the cell. The real problem was the mix being fed into the cell, and if the mix was not fixed, there would always be a problem with efficiency. There had to be a good variety of parts queued up for the cell and this was controlled by several upstream areas. By scheduling them to better feed the bottleneck, things would improve. Some changes might have been necessary in the cell anyway, but changes had to be made upstream too. This factory was not unique. Often a scheduler will be focusing on one area and will not have the time or the tools to see the larger picture and the patterns of cause and effect. Given time and support, they would see the issues, but in the stress of the moment things get away from you. Planners and schedulers should be given the encouragement, access, and time to review material relating to production control periodically and to learn about other approaches and techniques. Associations such as APICS are good sources for this type of literature. If the planners and schedulers view the job as a career with the appropriate remuneration and recognition, it is also reasonable to expect some self-learning and self-improvement. Professionals should be expected to keep up with their fields and to improve their skills without the aid or constant direction of their superiors.

If the schedulers and planners are using a scheduling tool, they will need to know how to use and manipulate the system to their benefit. They will need to know and understand why any automatic sequence was recommended; why one job of apparent equality was recommended ahead of another. The internals of the algorithm do not need to be understood, but the basic issues and trade-offs should be. The planners will need to know how to sort out problems if data downloads fail or have faulty data. They will need to know how to deal with upload problems and know what to do when the scheduling system gets out of synch with the main system. At a minimum, they will need to know how to change the resource profile, adding resources, changing capabilities, and the demand load, jobs, quantities, and due dates. They will need to know how to interpret any displays and reports in order to detect patterns that predict problems.

As the training proceeds, it is important to establish targets and feedback mechanisms for the schedulers and planners. For example, are there less communication problems and miscues with support departments? Are there fewer problems attributed to scheduling decisions? Are the schedules getting more feasible and are they making better use of the resources?

PERFORMANCE EVALUATION

The basic ideas of evaluation extend the types of things you can look at when hiring a scheduler or planner. During the hiring phase, the evaluations will be focused and of limited duration. Once someone is hired, the evaluations will become periodic, if at all. In addition to the ideas in the section on evaluation and probationary periods, there are several suggestions for how to evaluate planning performance over the long term.

The long-term evaluation process is important. Schedulers should know what they are doing and how much they are doing that is wasteful. They should know if they are creating good plans and good schedules. Their superiors should know the same information. This is hard. What can be measured?

For example, given your production forecast and normal production order size, you can look at how many setups you should have for the year, for the month, or for the week. How many setups are you doing? Can you explain the difference? You can estimate this type of metric and measure it. You can determine the minimum or maximum, compare it to your performance, and this gap is likely to be what separates you from the best performer. Jake does not track setups, does not know what they cost, and does not realize where capacity goes. If the number of unnecessary setups increases suddenly or as a slow trend, this should be a management issue or a issue for discussion. This can indicate other problems.

If you are in a repetitive situation and have regular cyclic production for the majority of your parts, you can also look at the inventory mix in work-in-process goods. If the inventory banks are healthy, certain ratios should exist between the parts if upstream resource conflict is to be avoided. For example, you determine the basic load on a cell or line based on yearly demand and how long it takes to make each part. In theory, the machinery has enough capacity to do the year's work, with time left over for good preventative maintenance. This assumes that you have enough of A while you make B, and you can do this without preempting B to make more of A quickly. This type of balance and control is not needed in "Wild West" situations, but is when you have competition and you need to avoid wasting resources. We call this type of balancing, managing *inventory health.*

Mathematically, you can figure out the desired proportions of each part relative to each other to avoid as much conflict as possible in the supplying areas. If you have sufficient capacity, you will have enough time to make each part in its cycle without preemption. In more general terms, inventory health can be viewed as your having so many parts or so many tons of parts in your work-in-process inventory. The tonnage or part count is OK, but are they the right parts? If the mix is not healthy and balanced, you will be preempting, expediting, outsourcing, and generating chaos. One study showed that over half of the inventory bank was substantially out of synch. There was a lot of chaos and expediting.

Consider using the inventory health concept as a way to measure the scheduler's performance if you have the repetitive build profile and if the manufacturing system is a reasonable performer. Not even Ralph would be able to keep the inventory bank in balance if the production lines and cells are not capable of decent predictable and reliable performance. Ralph would not have been a star at Jake's factory. However, if you can measure and track inventory health, it can be an indirect measure for smoothness, productivity, success in execution, and stability. If you cannot maintain a healthy mix in a repetitive situation, then you need to address basic manufacturing principles and fundamentals.

Planner performance can also be evaluated in a JIT situation. JIT and kanbans give automated scheduling on the factory floor, but there is still planning and thinking to do. For example, when the line is set up initially, you do not put the same number of everything everywhere and have all kanbans trigger at the same time. You analyze the situation and stagger the amounts so that a percentage of the parts will be pulled in a cyclic fashion and in a smooth, versus lumpy, way. As production demands change and process flows evolve, the kanban numbers need to be recalculated. The smoothness of the resulting manufacturing flows can be analyzed and planning quality judged. In a JIT situation, the planners must be able to detect a rising imbalance and know how to rebalance the number of bins and quantities per bin.

REDUCTIONS: RETIRING, FIRING, DOWNSIZING

Although this was a chapter on hiring and training, it is also important to reflect on what happens when a planner, scheduler, or production control supervisor quits, is fired, or is eliminated when the department is downsized. In many cases, the immediate response is extreme doom and gloom. How will you ever get anything out the door now? At one factory, management and other personnel noted no difference in production after a key person left or when the number of people in production control was further reduced. Take the output from the ERP system, generate a hot list of what is needed in the immediate future, and give it to a clerk to deal with. Why have a planner or scheduler? Obviously, the department was overstaffed to begin with.

Maybe, maybe not. It is possible that there were too many people in production control, but it is more likely that there were not enough, or not enough of the right type of person. Not everyone can be an effective scheduler; "anyone can do it" is a fallacy. It is also possible that the situation was so far out of control that no one, and no amount of effort, would make a dent in the chaos. It is possible that the person who was no longer in production control was inept and was part of the problem and not part of the solution. On the other hand, it is possible that the people making the observation did not see all of the picture and did not understand what the person really did. It is hard to judge and notice problems that are avoided, indirect costs that are not incurred, or reductions in expediting. These things are buried. It might appear that product is still being shipped "OK," and production is continuing to run "OK," but does this capture all of the things that a planner, scheduler, or production control supervisor really orchestrates and fixes? For example, a decision by a scheduler may save costs in maintenance and tooling. Another decision by a scheduler will avoid an unnecessary setup. Are setups tracked in factories? Not usually. Yes, production will continue to run through a plant without a planner or scheduler, but at what cost and at what level of chaos?

SUMMARY

We have tried to address how schedulers and planners can be hired, evaluated, and trained. This is one chapter where a self-assessment quiz is a bit tricky. We do not have one.

Our advice is to use this chapter as a checklist for what you do in your factory and production control department. When you need to hire a planner or scheduler, do you consciously think through all of the skills needed? Do you have training and education programs for planners and schedulers? How do you evaluate or track scheduler performance? Have you ever thought about doing it? If you are a planner or scheduler, how are you evaluated? Do you have a personal training agenda? How do you plan to keep your skills and knowledge current?

The next chapter looks at what information is used in production control. A planner or scheduler cannot do anything without information!

7

INFORMATION USED IN PRODUCTION CONTROL

PREDIGESTED THOUGHTS FOR THE BUSY PERSON

■ There are two main categories of information — official and environmental.

■ Official information is what is found in the bills of material, material masters, engineering documents, and the policies and procedures manuals.

■ Environmental information is all of the information not in the computer or on paper. It is the information about the people, culture, weather, attitudes, informal policies, possible issues with the workforce, knowledge about the vendors and customers, and much more.

■ For the hard or middle-of-the-road situations, the environmental information is far more important than the information found on hard drives or on the shelf.

■ The official information can be used for mechanical or rote scheduling.

■ The acquisition and interpretation of environmental information is a cognitive skill.

INTRODUCTION

This is the last of the *what* chapters. What information is used in planning and scheduling? In previous chapters, we tried to give a broad and practical definition to production control, discuss the functions and tasks of production control, and talk about personal characteristics that are important when hiring and training people in production control. In this chapter, we will discuss the type of information that is important to consider for production control decisions in more detail.

OFFICIAL INFORMATION

The official information typically used in production control consists of the data associated with manpower planning, material records, process routings, bills of material, current inventory levels, purchase orders, shipping and receiving records, firm orders or deliveries, and projected or forecasted sales. These are the primary data and are technically sufficient to make a scheduling or planning decision. Secondary data are associated with holidays, preventative maintenance schedules, and processing impacts like engineering changes.

It is easy to say that all modern MRP and ERP systems have this primary and secondary information. Many scheduling systems also have the data. However, aspects such as the options and combinations of options, units of measurement, format, method and style of representation, interpretation, and degree of detail vary dramatically between solutions. The degree of variation can be quite wide between systems. It can be likened to comparing a toy remote-controlled car versus a real Formula-1 race car. Both can have four wheels, a propulsion system, a steering mechanism, windows, lights, steering wheels, dashboards, and gauges. In simple text and with superficial analysis, the two are equals and even in photographs the differences may be hard to tell. However, when you attempt to climb into both and be transported, the differences will be revealed.

The information systems used in manufacturing are not designed to fit any situation 100 percent. It is probably impossible to do it. System configuration and usage is a compromise, and it is not reasonable to assume that any commercial, off-the-shelf system can accommodate all types of manufacturing processes and requirements. In the early 1990s, a survey was done that focused on leading manufacturers and scheduling technology vendors. The survey was described via a case study approach and documented several hundred production control concepts and requirements. The situation in the benchmark was also restricted to what can be considered the official information or representation of manufacturing. The benchmark did not include any of the information that we consider environmental. Environmental information is all of the information not in the computer or on paper. It is the information about the people, culture, weather, attitudes, informal policies, possible issues with the workforce, knowledge about the vendors and customers, and much more. The case study left all of this stuff out. It was full of routings, interdependencies between operations, issues about resources, and similar requirements that could be represented in a computer. The global manufacturers who funded the study indicated that the case study was representative and would be for the foreseeable future. Some of the scheduling solution vendors affectionately called the benchmark *The Factory From Hell* and the name stuck. Imagine what it would have been called if it had included environmental information as well...

The difference in opinion between the manufacturers and scheduling vendors was enlightening in itself. The two parties were not on the same page. The results of the study were confidential and restricted to the sponsors and respondents, but there was an interesting chasm between the two. This chasm related to what each party thought was important and what should be implemented in a software solution. Some vendors were closer than others, but a chasm was still evident. At the time, the data suggested that the scheduling software was technology that was being pushed and it was not being pulled by well-researched market needs.

There was another lesson in the survey. It was clear from the benchmark requirements that it would be silly for any vendor to even consider developing a prepackaged solution for 100 percent of the requirements. The resulting beast would be excessively dysfunctional as a whole. The question was always how much of the benchmark could be covered and where were the compromises? The survey results suggested that any solution capable of addressing many manufacturing situations to near completion would need to have a very tailored user interface, a scheduling grammar or language, and a very flexible approach to representing constraints and production logic.

In any event, the difference is in the details. If you are modeling the factory at a very high level and using aggregate concepts and data, many sins can be buried. However, once you start scheduling and dispatching, the details surface rapidly. The degree of fit will range from "close enough" to "you have to be kidding." If any kind of automated scheduling and dispatching is desired, the fit better be close or else the computerized systems will be generating infeasible schedules that even the sweeper would laugh at. Before we get into this any deeper, let us review the primary and secondary data.

The manpower planning information can indicate shifts, numbers, and skills. The material records can provide information about any special ordering, substitution, or processing of the material. This can include reordering control information and any controls on the vendor. The process routings specify the operations, resources needed per operation, setup requirements, and any unit-processing information like time per piece. The bill of material is very important of course and lets the production personnel know what goes into what and in what quantities. The MRP netting or explosion is obviously a critical aspect of any manufacturing process. The current level of inventory is usually straightforward, as is the awareness of any scheduled receipts or outstanding purchase orders for raw material or purchased parts. The most recent and historical information for what has been shipped or received is also not a challenge. If we ignore issues associated with accuracy and stability, the future forecasts and shipping requirements are also easy.

The secondary data relate to support roles like tooling, maintenance, and other information such as plant shutdowns and statutory holidays.

There are a lot of data and many fields in the MRP and scheduling software tools. There are many options and settings. This implies that they can model or represent many situations. This is true. There are many situations they cannot, even with all of the options and settings. Here are three, mechanically sound, manufacturing situations that are hard for MRP type systems or scheduling tools to handle and turn up in a number of industries ranging from metal bashing in the automotive sector to wafer fabrication plants in the electronics field. To model these types of issues, various workarounds are usually needed.

- **Case 1.** There are two independent subcomponents being made. They are triggered by different demands and are used in different products, perhaps in different quantities, rates, and times. For any one of a number of perfectly good reasons, these two seemingly independent subcomponents must be scheduled together, at the same time, on the same machine, or on two very specific machines, in the same quantity, or in a quantity that balances each other. Have fun. Is there a direct representation that helps model and control this or do you need to do a number of workarounds and kludges? How are two independent routings linked together to control resource allocation and start/finish times?

- **Case 2.** A product uses a subcomponent. The subcomponent is made from the waste product associated with the primary manufacture of a different subcomponent. There is now demand for the product requiring the by-product subcomponent and there is none in the inventory. There is a lot of the main subcomponent, but none of the by-product. There is also no immediate demand for the originating subcomponent. What is the system going to do?

- **Case 3.** There are multiple machines to choose for the first operation. One is chosen. After a number of subsequent operations, a similar operation to the first is required and the first machine chosen must be chosen again. The future sequencing decision is controlled or affected by an earlier sequencing decision. Does the system have the ability to remember and set the previous machine as the preferred machine for another operation automatically?

These three cases have focused on the dispatching and scheduling levels, and are only intended to illustrate the complex issues found in manufacturing. Equally difficult problems exist at the planning level if decisions must be made about complicated and interdependent relationships. For example, a small foundry had several furnaces of various power. Whenever they were considering work to accept and the plant's workload, they also had to consider the impact on the energy draw and how many furnaces could be turned on at the same time. The local energy provider was always quick and willing to bump the firm into the next costly category and reluctant to reduce its category. Have you noted an energy consumption index and rating scheme in your MRP or ERP package? Or any form of usage table with indexed costs that are used in loading, planning, or order acceptance? There are hundreds of these types of complex relationships that can be found. Note that we did say types and not individual examples. Some are not important enough to be included in a system, but many are. Often vendors have thought we meant a specific, weird, one-off example of an extreme situation that should not exist in the world at large, but if it did, they would simply add another option or provide a hard-coded solution for it. Have you ever seen a software package where features and options are added one at a time over a number of years? Not a pretty sight.

Where are we with all of this information? There is indeed a lot of information in a modern MRP or ERP database. Probably any single installation uses but a fraction of the features and functions, yet amazingly, the tools are unable to represent the complex interrelationships that exist in many firms. To determine how well your existing system is able to use the information it has, consider the following test.

Do you think the information in your MRP, ERP, or planning tool is sufficient in its thoroughness and accuracy to create feasible and realistic schedules and plans? Too vague and too absolute? Let us try a different question. How often do people correct errors in the official information that resides in the database? The bills of material? The routings? The plant's production reporting and tracking data? Inventory counts and levels? At one extreme would be almost all topics and all areas perhaps multiple times a day. At the other extreme may be a correction once a month to some information. Where are you?

If you are correcting data too often, you have a problem. Your processes or systems are insufficient. But are the data, even if accurate and timely, sufficient along with the planning logic to generate good plans? This is another one of those vague questions. If the computer system generates an initial schedule or plan with a priority sequence — do this on that machine next, followed by that other job — how often is this sequence actually followed? Are some jobs resequenced manually by the planner? Are the plans edited manually? Processing times lengthened or shortened? Setup times modified? Work moved to different machines? How much time is spent each day or each week manually rethinking the software system's recommendation and tuning it? If you spend very little time, this is a good sign. If you spend more than a few minutes each day at this, it is a sign that the manufacturing system is having trouble representing your situation.

ENVIRONMENTAL INFORMATION

We have mentioned environmental information, but did not really explain it yet beyond one or two sentences. You probably know what it is, but might not be aware that you know. If you were one of the lucky people to answer the above questions and indicate little modification to the computerized recommendations, odds are that you have little environmental information to worry about. You do not likely know, nor do you need to know, about environment information, so you can skip this section.

Just ask yourself why modifications were made to the schedule or plan. Was it because Sarah was not working that shift and you really wanted Sarah, and not John, to perform that key operation? Was it because the machine was just repaired and you do not trust it yet, and want to put something low risk on it first? Was it because the last time the part ran, there were problems getting a quality part and you want to give it more time, just in case? Was it because there was a vacation weekend and you know that the senior personnel will take priority for extra overtime on the weekend and then take extra days off during the week? Does this mean that the days just before and after the weekend will be less productive? Was it because you heard that a winter storm was approaching and this will foul up the shipping? These are all examples of environmental information.

Sometimes environmental information has no impact or a different impact than last time. This is what makes it hard to grasp, understand, and learn from. This is the type of stuff that makes a sequence thought good on Monday considered mediocre if considered for Tuesday, and a schedule thought good for the Tuesday, unacceptable for Friday. It could be the same jobs scheduled each day, but the sequence and resource assignments would be different.

The information may also be related to a person's attitude or emotional health; for example, issues at home, with other workers, or the general work situation. One scheduler noted the poor attitude a team had during a training session and made sure critical jobs were not scheduled for their team on the night shift. The scheduler wanted to make sure that additional support people were around when the critical jobs had to be run. There are many examples of this type of environmental information. The information may perhaps be quantifiable, often is not though, and the majority of it is fleeting, obtained from mobile sources or through multiple senses. Schedulers have tweaked on the decrease of production based on the way parts were piled around the machine. The look of a worker, the muttering, the smiles, the thumbs up; this is all environmental information. Some of the information may be captured and specified in a custom package, but there might be legal issues with putting some of the information in a corporate database. For example, until Bob is done with rehab, you do not want him doing any critical work. Try to get that one by your privacy laws, through your Human Resource department policies, and into the routing file. And that is a tame one.

In some ways, the environmental information is far more crucial and important than the official data residing in the corporate database. This information is the stuff that provides you clues about the future troubles that production control is supposed to avoid, minimize, or otherwise discount! It is used in a small number of the decisions, perhaps no more than 10 percent, but they are the key decisions. They are the decisions that we discussed in Chapter 5. These decisions relate to the recognition and handling of special instances in the immediate and foreseeable future.

There are various categories of environmental information that you can consider. These are:

- Information about vendors and key customers. What is going on at their plants, in their geographic region, their products, processes, personnel, and facility?
- Information about transportation or distribution network in which the plant finds itself. Are there any road reports, traffic issues, or major construction projects planned to start next month?
- Culture and organizational knowledge about the general patterns of what happens or does not happen within the plant. What happens before, during, and after tours? Vacation times? Plant shutdowns? Changes of the seasons, beginning of skiing or hunting season? School breaks? How does a product, process, or resource upgrade affect supervision, support staff, and meetings?
- Physical impact of the environment. This is the weather and its components: temperatures, humidity, snow, rain, and hurricanes. Do the seasons imply different processing times, yields, or setups? Are dies and fixtures stored in heated sheds? Are there different traffic patterns and

delays with the seasons? When the seasons change from one to another, does an impact occur?

■ Current information about the factory within the four walls. What do your five senses tell you? Sight, smell, touch, taste, and sound provide additional information to you beyond that found in the computer system. Taste might have limited application in some industries and the benefits of smell might be limited in others, but the point is the following: You use a lot of information from all kinds of sources to make a decision. Why do you think so many schedulers do walkabouts when they first arrive at work? For their health?

SUMMARY

There is official information and there is what we call environmental information. To have effective and efficient production control, you need both to be present. You need to have access to the information and you need to know how to interpret it. You also need to know how one piece of information is related to other information. This is not easy and is dismissed by management frequently as being unimportant.

In top factories, the environmental information is sought out actively and the information network consciously cultivated and maintained. In the more challenged shops, the planners and schedulers are sensory deprived and are kept in the literal dark. This darkness might be by choice or by situation, but the end result is the same: many unpleasant surprises each and every day.

Typically, the environmental information is processed first, looked at before anything else. Ralph and his kin assess it for risks and issues. This information will guide you to the key or hot problem areas. Schedulers often talk about scheduling the areas that need scheduling and just letting the other areas get on with it. If there is not a problem, why interfere?

The next chapter begins the discussion on scheduling tools with a short review of the concepts underlying capacity analysis.

8

MRP AND CAPACITY ANALYSIS

PREDIGESTED THOUGHTS FOR THE BUSY PERSON

- Infinite capacity analysis can provide some insights at the planning level, but provides little help for the detailed scheduling and dispatching tasks.

- Finite capacity analysis is a core element for any improvement in planning and scheduling.

- The standard MRP approach to scheduling is useful in some plants, but not too many.

INTRODUCTION

Almost all factories have some kind of MRP running. Either a legacy MRP, an updated MRP-II, or ERP. The program might be home grown, heavily customized, or off the shelf. The internal concepts will be largely the same. They have been the same since the early 1960s. There might be some new options and some new fields, but the philosophy and techniques have been mature for a long time. In this chapter, we will briefly describe the main concepts behind the MRP approach to capacity analysis.

INFINITE CAPACITY LOADING

Traditional MRP logic and capacity planning tools use backward scheduling and infinite loading when generating scheduled receipts and requirements. At the top level of the bill of material, the requirements may be driven by a specific demand or the desire to maintain a specified minimum level of inventory. This sets the due date and quantities. The release or start date, or due date for subcomponents at the next level of the bill of material, is determined by either a fixed lead time or a calculation that uses setup and processing time. A queue time or movement time can also be included to move the date earlier. Doing this throughout the bill, looking at on-hand inventory and scheduled receipts, will determine a schedule. Some call this the master schedule. Some people call the dates at the highest level in the bill of material the master schedule. Terminology will kill you. One survey on production control practice was sent to approximately four dozen factories with about two dozen questions on the survey. It is not a stretch to say that each question was interpreted differently, some small, some large differences, by each respondent.

The result of the MRP activity resembles a schedule. It says when things should start, when they should finish, and how much should be made. Calendars for vacations and holidays can also be used in the calculations to ensure the right number of working days is taken into account. According to this definition, the MRP-II and ERP systems schedule — just like someone who is in the water and flailing his arms and legs — is swimming, regardless of forward movement.

Unfortunately, the MRP logic does not pay attention to what the resources are actually doing and is quite happy to have the same machine work on two, three, or more jobs at the same time when this is physically not possible. There is no sequencing logic that determines what job to work on when there is a resource conflict. This is the assumption of infinite capacity. If you have dedicated lines for each product and building to a rate, this is not a problem. If you also have so much extra capacity, in house or through outsourcing, that there is never a conflict, this assumption is not a problem. In every other situation we can think of, there will be some level of inaccuracy and infeasibility in the schedule. The degree of inaccuracy and infeasibility is the kicker. If there is very little conflict and the conflict can be sorted out without much fuss, then the MRP schedules are quite adequate. If there are many conflicts implied by the schedule, the schedule is not of much use. It can be used to set the final due dates for the highest requirements, but the intermediate dates are useless for the most part.

Why do MRP-based systems do this infinite load thing? There are a number of contributing factors. We will try to explain some of them.

- One of the initial goals was to create a unit of work. In the late 1950s and a couple of decades following, the unit of work was week or month oriented. Perhaps even a day, but week units seemed pretty common. A common term of the unit of work was "bucket." The buckets of work would be separated by work-in-process inventory and the departments and subdepartments would be responsible for the detailed scheduling of the work within the bucket. It is not clear if this was an objective or a result of the system. The initial processing time and turnaround in the mid twentieth century of the early MRP systems meant that daily and within-day scheduling and rescheduling was infeasible. In many firms, it took a week to get the next weekly plan together. The due dates generally were phrased as week-of; it could be done anytime during the week, just get it done by the end of the week. Infinite loading works really well with the bucket concept.

■ Doing week-of scheduling, infinite loading, and bucket grouping meant that less data were involved and less computations were required. This reduced the shop floor tracking requirement, information input requirement, and the associated data maintenance overhead. Expensive computing time was also conserved, as was data storage.

■ The infinite loading meant that the software did not have to keep track of what was already scheduled and what the resources were working on when, and for how long. The software also did not need any logic to determine what resource to pick out of a set of similar machines.

These factors directly related to the cost and the power of computers at the time. With computer cards, magnetic tape, and limited memory, you could not reasonably do more than use infinite loading assumptions and bucket grouping. It made sense in the 1960s and 1970s. The implementation of the concept limited the functionality. The groundwork was laid for the future.

Most MRP systems provide capacity analysis tools and loading tools, such as capacity requirements planning (CRP), rough-cut capacity planning (RCCP), or input-output planning (IOP). These tools help the firm deal with the infinite load assumption. Right?

The help is only partial. These tools usually project the expected loading that will result on the resources. For example, two centers might show 80 percent utilization and 120 percent loading, respectively. You are then expected to guess what should be changed in the various dates and quantities to increase utilization on the one center, and reduce it on the other. After you change your dates or quantities, the loads are then recalculated to see if the utilization went up or down. By moving one set of dates and quantities, you might have now discovered 110 percent utilization at another work center. You then try to fix that work center's loading by altering other work. In very simple situations with few products and few resources, this iterative approach is adequate. Today's systems can provide many summaries and charts showing the projected capacity utilization.

However, even if the processing and setup times in these systems are correct and thereby the loading figures make sense, the systems cannot recommend what to change, either at the single-order level or set of orders. For example, consider what might be necessary to do if parts A, B, and C are all scheduled to run on the same resource two months from now. If the parts are repetitive, more of A could be made this month to move its next demand date later in the second month and away from B and C. If B is also in rotation and scheduled for this month, less could be made, pulling its second-month demand earlier. Hence, two orders or scheduled jobs have to be altered to resolve the resource conflict. The system recommends to do A, B, and C at the same time, the problem has to be identified, and that is good; that is what the MRP tool tells you. You make the changes for A, B, and C, but discover that by doing so, other conflicts are made elsewhere. Oops. Now, fix them. And on, and on it goes. Few machines, few products, not a problem.

Now, imagine hundreds of resources and hundreds of orders, even thousands. Get the picture? If you have a larger concern, the MRP capacity analysis tools are usually unwieldy. However, they do tell you how much extra capacity you need that day or week. If you can schedule in 10 percent more overtime easily, or call in some contract labor, or subcontract the work, the solutions are easy to do and the capacity planning tools are helpful. In the above example with A, B, and C being asked for at the same time, the capacity requirement is 300 percent, not 110 percent. This is a 200 percent shortfall. It is difficult to schedule 200 percent by overtime. A complete extra shift may be required. Even two shifts. But what happens when the shop is running at peak load already or the problem resource is the bottleneck? Most shops do not have the type of elastic capacity implied by the capacity analysis tools. The factories do not have the easy options. The factories have to move the work around, alter dates, or alter quantities.

FINITE CAPACITY LOADING

Finite capacity loading helps with this shell game. This is the second type of scheduling that you might encounter and it is not rocket science. The finite capacity approach will not allow two things to be done at the same time on the same resource unless the resource can actually do it. Furnaces, multifunction work centers, burn-in racks, and other similar resources can handle multiple jobs at the same time. Most machines cannot. You want to be able to model what a machine or work center can do; for example, the number of parts, the arrival of departure criteria for each part, if parts come in batches, at timed intervals, if the parts leave together, leave in batches, or leave singly.

There are usually two strategies used in crafting a sequence using finite capacity analysis:

- If the work is forward loaded (i.e., starting from the earliest release date and pushed through the system), one of the jobs will be delayed until after the other is done or an alternate resource searched for. If there is enough slack, queue, safety time, and future capacity in the schedule, this delay will not cause problems to downstream operations and due dates. If there is not enough time or capacity in the future, the job will be late and its scheduled receipt date blown.

- If the work is backward loaded (i.e., starting from the due date and pulled from each previous operation), one of the jobs will be started ahead of the other job and have its inventory sit around a bit longer. This is OK if there is the inventory, time, and capacity to do it earlier. If there is not, then some part of the job had to be started before today and that just cannot happen.

This is the key benefit: The finite capability of the system is recognized and work is delayed or started earlier than what an infinite analysis would indicate. Utilization on the main resources will not exceed 100 percent. Sometimes it is necessary and possible to mix infinite and finite views of manufacturing when a decision support system is built. You can model or describe aspects of the system that have little elasticity as finite and tightly constrained, and aspects that have usable elasticity as infinite. This allows the scheduling system to enforce real constraints implied by the main resources without the user having to tune everything. You can then look at options for relaxing the minor constraints that might arise, the ones with elasticity. For example, if the shop is running flat out, three shifts, seven days a week, the main lines might as well be modeled as finite. There is little anyone can do to increase capacity. There is no more overtime or weekend shifts. However, the number of setups and support tasks might be noted as infinite resources utilized by the work. There might be a soft upper bound on the number of setups that can be done per shift (e.g., four), but it is known that with some negotiation and creative crew scheduling that the number can be six or even eight. Hence, it makes sense to let the number of setups float, but with monitoring to indicate when overloading is occurring.

The finite capacity tools give you various options. You might be able to intermix the forward and backward load ideas. One factory would first forward load priority work that needed expediting, then backward load firm customer orders, and then fill any remaining time on the schedule with stock or service parts. Do not just use the tools blindly, think about the strategies and tactics you can use. Finite or infinite. Forward or backward. These are you your main choices. You can also use simple scheduling rules for resolving the sequence order at any machine or work center.

Finite capacity scheduling has been performed traditionally as a separate system task with software supplied by a third party or the MRP/ERP vendor. In recent years, some of the ERP vendors are including integrated finite load analysis tools with interactive Gantt charts and a relatively small set of functions for manipulating orders and functions. For some cases, this small suite may be sufficient, in others, no. The ability to model complex routing and finite relationships is often absent in ERP/MRP and a separate tool is needed. It is hard to create one tool that is good for all purposes.

In almost all systems with finite capacity scheduling, late jobs or jobs starting earlier than feasibly possible are highlighted. This gives great benefit to the user. The highlighted jobs or tasks are the ones to worry about; they are either earlier than possible or later than desired.

SUMMARY

In this chapter, we described the main strategy used by MRP logic for determining what to do when — infinite loading with backward scheduling. We have also described the finite loading concept that respects the capacity of resources and the basic ideas of forward and backward scheduling. Depending on your ERP/MRP system, you may have some finite capacity analysis capability. Most do not. The finite capacity approach is tightly linked with planning and scheduling systems. The core concepts behind planning and scheduling systems are described in Chapter 9.

Web
Added
Value™

ADVANCED PLANNING AND SCHEDULING SYSTEMS

PREDIGESTED THOUGHTS FOR THE BUSY PERSON

- APSs are not magical entities with wizards imbedded in them. They can be very useful and very helpful, but they can also be as useful as a golden tree stump.

- Getting the right APS in terms of fit may be one of the biggest problems.

- Mixing high-tech algorithms and technology with low-tech manufacturing or production control is difficult to do. It will cost more, take longer, and require patience.

- An APS working at one level does not imply that the same tool or a sister tool can be used with the same success at a higher or lower level. The details, level of detail, planning horizon, and subtle interdependencies challenge systems differently.

- What works at another company or plant, or during a demo, does not mean that it will solve your problems or help you!

INTRODUCTION

Chapter 8 gave an overview of the MRP approach for infinite capacity analysis and finite capacity alternative. The finite capacity view is the heart and soul of advanced planning and scheduling (APS) tools. Older or slightly less functional versions of APS tools might be known as finite capacity scheduling (FCS) or finite capacity planning (FCP) systems. While there are some differences between APS tools and the FCS/FCP tools, they are close cousins and this chapter can be used for both sets of tools. These advanced software tools now number over a hundred with some ERP vendors supplying their own, other ERP vendors packaging their ERP software with a specific vendor's APS, and other APS vendors acting as independents. Organizations such as APICS have conducted regular surveys on planning tools and are good sources for contact information. The surveys also provide information about main features and functions.

APS CONCEPTS

It is a very confusing world out there. Depending on what salesperson you listen to, APS solutions will solve all of your production control problems, from lowering inventory levels, to reducing lead times, to improving equipment utilization and improving maintenance. They will do this magic within the four walls of a plant, throughout the supply chain, and for all types of factories and industries. Others will restrict their benefit claims to specific industries, types of production processes, or types of factories. There are many claims and the scope is quite wide. If possible, get the real information from an existing customer, not one who just installed it, but one who has been using it for two to three years.

Conceptually, an APS is a software system that is able to generate schedules for part of a value chain. In some cases, an APS can address the complete chain. Figure 9-1 shows a simplified view of the architecture of an APS.

Technology tells you something about architecture, platforms, and possible types of interfaces. The data model is, or should be, the representation of your real world. The design of the data model more or less determines if the system fits your company or not. The algorithms and functions use the data model to offer functionality and should support you in doing your work.

There are many phrases that are used to describe the scheduling functionality: genetic algorithms, tabu search strategies, beam searches, hill climbing, linear programming, branch and bound, simplex, and constraint directed search heuristics. Many APS vendors make a big deal out of this functionality and the sophistication of the algorithms; how one algorithm can generate better schedules than another or how one algorithm is faster than another. The algorithms are definitely necessary to find better schedules out of the vast number of possible schedules. We will return to the scheduling functions later.

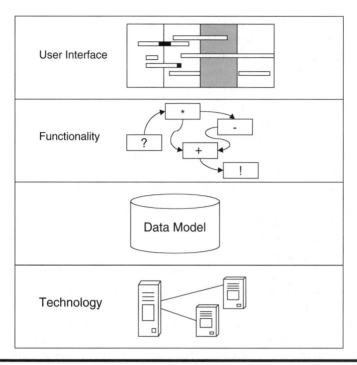

Figure 9-1. APS Architecture.

Lastly, the user interface is what made APSs famous in the early years. Most use an interactive Gantt chart interface that helps planners to get an overview of the mess they have to deal with. The history and ideas behind the chart were described in Chapter 2. With the computer software, you can click, drag, and drop the activities on the chart, and almost all information is at your fingertips.

In production control, there are five traditional objectives of better sequences: high service levels, lower throughput time, improved efficiency, lower inventory, and higher utilization. These objectives are hampered by production uncertainty and the sheer number of possible schedules to consider. Normal production variability in terms of yields and processing times can be addressed by algorithms that include advanced ideas of where to place slack time in the schedule or where to have extra inventory reserves. Uncertainty is also addressed by the ability to reschedule and react to the changing situation on the factory floor. Most systems are fast enough for rescheduling and some tools will allow partial rescheduling. Rescheduling is necessary when the variance in production is large enough to damage the planned work sequence.

The sheer number of possible sequences and schedules makes it hard to craft manually, or with simple mathematics, what would be considered a good schedule. The APS algorithms for schedule generation and searching help to address this problem. If the APS can model your situation, it can reduce some of the complexity in your production control decision making. This should enable you to make better schedules quicker.

There are some factory situations that can be modeled at the feasibility level and for which there are clear objectives. For example, process industries have had good success with scheduling technology. The process manufacturing methods are usually stable, consistent, and predictable. They use rates, volumes, fixed size tanks, and have shipping schedules. They work in bulk and their main concerns are mixes, blends, and changeovers. There is also heavy automation and insensitivity to individual operator variance. They also have a lot of historical data that can be fed into algorithms and software tools. Another important aspect is the degree of physical connections in a process situation versus a discrete part factory. This latter point is related to the amount of human interaction and intervention there is in the actual production. Process situations generally have less variability and chances for operator-introduced variance. One factory was experiencing high variance on an assembly line. They had operators doing a number of functions before a heavily robotized part of the line. Robots do not like variability. They expect to find things at certain places, very specific places, within very specific tolerances. They do not appreciate it when tools are left where they should not be or tolerances are exceeded. Humans have a tendency to increase variance and the processes should be designed to avoid introducing high-variance operations before low-tolerance operations. You get these types of situations in discrete part manufacturing, rarely in process.

A second area of success for APS has been the larger supply chain views. This is where the details can be ignored and the objectives are clear. For example, success stories exist for inventory reduction at the warehouse level, the distribution center, and what is in transit. The ability to synchronize multiple plants and control the general flow of goods at the week or month level is a substantial improvement over the traditional methods. If there is enough predictability in the supply chain, the synchronization can even achieve the day level. The manufacturing operations are grouped together, details dropped, and the supply chain modeled as producers and consumers.

A third type of situation that can benefit from software that can provide better sequences is that with sequence-dependent setups. In such a case, the software can remove the burden from constantly trying to juggle the benefits if you do A-B-C, or A-C-B, or B-C-A. There are many industries where significant savings can arise with smarter sequences. For example, if you have a variety of inks and colors, there are usually preferred sequences to reduce setup times. If you are dealing with material that goes from wide to narrow, there might be savings if you schedule the work in a way that exploits the savings.

A fourth situation for better sequences is a dedicated, automated, or semi-automated packaging or assembly line. This type of situation is predictable enough, and usually simple enough, for software to model. Better sequences will help.

Note, these are better sequences, not optimal. It is possible that you can also craft better sequences if you had enough time, but you usually do not. You do not have time to think about all of the color changeover issues for all of the jobs, for the complete time horizon. The software can do this. The goal might be called optimization, but there are many gains to be had from slightly better, or substantially better, sequences. In many cases, you can dial knobs, vary preferences, and fine tune the results; the assumption is that the software and system can get the schedule close enough to something you like and is still good mathematically. They hope that you do not simply delete all of the software-generated schedules each morning and start from scratch in a manual fashion. We have heard of at least one scheduler who does this.

ORGANIZATIONAL COVERAGE: SUITES AND MODULES

We can make a distinction between an APS module and an APS suite, which contains the modules of one vendor. Each module has an application area. An overview of the most common application areas is shown in Figure 9-2.

APS vendors may have modules for each application area and even more. The common theme in planning is allocating tasks to resources in time and the

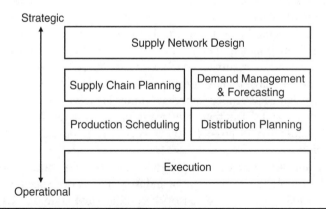

Figure 9-2. Common Application Areas.

common theme in execution is workflow and registration. There are vendors that focus on planning and there are vendors that focus on execution. This book focuses on production control and planning, so we will restrict our attention to that part of the organization and process. Some vendors also focus on warehouse management. There are even vendors that focus on control versus planning and execution; they concentrate on getting feedback from execution. This latter type of control application is referred to as supply chain visibility or supply chain event management.

THE VENDORS

There are roughly three kinds of APS vendors: large, small, and your ERP vendor. The small vendors can do an excellent job for the common APS functions for a fraction of the costs that you would pay to a large vendor. However, if you need a global scalable system, you might not have much choice. Most consultancy firms that are able to do global rollouts do not support smaller vendors. When dealing with a large APS vendor or one brokered through a consultancy, the cost will be substantial.

To balance the APS vendor, there is your ERP vendor who suddenly draws an APS brochure out of his or her briefcase. If you go and select an APS, somebody in your organization is going to argue that you should look at the APS product of your current ERP vendor. Your ERP vendor is going to argue that interfacing will be much easier with their APS module compared to integrating an APS system from another vendor. The easier interfacing argument is a bit overblown these days. It is safe to assume that all of the major APS vendors can interface cleanly with all of the large ERP packages. There is little difference between them on this point; the individual APSs or the APS from the ERP vendor. There are many other differences, but technical interfacing issues will not be your biggest concern. The biggest challenge will be matching information from bundled functionality A to bundled functionality B. This problem always has to be solved, no matter where the APS solution comes from. The ERP vendor may or may not have the advantage here. Do not assume automatically that ERP vendor–supplied options are always easier to use or will generate better results. The main advantage of licensing an APS module from your ERP vendor lies in possibly lower license fees and having to deal with only one party.

Apart from the range of modules that vendors offer, the main difference between APS tools lies in the type of industry the vendor specializes in. This will be reflected in the data model of the product and style of user interface.

For example, if you are in a batch chemical plant, an APS should be able to model your by-products, product quality, sequencing rules, changeovers, silos, tanks, and any special sequencing rules stipulated by environmental, governmental, or physical restrictions.

IN THE BEGINNING

In the mid 1980s, in Germany and other countries, developers were beginning to exploit workstations and the personal computer. They combined databases, interfaces to manufacturing systems, some production control logic, and electronic Gantt charts. In Germany, these systems were called Leitstands (which roughly translates as control post) and in North America they were the FCS systems. AHP Havermann was an early entry in Germany and systems from Cornell University and the University of Waterloo were early North American entrants for the discrete part industries. There were others being developed in the same time frame for process and continuous flow. By the late 1980s, there were several dozen systems on the commercial market and many more custom systems built within firms. While there were and are differences between each scheduling tool, many have relied on the Gantt chart as the way to present a schedule to you.

These new computer aids were generally the FCS or FCP systems. For most purposes, you can consider FCS and FCP one and the same. The key word is finite. These early FCS and FCP systems were focused on scheduling on a low organizational level. They took the output from MRP as a starting point and would generate a schedule. The output from the scheduling system would then be transferred to the shop floor to be executed. In a sense, FCP systems were used as a bandage or fix for the MRP systems.

There were two major groupings of the early tools: process industry and discrete part manufacture. Situations such as chemical processes and continuous flow areas like assembly lines or bottling lines were reasonably easy to model and support using the computer systems. These have been areas where there have been repeated successes over the past decade. The discrete part situations were also easy to model if the work was simple, predictable, repetitive, and relatively stable. By 1990, there were some early successes in discrete part factories, but in these factories, there were not many detailed constraints or interdependencies between the constraints.

The simple and easy sales were taken care of quickly and then the vendors were faced with a problem. There were still many factories without their tools. Unfortunately, this huge potential market for detailed scheduling and planning was within unclean or unsavory factories. These were the difficult ones where things were not predictable, repeatable, stable, or well run. To install production control software in these situations was painful, time consuming, and problematic. In the 1980s, almost all of the tool vendors, many still in existence with APS products, claimed that they could indeed handle the problem children, but one by one they quietly stopped making the claims and focused on the simpler situations. According to one APS vendor, they tried hard to avoid the problematic factories, the dynamic job shops with great uncertainty.

What were the vendors to do? They had their lovely software capable of modeling relatively simple flows through factories and they wanted to make some revenue from this investment. At the same time, manufacturers were becoming aware that the supply chain was important and that some high-level planning was necessary to make the firms more efficient and effective.

This was a fantastic opportunity for many of the early vendors. With some relatively simple extensions, the vendors were able to model the larger problem at the plant or major department level and ignore all of those ugly details. Remember the old saying: The devil is in the details? Never more true than for production control software. Since the problem was so huge in the supply chains, the vendors and manufacturers were able to get big gains in the overall picture, while letting the situation within the four walls sort itself out. It is easy to get big gains when you first enter a situation, encounter sloppy practices, and find a lack of common sense. Any conscious rationalizing and reorganizing was bound to pay off and the vendors had tools that would help or facilitate the process. The vendors could also charge larger amounts of money as the whole supply chain was the target, not just the assembly line in one factory. Of course, there would be some general plans for the individual plants or departments, but since the details were not modeled, it was hoped that things made sense — or sense enough.

Once the dust settled, the new APS solutions became visible, easy to see with all of the marketing literature and large type.

APS BUZZ: THE SCHEDULING ENGINE

This is the black box. This is the area of black magic and wizards. There are hundreds of scheduling techniques. Why so many? The problem of finding or generating a good schedule is so difficult that there have been many different ideas about how this can be done. It is impossible to calculate the optimal schedule for a given problem unless it is very simple. The common approach for nontrivial problems is to generate many alternatives and select the best one.

Unfortunately, for any realistic scheduling problem, it is impossible to generate all of the possible schedules and compare them.

The scheduling engines of the APS tools use search techniques that are designed to find the best schedule possible. This is based on how long the search is allowed to go on, how many schedules will be generated, how the various work sequences are generated, and how the search is done. This is what search techniques do, they try their best, but cannot guarantee optimal or the very best. The words optimal and optimized are overused and abused.

There are five big problems with optimization:

1. Optimizing in the strict meaning of the word is impossible except for the simplest and smallest of problems; for example, few machines, all similar jobs. Any real factory problem cannot be optimized. Some parts of a scheduling problem might be optimized, but this is only possible if the problem is narrowed down sufficiently, leaving a larger part that is not optimized. Different techniques can yield different levels of goodness, but optimal is not possible. You might be able to get better schedules and plans, but they cannot be guaranteed as being optimal.

2. You need operational feasibility before optimization or before any kind of trade-off with traditional objective metrics such as late jobs or tardiness. If you cannot first project an amount of work to resources in a way that is considered feasible on the shop floor, why worry whether one schedule reduces the number of late jobs by 2 percent compared to another schedule? If the schedule cannot be executed, who cares?

3. You are always trying to optimize something with the software packages. What is that something? Even if you cannot optimize it, you are trying to get it as best you can. Depending on the firm and industry, there can be some easy things to strive for. You can try to reduce the number of late jobs or reduce the amount jobs are late by. In today's world, there are also supply chains and customer-supplier relationships where late is not part of the vocabulary. There are huge penalties and creative manufacturing is used to avoid any late job. These manufacturers do not want to hear that a scheduling solution will have 10 percent fewer late jobs and the average lateness will be reduced by 15 percent. They want and demand zero late jobs. The scheduling solution can give some boundary conditions or insights, but would not be considered as an operational output. How can you always satisfy objectives like no late jobs through the sole use of sequencing logic? You cannot.

4. What is best now will not be the best in five minutes when that large order is cancelled or changed. A company cannot simply generate new

schedules every minute as a reaction to every change. This would lead to "nervousness" in the schedule and general confusion on the factory floor.

5. What is best for your part of the factory, or your part of the supply chain, is not always best for your supplying/demanding side of the factory or chain. Schedules are usually constructed for a part of the complete problem or system. In one part, it might be best to pull certain work forward, creating huge problems in another part of the system. Because there will always be parts making up a whole, there will always be schedules that need to be aligned.

The way an APS generates possible schedules and searches for the best schedule can usually be determined by the name of the technique. For example, an approach called "genetic algorithm" generates and looks for the best schedule in a fashion different from an approach called "branch and bound." It usually takes an advanced university degree to understand what the differences are and how the differences will impact execution and quality. The differences between techniques that you may notice are speed, possible quality of the solution depending on how you look at it, options and parameters for tuning the technique, and possible interactions with the technique as it homes in on a possible sequence. In this book, we will not go into the details of these techniques and if you are interested in them there are some references at the back of the book that will help you.

It can also be difficult and quite time consuming to create the appropriate data models for the mathematics. While most users get some form of model operational, some will find that the process will be long and might never be completed. These latter cases are likely to be those where there has been a mismatch between what is needed in the factory and what the tool can model.

There are many more issues that relate to the design of scheduling engines, what data are needed to describe the scheduling problem, and how to craft schedules that make sense and are good. The technical and development issues relating to scheduling tools are the focus of an imminent book by Richard Conway (Cornell professor and co-author of the 1967 classic *Theory of Scheduling*). This book will be of interest to people who want to know why scheduling tools are hard to create, why scheduling requirements are hard to represent and satisfy, why scheduling tools are hard to install, and what happens when they are used. It explains why any claim of optimality in scheduling is, at best, deceptive. The title of Conway's book is *The Practice of Scheduling* and is very complementary to this book.

SUPPLY CHAIN MANAGEMENT

Without APSs, modern supply chain management would be different. APSs enable you to make more complex decisions and APS suppliers have added much to the supply chain management vision.

Supply chain management may sound more ambitious than it is. Are you really managing the whole supply chain? Do you find the mine, the boat, the trans-shipment terminal, the steel making company, the spoon factory, the wholesale distributor, the retail company, and the consumer making production plans together? There are very few such situations. A clothing retailer may actually have its own flocks of sheep for wool, manufacturing processes for its own production, and supply the latest desires in a JIT fashion, but this is one of the rare examples. These rare firms can control and plan a large part of the supply chain, but it is not the entire supply chain. Do they plan medical supplies used in the sheep farming with the actual drug companies? Unlikely. There are always boundaries.

Supply chain management is about partial supply chain management. You need to be realistic as to the boundaries and where the need for coordinated planning exists. The more links in the chain can create scope of control problems. There will be a balancing act between the coordinated behavior of the chain as a whole and the independent behavior of each link in the chain. For example, who decides that a plant in the middle of the chain will introduce a new product, entertain new contracts, embark on an expansion program, and otherwise focus on its own return on capital? Each of these activities can create variability in the production at the plant and who decides how this translates into lead times, inventories, and costs? There has to be some single driving force for the chain, but there has to be some decentralized control as well for each link. There might be one big link in the chain that is driving the whole chain and that link might have a hierarchical planning mentality. Hierarchical planning only works when fitted into a power structure that is formed accordingly as a true hierarchy. Unless all factors are known and all plants in the chain report to the same master, it is possible that a purely hierarchical situation may be heavy handed. The chain will be driven from the perspective of the single link, perhaps the final assembly plant, and all other links may be forced into uncomfortable compromises.

As many supply chains have a somewhat decentralized power structure by necessity of various corporations being involved, the corresponding production control structure should also be decentralized partially. Partially decentralized means that not all of the planning decisions are made from one centralized group. Some decisions will be made that drive the chain, but localized flexibility may be necessary. A hierarchical production control structure assumes many things; for example, that you can simplify the problem on higher planning levels and direct and constrain lower levels. Partially decentralized production control structures can likely yield better performance in most supply chains and there must be clear ownership and authority between the links. For example, one large corporation established corporate-wide purchasing agreements with suppliers at the start of the supply chain. This established good prices for the corporation. Unfortunately, the suppliers in the middle had no influence with their suppliers. The corporate-negotiated suppliers had no interest in the individual plants, a different corporation, pulling from them as long as the big corporate headquarters was happy. There was no leverage or influence at the link level. The individual plants pulling from the supplier were not on equal footing. This is an example of the centralized control ignoring the decentralized decision making, and what this means, throughout the chain.

Supply chain management is all about trust and true cooperation between parties; or one party dominating the chain and simply telling others what to do. Domination usually yields terrible customer service. Working together is mandatory and a mutual win-win attitude is important. Is the large customer with the assembly plants perceived as a big bully or is it actually helpful in creating better solutions and profits at the suppliers? It is difficult in a supply chain to have each factory or link make an appropriate profit as an independent party. Everyone wants to make a certain percentage of profit based on revenues and capital investment. If there are different corporations involved, it is hard to do anything else. If the supply chain is integrated vertically with many of the plants within the same corporation, there are different options, albeit rarely used. Usually, each plant is viewed as an independent entity for profit purposes and the supply chain is not viewed as a single entity. Henry Ford had a vertically integrated supply chain. He still outsourced many items, but the key and critical components were controlled. He did not take a profit at each link he controlled. He took a profit on the final car and viewed the supply chain as a single manufacturing process. This enabled him to focus on the manufacturing job, some processes added higher value than others, and he did not expect each of his feeding processes to hit a specific return on investment. As he put it, he did not take a profit on the coal he mined, he took the profit on the final car. Each link could concentrate on production! Would his approach work today? Ford is often pointed to as the example of mass production and lean processes; he should also be viewed as an innovator in the supply chain management area. It was not just the vertical integration, it was how he did it.

In many cases, there are so many incredible inefficiencies in a supplier-customer relationship that just by analyzing them based on common sense can yield enormous results; for example, using the same standards for pallet sizes or using multiples of common load sizes. Other examples are shipping via one warehouse instead of two or shipping via milk-runs, consolidated shipments, or strategic use of cross-docking and inventory control at large assembly plants.

If you have a supply chain within your own company, an APS could certainly add value to your supply chain; for example, to manage inventories more centrally or to make sourcing decisions, what to produce where. Be aware of the fact that many opportunities for improvement on the supply chain level depend on the organization's capability to centralize strategic and tactical functions, and then have decentralized operational control. You may have to deal with reluctant plant managers or you might get stuck in the power struggle between sales and business lines.

IMPLEMENTING APS FOR SCM

There are many differences between implementing a detailed scheduling system and a supply chain APS. There are also many differences between implementing an ERP system and a supply chain APS. The most important difference is that in an APS implementation, the good old physical/control/information (PCI) model should be taken out of the cupboard, dusted off, and used again in full glory (Figure 9-3). There are many elements in the supply chain situation that imply geographic distances, delivery issues, lead times, and plant-wide capacity usage. At the highest levels, you are not just moving a few jobs from one work center and assigning them to another work center in the same department; the impact on the factory as a whole is minimal. In a supply chain, you might be moving demand and product mixes about and these can have far-reaching effects. No longer a 10 percent impact on a single machine, the decisions can be 10

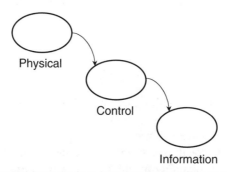

Figure 9-3. Physical-Control-Information.

percent on a factory. You need to really think and think hard before you start anything drastic. The software better be a good fit and do what you want it to.

The model should be read as follows: The design of the physical system leads the design of the control structure and that again leads the design of the information structure, which contains the ERP, APS, and other information systems.

This may seem trivial, but in many projects the consultants start to draw up control processes without understanding the primary process. They may even specify the information systems before thinking about the control structure or the physical problem. This habit stems from the ERP world where the financial reporting structure is often seen as being more important than the physical process. Who drove your ERP selection? The financial and accounting people? For Y2K? In the APS situation, this backwards focus can lead to an inefficient implementation process: questions hang in the air for weeks, erroneous assumptions are made, and costly corrections have to be made. Moreover, the information structure inherits the errors made in the control part. If you enter the project room for an APS implementation and you do not see a flow chart of the primary process on the wall, start worrying!

Creating an architectural view of the allocation of functions and information between the ERP, the APS, and other functions is certainly a mind teaser. It is hard when you have to bridge organizations and processes along the chain. And, it should be done early on. You do not have to wait until an APS is selected because the problem is largely supplier independent, even if you buy the APS from your ERP supplier.

You and others in the production control department need to be on board early and participate from the beginning. You understand the physical and control flows better than others in the company.

If you are interested in an extensive analysis of supply chain management and APS concepts, the book by Stadtler and Kilger, *Supply Chain Management and Advanced Planning: Concepts, Models Software and Case Studies*, is a good place to start.

SUMMARY

Let us try to summarize our thoughts on APSs.

What can an APS do for me?
- In general, make things visible and transparent
- Clean up your planning data along the way, during the implementation
- Make decisions faster (replanning, shorter planning cycles)

- Get feedback about your performance
- Reduce errors in the plan
- Possibly generate good suggestions about where your inventory should be and when it should be there (supply chain level stuff)
- Possibly generate good suggestions for loading and short-term sequences

What can an APS not do for me?
- Automatically optimize your supply chain, in every case, every time
- Eliminate disturbances in the physical world
- Change the way of working, in production control and throughout the production flow
- Improve your inventory accuracy or material variances
- Improve your processing times or your production consistency
- Make planners and schedulers redundant

The following chapter discusses a number of strategies and tactics for acquiring planning and scheduling software.

ACQUIRING A PLANNING AND SCHEDULING TOOL

PREDIGESTED THOUGHTS FOR THE BUSY PERSON

- Best proof of being able to handle your problem: similar plant using the tool for several years and you get to see the scheduler use it under a stress condition.

- It will likely take a year in the best cases to get a system and get it fully functional regardless of what people say.

- NEVER let people who do not know what really happens in production control specify or buy the system, even if they think they know. They can be part of team, but they should not have the final say.

- Buy standard, buy and tailor, buy and do a little customization, a lot of customization, totally custom. Those are your choices. Start with the simplest option and see if it works. Go for the standard if possible and avoid custom unless you have no other option.

- Implement a system on a limited scope as a pilot. Try one line and a few products before trying to scale up. Then iteratively scale up.

INTRODUCTION

Chapter 9 provided an overview of planning and scheduling software systems. How do you get one? Which one? In this chapter, we will describe some typical steps that can be followed when you desire to acquire increased support in production control. The details and specifics are always a bit different from site to site, but the types of issues are similar.

THE BASIC REQUIREMENTS

Always try to do this first step of requirement analysis regardless of what you think the final solution is: Understand the problem as best you can. The amount of effort and time invested in understanding and documenting the requirements will depend on the importance of the system, complexity of the situation, and the possible downside or risk of requirement misspecification.

Do not advocate or be a slave to any particular method or notation scheme for what you discover or how you discover it. Too often, methodologies become mythologies and people come to believe that just because a specific method or style is used, the solution and answer are correct. Wrong. It simply means that a level of consistency exists and whatever solution was derived looks like other solutions. The quality of the solution is more dependent on the individual problem solvers than on the method. There is good in methods though. Various methods do help contain and control group dynamics, and help facilitate the discussions. Other methods help document different types of problems. Having a consistent method can help reduce issues with communication, but there is no one method or one way of doing problem-solving or requirements analysis that will work in all situations. Excellent problem solvers have multiple tools at hand, know when to use them, know the strengths and weaknesses, and know when to run like hell away from them. They are not caught in the religious cult of a particular school of thought at the expense of the solution.

Having said that, we find ourselves being hypocrites on at least two counts. First, it is something of a cult about not having to be a slave to any cult. Second, we are advocates of systems thinking, ethnographic research, proactive concepts, mistake-proofing, and focusing on value-added aspects of information systems; all of which could be cultish if you allowed them to be.

You should consider the following facets in any requirements analysis of production control. The following list is a rather full, but incomplete, shopping list and should be modified based on the need:

■   What information is used to make dispatching, scheduling, and planning decisions? At the planner's desk and in meetings?

■   Where does this information come from, when is it gathered, how is it used, how is it validated, how does it change over time?

- Where does any decision go? Reports, any form of dissemination?
- How are the reports and data to be distributed?
- If there are multiple people involved, who does what?
- What are the usual, mechanical types of decisions that are made? When are they made? How many times is the decision made? What is the frequency of decision making? Who uses the result of the decision?
- What are the updating or data manipulation functions? How many items (jobs, operations, batches) are considered or looked at? What needs to be updated at the start of day, during the day?
- What are the special, exceptional decisions that are made daily, weekly, monthly, quarterly, yearly?
- What information is needed to model or represent the factory? The processes, routings, resource characteristics, and product characteristics?
- How often are the fields or values for products, machines, work, and routings updated?
- What are the reports, formats, content? How is each value derived? What are the formulas, calculations, and data sources?
- How are decisions changed or aspects modified after the fact? What are the requirements for rescheduling? What manual changes are made to the schedule?
- What is done now? Why is it being done? Can it be eliminated? Reduced? Done otherwise?
- What functions will be needed in the future? What functions are needed now?
- What are the currently perceived problems with production control? Why is enhanced support wanted?
- What are the quantifiable goals and objectives expected from any improvement effort?
- What are the warm and fuzzy qualitative goals and objectives?

This set of information is definitely required for any basic implementation of a decision support tool and is also likely a good list to revisit before advanced tools are considered. Without some understanding of these areas, you are making decisions without a full deck of cards. Many firms make decisions without knowing what they are doing and what they want to do. Many firms also fail in their attempts at introducing support systems for schedulers and planners. The milestones are missed and the costs balloon.

You do not need all of the data and information in one fell swoop. It is possible to do the requirements analysis in an onion skin fashion. You deal with issues and concepts that have a similar granularity and importance at each layer.

You can determine rough estimates or ideas quickly and know in what direction to head. For example, you can first lay out the basic structure of the area to be scheduled, what work will flow through it, and what the most significant characteristics are of the work and resources. You do not need part weights, precise measurements, or the industrial engineering estimate for processing times. However, before pen hits paper on the contract and the cash starts to flow, you should do a decent amount of thinking about the key characteristics and any relationships that affect sequencing decisions. In any problem-solving situation, a problem understood is a problem half solved.

If the list seems onerous and too much bother, think about what you are dealing with. Production control is the heart of the factory. Almost all information flows through it, almost all operational actions are derived from it. Resource planning and support areas such as tooling are dependent on the quality of decision making in production control. You want to improve the situation, not hamper it, slow it down, or create more work. You want to make life better. You want to make certain clues easier to see, to reduce manual data activities, and to create rough starting positions from which to work.

You will notice that at this point we have not talked about other technical requirements regarding the potential tool's implementation. The first requirements phase should be strictly focused on the problem and not hindered by any solution constraints. Usually, solution constraints such as operating systems, software options, and standards are elastic. They can be manipulated a bit depending on what the problem is, what the potential set of solutions is, and what the relevant gaps are in the fit. If there is a reasonable solution that also satisfies arbitrary technical requirements, that is good news. If there are no reasonable solutions that also satisfy the bureaucracy, then something has to give. Either the lesser solutions and corresponding compromises are accepted without whining, or the technical constraints (such as architecture, operating system, or database) are relaxed in favor of the better solutions.

It is possible that your requirements may change from the start of the project to the end. You have to think about what else is happening in the factory. For example, in one plant, senior management was dismayed by the high amount of inventory. After thinking about the problem, they simply sold half of the storage containers and forced the workers to figure out how to run the plant with less inventory. The throughput time decreased and the delivery reliability improved. You might not be able to do this in every case, you do have to be careful, but there are likely to be many practices and habits to challenge and improve before software tools or special aids can be considered. The tools being considered before the drastic inventory reduction were different than those being considered after! The reason is obvious. A tool you initially think you need might not be the tool you really need after the dust settles. However, it is also possible to plan ahead to when the dust is expected to settle and have a reasonable set of tools in place.

UNDERSTANDING VARIABILITY

When you set about acquiring a tool, you must also take a hard look at your sources of variability. What types of variance you have, and what you think you will have in the future, will dictate in part what kind of tool you should consider. The degree of variability in the system will also dictate the level of results you can expect. There are two types of variability to worry about: variations and variance. Both can cause production control nightmares. While there are mathematical definitions of these two words, we will focus on the everyday interpretation.

Variation refers to the different types of things to consider (see Figure 10-1). It is always easier when there is just one of each type of thing — one kind of printed circuit board, one kind of battery, one type of drilling operation, one type of bolt, and one type of wrench to use. It is easier to plan if there is just one type of order stream hitting a group of resources; for example, three hundred of the same assembly each and every day. It becomes difficult if the quantities or the batch size vary. It also becomes difficult if the products vary. If both vary, the problem becomes more than twice as hard.

Variety and the resulting complexity is not a linear, or one-to-one, relationship. It is like building something out of building blocks. If all of the blocks are the same size, the number of options is reduced, and you can always be

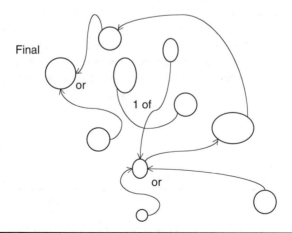

Figure 10-1. Variation — Many Relationships.

assured that a block will fit. You can also be assured of building the same structure if you start with the same number of blocks. If the blocks are not the same size and if the number of each block size changes with each day, you will have a hard time trying to make the same structure or to use the blocks wisely. More planning and designing is necessary in these cases. You may know in advance the number of blocks and their type, but you cannot just start piling blocks on top of each other. It is the variety and number of choices that creates many planning problems. The requirements need to specify clearly the types of variation that exist in your factory. The vendor needs to know the types and numbers of blocks. They need to know the possible variety in types and quantities. One system will be able to handle a greater variety in one area than another system. One system is unlikely to handle all forms equally. Without specifying it explicitly, you might end up with a system that is very laborious and painful to use. It might not be able to model or visualize what you need. High variation implies a lengthier implementation, more data to convert and check, and possible changes to forms, reports, and displays.

Variance is the difference between what is expected to happen and what actually happens (see Figure 10-2). Variance is not the same as variability. You can have a lot of variation but little variance, or have little variation and a lot of variance. They cause different problems. When both are causing problems, you have very big problems. Almost everything in manufacturing will have some degree of variance. If the variance is within tolerable limits, the variance is OK. It is planned for by using less than 100 percent efficiency, utilization, and yield estimates. If you cannot tolerate the level of variance, the uncertainty becomes a headache. How certain are you about what will happen? Do you predict the batch run length to the minute? The second? Half hour? Or, how long does each operation take? What is your yield? Every time? Are these estimates always close? If the variability is absorbed or does not matter, all is well. If you only have a few sources of undesired variance, it is also not too bad. You can manage this. If you have unwanted variance on almost every facet in your factory, your name might be Jake. If you cannot predict when something

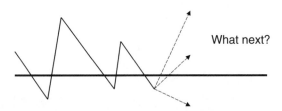

Figure 10-2. Variance.

is to start, how long it will take to be set up, how long it takes before the first part is checked by quality, how long each subsequent part takes, and how many parts you get, how can you schedule?

If you cannot have reasonable predictions and expectations, it is impossible to coordinate your resources effectively. There are many things that will be difficult to do. For example, you cannot start parallel setups or do hot changeovers if you cannot predict when the changeover will take place. Many hot or quick setups require an orchestrated effort and you are not going to have everyone just standing around waiting. The uncertainty affects the immediate situation and the future. You cannot schedule the next production for a part confidently if you do not know how many good parts are going to made in the current batch. If you do not make enough, the next batch will be pulled ahead by the MRP logic. This might be OK, but if you are trying to keep certain products being built in rotation and on cycle, the plan just got messed up. Variance is a problem when trying to pull work through the plant while trying to have low inventory levels. You cannot rely on a smooth build of three hundred per day if the pulling department varies from zero to six hundred per day. The pull per month may be a steady six thousand, but the daily variations can kill you and prevent low inventory levels from being reached. The possible examples are endless. You should try to reduce the variance, all of it, all types. This will make your life easier. There are many factors that will determine how much variance can be reduced by and you might have to accept fate; what you see now might be what you will have in the future.

If you have high variance in many areas, simple finite capacity analysis is about all you can hope for, perhaps not even that. Do not try for finely crafted sequences until the variance levels are relatively low. You should put the variance in the requirements document. This would include the existing and future expectations after all of those continuous improvements the plant is doing. The vendor needs to know how variable your process is, they need to know what solutions may work, and they need to know if they should quote on your request. The amount of variance will also affect the duration of the implementation since high variance may imply confusion, loss of focus, and reduced project time on the part of the people supposedly dedicated. The amount of variance can be perceived as an embarrassment, but it must be on the table and the knowledge shared.

Variability comes in many forms. Look for variation and variance in:

- Demand — mix, timing, quantities
- Demand — peak situations, product introduction, build or balance out
- Jobs and operations — number of operations, jobs, batches to be scheduled and tracked

- Jobs and operations — normal times, special times like yearly shutdowns
- Process — setups, processing times, first-off inspection, teardowns
- Supply chain aspects — lead times, quality, quantity for the material, subcomponents
- Execution — the durations and yields, inventory accuracy

When talking about variability, you and your friendly consultant or vendor might discuss averages. The number of product families is three, the average number of different products in each family is five. You can have an average of "5" from "4,5,6" or from "1,5,9." There is a big difference. Whenever looking at an average, consider the range of values that make up the average. If it is a single grouping like the number of products in the three families, thinking about the range is sufficient; "4–6" and "1–9." If you are talking about dozens of product families and hundreds of products, then you need more information to make sense of the average. If you are talking about average processing times, average yield, average demand, or average lead times, you need more than just the average and the range. For these types of numbers, you need to think about the *standard deviation* associated with the average or mean.

If the numbers come from a tight region around the average, you can use the average for planning and be confident about it — 4,5,6. If the numbers are widespread — 1,5,9 — placing a lot of faith on 5 is only wishful thinking. The concept of standard deviation helps you think about this idea of tightness around the average. If we had an average processing time of ten hours for one hundred parts, you can reliably plan with 10 as the mean or average with plus or minus one-half hour, 68 percent of the time. It is darn hard to plan when the mean is 10 with plus or minus five hours, 68 percent of the time. This *plus or minus number 68 percent of the time* is the basic interpretation of a standard deviation when something is assumed to have what is called a normal distribution. This type of assumption requires a large enough number of events or samples (i.e., the population) for the math to work and you get a distribution of values that looks like a bell curve. Most spreadsheet programs have functions you can use to analyze a bunch of numbers and determine the mean and standard deviation. If you are doing continuous improvements and focusing on repeatability, you should see the standard deviation decrease as consistency increases and repeatability increases. You want the standard deviation to be small. You might have met the concept of standard deviation in inventory theory, setting safety stocks. You might have also seen the concept in statistical process control when you set limits at three sigma to allow for random results. The concept is also buried in philosophies or programs like Six Sigma. The word sigma is used as a substitute for the standard deviation phrase and comes from the Greek letter used to frequently denote the standard deviation in equations. Thus, six sigma is talking about six standard deviations.

The terms standard deviation and sigma are rarely used in meetings. Everyone talks about averages. The spread or dispersion of the numbers that represents the variability is rarely, if ever, talked about. Consultants come in and try to drive down the average from eight to four hours per setup while not affecting the variability and in some cases increase it. It would be better to start off with reducing the variability and getting a consistent eight-hour setup; then you can plan. Then you can also look for ways to reduce the setup time systematically in a controlled way while maintaining low variability.

Two last notes on averages and variance. First, some people do things like average averages. You cannot simply average averages, it does not make sense unless you do more math and more thinking before you use that single number as representative of all things being averaged. If every average being averaged has the same number of things being averaged, it is OK from an equation viewpoint. However, without knowing the dispersion of the numbers, the usefulness will always be suspect. If one average has three numbers in it and another has two hundred, the average of the averages does not make sense. Second, some fail to look at variance during the month each day and just use cumulative analysis each day as they track towards the end of the month. As you put more and more numbers into the calculation during the month, the overall variance is reduced. You can have wild variance each day, but the number for the month looks OK. Someone who is busy and is only looking at the monthly number sees nothing wrong. The variance for the month looks low and good scheduling is expected. However, you have to plan and schedule with the daily variability.

If you want to do a really good job on understanding your problem and be able to document the dynamics and issues, you should consider calculating the variances you have and itemizing the variations. Calculate the standard deviation stuff, not just averages. This information should be included in the requirements specification.

PULLING THE REQUIREMENTS TOGETHER

How can you get a handle on the requirements? There are a number of issues associated with this topic:

- Who generates the requirement specification?
- How long will it take?

■   How are the requirements discovered?
■   How are the requirements documented?

Answering this list in detail can be another book in itself. However, we will try to give some short answers that still have some meat.

Who Should Specify the Requirements?

A vendor of scheduling systems, or a consultant tightly aligned with a vendor, is not always the best choice to do the specifications for you. You might be lucky, but you might be inviting problems and a possible vested interest. A team made up solely of people from the information technology department may also be problem, as they may not know the real problem. Neither should the system be solely defined by management or by corporate gurus. A team should be used. It should have people from production control, like you, management, and information technology. If sufficient technical or specialized knowledge does not exist within the plant, corporate expertise or an outside consultant might be needed. The key is to have:

■   Someone who knows what really happens in production control, e.g., the planner or scheduler
■   Someone who knows what should happen in production control, e.g., someone who knows best practice, what is feasible, and what is reasonable
■   A management representative, e.g., production control manager
■   Someone with a systems approach and experience with software requirements analysis, e.g., a body from information technology

You certainly do not want a fresh graduate who is book smart, but does not know a job shop from a flow shop to be your main lead. They can participate, but should not lead.

How Long Does It Take
to Determine the Requirements?

The type of situation, goals, and skill of the requirements team will dictate how long it will take to determine the requirements. Probably a minimum of two weeks is needed for any decent-sized shop. Expect to spend up to ten or twelve weeks for a really big job shop with many issues and unique aspects. Be careful, when this phase is prolonged too long, people will tire and they will need to see something physical or concrete before they can provide more details. Therefore, it is not always a bad thing if not all details are specified beforehand. It is a compromise and a risk. The balancing act is between trying to specify too much and making sure that the important stuff is specified. Make sure that you specify the must-have type of requirements first, in case you have to push the specification out early.

During the implementation, there should be room for small changes to the system. The reports will never be 100 percent or match your requirements exactly. Being able to tailor and customize reports is a way to reduce risk and deal with unknown or changing format requirements. There should also be some simple way to add or associate unique information to the jobs, operations, and resources. The information may be descriptive and textual, or the information may be quantitative. The quantitative information may be special values per piece, job, or operation. The values should be accessible for rolling up into aggregate statistics and appearing finally on a report. If you have this type of capability in the software, less risk exists when making compromises in the requirement specification phase. It is harder to make routings flexible or to specify relationships between work, operators, and resources. It is more important to take sufficient time on these topics than it is to worry the poor reports to death. The analysis needs to make sure that the basic concepts of the system will be right. Can you generate, or represent, the schedule you need? If you do not take the time needed for the main concepts, you will end up specifying a car when you need a truck.

How to Discover the Requirements

The best way we know of to discover the scheduling requirements is to have one or more team members sit at your desk during the first and last weeks of the month. This suggestion is in the spirit of ethnographic research. In this methodology, observers spend a significant amount of time with you to learn from you, understand your needs, and develop solutions with you. They take the time to see, hear, and listen.

The observations are taken from the time you start work until the time you are done for the day. Watch, observe, document, and ask. Who was on the phone? What is being done now? Why? Is it not enough that you might be on the committee? No. There are many things that you do that are second nature and automatic. You are not aware of everything you do. One study showed that about 10 percent of the activities tracked were of this type. All of the schedulers insisted that they did not do these 10 percent of actions or at least had no recollection of these activities. In the heat of scheduling and working, it is hard to step out of your skin and reflect on what is actually happening, what information is used, what questions got asked, what was done in response. Another individual can make these observations and then discuss them with you.

The first fifteen to thirty minutes of your day is a diamond mine. There are other times that are also special. For example, the last week of the month is when all hell breaks loose and the first week of the month may be when planning is done for the longer term. The first of the week illustrates what happens after a weekend and Friday shows the preparatory work needed for the weekend. This is the minimum study, two weeks bridging the month boundary. Ideal studies typically last longer than two weeks and they try to capture changes in products, processes, and the year-to-year planning.

Special scheduling requirements can occur for:

- New product introduction
- Engineering changes to the product, manufacturing process, or material changes
- Prototype parts, past service parts
- Product deactivation — balance out, build out, service part banks and inventory
- Machine or resource acquisition, individually or complete cells or lines
- Machine or resource upgrade, minor maintenance, major maintenance
- Machine or resource breakdowns and repairs
- Facility upgrades or improvements that require work to be built ahead and banked
- Manpower training, hiring, and learning curves
- Weekends, holiday weekends — the days before, the days between, the days after
- Regular, extended downtimes — summer shutdowns, December–January holiday season
- Differences in the seasons — winter, spring, summer, fall
- Changes between the seasons — winter to spring, spring to summer
- Cultural events or phenomenon — start of hunting or skiing seasons
- New corporate policies and activities — creating a focused factory, introducing JIT, continuous improvement activities
- Government regulations for production and distribution — when and how things are made or moved
- Differences in shifts — duration, sequences, day or special time of year dependencies
- Differences in crews — numbers, movement, productivity
- Differences in operators — efficiency, quality, skills
- Differences in operators — preferences, any restrictive union policies
- Processes — anything that forces things to work together at the same time or on the same resource

- Processes — anything that prevents things from working together at the same time or on the same resource
- Processes — anything that forces tight control of work, with regard to one operation's finish time and the next operation's start time
- Processes — anything that forces tight control of quantities or material movement with regard to what is made when
- Processes — anything that indicates that certain resources are selected over other seemingly equal resources
- Material — arrival quantities and units, variance issues
- Material — common or shared material, parts made from scrap

This is a good starting list, but is not complete. You cannot assume that every, or any, scheduling system can deal with your weirdness. You need to sit and ask if everything is scheduled without any special consideration or if some jobs have special sequences or information involved. Not all of these matter to all plants. Some plants are isolated from the effects or issues. These are the lucky plants.

For the other plants, each of these should be reflected on. The reflection is necessary to know how much manual tuning or adjustment of the schedule might be expected each day or how feasible any computer-generated schedule will be. This is important for judging how long it will take to get a good schedule generated before it can be distributed. It might be that the special scheduling is rare, or easy enough, that it can be done through manual tuning or just ignored. Or, it might be that the issue is so common, or troublesome, or so important that it needs special functionality in the tool. One problem with the special types of scheduling decisions is their frequency and possible impact. It can be easy to forget about them or miss them during the daily or weekly routine. It can also be that the download from the ERP resets the tuning each day or the scheduling logic does not maintain the manual tweaking and the special scheduling has to be repeated each day until the activity completes. For example, if you move 20 percent of December's forecast into November to allow for a longer holiday break, will this forecast movement be retained or performed automatically each week when the customers transmit a new shipping schedule? Or, do you have to adjust the demand manually each week through the summer and fall as you do a six-month plan? If you need to align two operations with a specific spacing between them, will the system protect this spacing when the next rescheduling is done, allowing the pair to shift in time, but with a fixed spacing between them? If the operations are not part of the same routing?

It is best to think about all of the regular and special scheduling issues.

How to Document the Requirements

The best way to document the requirements is to build a partially working prototype in something like a spreadsheet and use that in conjunction with some written descriptions. There is nothing like building a prototype to shake the apples off the tree, ensure that terminology is understood, and know what information is used, what calculations are necessary, and what the reports are like. Unfortunately, such a prototype will take four to eight weeks to craft. These prototypes usually can find ambiguous information and definitions that at first blush look rock solid, but when actually worked with, have the firmness of a cooked piece of pasta. For a small firm with a small problem, the cost and effort of such an activity is hardly warranted. Should be done, but it cannot always be justified. For a larger firm, it should be done. It acts as an excellent way to describe the problem and provides any vendor something solid to analyze when presenting a bid. Misunderstood requirements and meanings have killed many projects after the deal is made and work started.

If a strictly paper approach is used, then the requirements should be stated clearly, with examples whenever possible. The questions and topics listed in the first subsection of this chapter can be used to help organize the document. Copies of existing reports marked up are useful. Screen captures with annotations are also good. A flow diagram can also be useful that indicates when during the day the scheduler or planner does certain things, what the information is, what is done to the information, how the information is used, what manipulations are expected to take place, how often things are done, and what any reports might be. Any interaction with other systems, such as data from the shop floor tracking system, should be identified clearly: when it occurs and any timing or accuracy constraints.

In the paper file, the most important pages are a sample set of jobs, processing routings, tracking and updating examples, report mock-ups, data file formats for information exchange, must-have features, and an expected schedule based on the example demand input. And, do not forget the information on variations and variance.

The organization of the requirements should clearly include information important for the vendors. This includes what functions are done often throughout the day, throughout the week, and throughout the year. The requirements should also specify performance goals if you can; for example, how long it should take to generate a schedule, create routine reports, and download or upload data to the other information systems. For important functions that you rely on, it is not sufficient simply to state that a function is used, you should state how it is used. This will avoid misinterpretation and possible problems in the future.

Part of the documentation should be a clear and honest assessment of what data currently exist in the factory's databases and how good those data are. The vendors need to know if you have process routings for each part, that the routings are complete and accurate, and that the bills of material are accurate. This type of information is important to know as it affects how much work will be needed during the implementation and verification stages.

The documentation sounds onerous and a great deal of work. It is hard to specify and put together. You might also think that you are asking for too much and specifying too much. This is a natural feeling. Surely, no vendor can do everything and satisfy such a list? If you only specify what you think someone can do, then you are cheating yourself. You should specify what you want and what you need. Let the vendors respond accordingly. They should be responding to your larger set of requirements and indicate what they can deliver on. Seeing your larger set might also give them ideas for future features and functions. Internally, you should prioritize and rank the requirements and ideas:

- Must have — 100 percent support with no workarounds or kludges and the interface must be very fast and friendly because it is used frequently and is important
- Must have — 100 percent support with no workarounds, but a slightly awkward or slow interface would be accepted because it is not done too often
- Must have — 100 percent support, but done with workarounds or special fake or phantom resources or work; must be reasonably fast and friendly because it is done often and under stressful situations
- Must have — 100 percent support, but done with workarounds or special fake or phantom resources or work; can be slower and awkward because it is used infrequently, but important when it is used
- Preferred to have — a function that is not life or death, is done now, if not in system would cause extra manual work to be done off-line or with extra spreadsheets; not too much work would be acceptable; can be a tie breaker between almost similar systems — do not want too many of these though, can make the system unusable
- Nice to have — there is a dream or a wish list: we would like to, we have not done this yet, but if we had this function, we could go to places only dreamed of; there are always some of these, the senior managers have their dreams, the production control supervisors and managers have theirs, and the schedulers and planners have theirs; make sure that these types of requirements are recognized as dreams and wishes and do not prevent a good tool from being excluded

Think through what you need for 80 percent of the parts, 80 percent of the time. These requirements should be must-haves and available through direct functions and features. Reflect on the special cases you documented while thinking about the requirements. Which ones fall into this 80 percent category? Which ones are very rare, but if the requirement is needed, the impact is huge in terms of resource coordination? Do not ask for every one of your special babies to be a must-have with direct support. How many are that important? How many can be patched together reasonably? This is the type of rationalization process you need to go through when slotting the requirements into the categories.

Do not share the ranking with the vendors initially. You can ask them to rate each of your functions in your requirements as complementary to the above. You can give them a table to fill in for each requirement. The table can specify if the function exists, is supported 100 percent through a direct menu or option box, and completes in seconds, minutes, or hours; or the function can be done, but requires a workaround; or the function can be done by customization in tables; or the function can be done by unique programming. You then compare the various vendors with what you specified internally. When you narrow down the list of vendors for a demo, you can then share your must-haves and ask the vendors to demonstrate these features and capabilities.

If you are lucky, some of the vendors will challenge some of your requirements; you might be working on the symptoms of something and not the real problem. In this case, you will be challenged to improve and change some of your basic methods and processes, instead of just accepting the status quo. They might not support something because it should not be supported!

Does this whole documentation thing still sound like too much work? It seems that it just gets worse and worse. You need to think about return on investment. How much money is a system going to cost? How much labor and effort is going to be involved? How long is the system expected to be used? How much benefit is the system expected to return? How much will be lost if the system does not perform or fails? Pay now or pay more later.

There is a possible problem with the specification of requirements that needs mentioning. The requirements as documented might not make sense! Or, you might be asking for all kinds of things to help solve other problems. The requirements need to be reasonable. If you are only scheduling and planning for a month now at the detailed level, do not ask for the immediate delivery of something that can handle twenty-four months of detailed planning at the minute level, for all jobs, for all operations. If each scheduler or planner is currently dealing with a few dozen machines or resources, why ask for a system that will incorporate a few hundred or a thousand? First, you will need to grow into the situation. This would be a big change to the production control process.

A scheduling tool is not likely to eliminate a scheduler or planner. How many machines or centers can one person plan? With or without a tool? How far on the horizon is a reasonable time for planning? Second, it is possible that after you start doing several months of detailed scheduling, you will figure out what you really need and what you can really do. Related to this is the concept of linked systems. You might need a high-level planning tool that feeds a number of different detailed scheduling tools. You might need a special tool for the job shop and a different tool for the repetitive assembly area. Think about this when you are doing the requirements. If you have different problems, do not insist that one solution has to be the answer. If you are Jake, you can get a lot of benefit by hitting the problem areas individually instead of looking for one big magic solution.

TURNKEY, OFF-THE-SHELF SOLUTIONS

It might take two to four months from the time the idea is hatched until the time a vendor can be approached. The time is required to understand the requirements and to document them concisely in a form usable by a vendor or developer.

From a plant's viewpoint, the best scenario is a reasonably priced package that currently exists, that requires no customization, just parameter tuning and configuring. No programming, no extreme requirements for training, no hassles.

The types of systems described in the preceding chapter present special challenges to a factory. It is not reasonable for a single manufacturer, unless you are huge, to undertake the full development of a planning and scheduling tool. The cost and development effort is in the millions of dollars. The development time is years. It will be hard to obtain a return on the investment and you might end up looking for other plants to share the costs with or to license the tool. There are three other reasonable options for acquiring a software tool:

- Use one off the shelf, plug and play it.
- Tailor or customize a close match by working with the vendor or qualified third parties.
- Do it yourself, or with contract programmers, by utilizing a scheduling toolkit or software library as a starting point. While incurring some development costs and risks, hope that the majority of the messy stuff is already done.

As much as someone would like to create a custom tool or customize an existing one, the preferred option is always a turnkey operation. The second preferred option is the customization one. Vendors love the customization option; it smooths out their cash flow nicely. The option of last resort is the unique or custom tool.

Only after due diligence should a unique system be considered. For straight assembly situations that just run without many "yabuts" (person 1: "This is the sequence to run the jobs in.", person 2: "Ya, but..."), or for large automated processes, option one is feasible; you do not need a unique solution. There are many good tools on the market for these situations. Once you get into low volumes, high uncertainty, high mix, job shop flows, and many operational constraints, you are into options two and three. If the problem is not too unique, option two is a good road to follow. The vendor will make as much in consulting and contract work as what the product costs you, but this is still cheaper and better than doing it yourself. Option three is not for the faint of heart. It can be the best solution and the right thing to do, but everyone has to go into it with their eyes open. These are the factories where there are real or perceived exceptions to every standard or convention, and where creative routings are made each and every day. The feasible scheduling will depend on things like who turns up for work today, what is on the factory floor, and union agreements.

In any case of compromise or reduced functionality, it is very important to realize the impact on the function and task. If you decide to forego certain customized features or certain functions and reports, what is the impact? The impact can be reduced thinking time for you, greater effort and load on others using reports generated by you, more chances for overlooking potential problems, and the like. Or, there may not be any real impact and the feature is not really necessary or of value. It is important to think it out, to think beyond the immediate function, and contemplate the system impact. Sometimes an expenditure associated with a special feature or function saves a great deal of money. If you do not go for the function, you might save a few dollars at the expense of many. If an extra five minutes a day is needed to do clerical or nonvalued work because a function does not exist, then decisions that could have been made better with that five minutes will suffer. Trade off the cost of functionality versus five minutes of decision time. If the decision can impact the frequency of a $15,000 changeover several times a year, the cost of the time-saving function might be worth it.

Two or three vendors should be approached with the request for quote. It may be wise to have the vendor in for the quick presentation before a full demo to see if they are close and if you can stomach the solution. Key question: How many sites similar to yours are using their software and for how long? Be wary if you are the first in a category. Nothing wrong with being the pioneer, but ensure that everyone is wearing protective armor. Before wasting anyone's time beyond the initial presentation, ask for a reference and try to visit them for one to two days, preferably end of the month. Do a "Show me!" You want to see the system in operation and see how people use it. Everything else is suspect and can be smoke and mirrors. And we do mean visit, not just a short meeting. Visit from the start of scheduler's day until the scheduler leaves, preferably on a Monday or Friday, and at the end of the month.

For the short list of possible vendors, the main event will be showing you how they handle your challenge data. It should be based on your sample data and your challenge problem, not theirs. Find out how long it took to model your sample and put it into their system. This is always good to know. Then the fun begins. Does the system satisfy your requirements? If your requirements document is well prepared, the impact on your time will be minimal and it will be easy to check out the vendors and process your checklist. But if you cut corners, be prepared for many questions from each vendor and extended meeting times.

You can try a few small changes previously created, but not given to the vendor, and then placed on the table during the demo. Ask the vendor to do the changes or operations while you are sitting there. A list might include:

- Update any work in the current time zone to show progress, move a job ahead, delay it.
- Pause a job, preempt it, add a new order, copy an existing order, split a current job into pieces or stages.
- Move a job or product on the time horizon and lock it in, move the work to another resource.
- Alter a resource's capability, add a resource.
- Add a product, delete a product, change a product's key parameters.
- Add demand or a work order, change an existing job order.
- Show how an engineering change, new product introduction, and a balance out situation is done.
- Try to model a simple learning curve.

You cannot have very many changes or aspects shown, but try to get a few good ones in. A good idea is to try a fully loaded demo: the peak number of jobs, machines, personnel, and operations expected. How long does it take to initialize, load at the start of day, do the basic scheduling or rescheduling tasks? How easy and intuitive is the cutting, pasting, sliding, moving, or inserting of work? If you do things in the real world, can you do the same types of things? For example, can you just pause a machine for a shift or two and come back to the work? If you have more machines than people and have certain processes, this might be possible. Can you model a setup crew separately from the quality step separately from the operators separately from the tear-down and cleanup phase? In some factories, you need to model the setups on one shift and then the running on another. If the setup crews, quality inspectors, or similar resources are restricting forces, you might have to include the ability to model them and include them! If you can pause, otherwise delay, or simply split work into multiple batches, make sure that you can do the same in the computer system, during the demo. If you always try to align setups for the start of a shift, will the software also be able to do this automatically or will you have to manually adjust the setups on the schedule? Think through your normal day and the various things you do with jobs on the factory floor and try to get a demo of your typical day; one of each kind of activity.

Observe speed and performance issues. Some systems degrade in a linear fashion, others do not. Does twice as much work double the execution time or does it take longer? Some systems can handle more work easily and others will bog right down. If the schedule is full of jobs and work, do any of the functions slow down? Does it matter if you move or change something in the near future versus out on the time horizon? It is better to know this type of behavior before you sign the deal.

The vendor's demo will tell you a lot. The best demos will be those that focus on must-have requirements and show you how they are addressed in the tool, with real or simulated data. They will be able to show you a simple mockup of your factory, the processes, the routings, sample schedules, and sample reports. They will be able to show you how to use the frequently used functions and explain how to do the infrequently performed functions. If the proposed tool is weak, the vendor might deflect some functionality to the MRP/ERP system or might focus on other functions that were not on your list. At one factory, the advanced planning tool being proposed was supplied by the ERP vendor. The attendees were asked to believe words, not demonstrated capability. To make matters worse, many questions were answered in relationship to the ERP and not the planning tool. Planning and scheduling is hard enough without having to do parts of it in two systems. This was a weak solution. It was not clear that the people representing the ERP vendor really understood the difference between ERP and planning functions. At another factory, the planning tool vendor made all kinds of assumptions about the ERP and MES systems that were not valid. They also had a poor demo. There is no guarantee that a planning tool vendor will be better than an ERP/planning tool vendor, or the other way around. Rely on the demo, existing users, and demonstrated capability. Do not accept verbal promises as proof. One ERP vendor indicated that a certain type of feature could be added at the plant level, by plant personnel; it could be done. After the system was purchased, it turned out that the special feature could indeed be added, the promise was true, but the contract indicated that the warranty would be voided if such features were added unless many other conditions were met. The feature was never added. Get promises in writing and ensure that any special functions or features will be supported and not cause support problems.

VENDOR CHARACTERISTICS

If you are going for the off-the-shelf solution, ensure that you can get affordable support that matches your situation. Will you need seven days a week and twenty-four hour support for remote access support and reasonable on-site service? A production control system is mission critical and cannot be down for long periods of time. A very small vendor will be high risk and proper contingency plans must be in place.

If all else is equal, the larger, better experienced, and outfitted vendor is probably the logical choice. Especially if they have support in your geographic area and experience with your products and processes. That could be a match made in heaven.

The vendor should be able to get at your data and your current system from afar and also be able to update your system in the same way. This might be possible through your computer network or through dial-in access. To gain remote access might involve the information systems group and may require a variety of permissions. Special software and hardware might also be needed. Get this remote capability up and running as soon as possible, do not wait until you need it and the system is down.

The vendor should clearly understand the realities of production control and not be staffed in its entirety by naïve programmers who do not know manufacturing. You do not want to train them in manufacturing and production control.

You also do not want them giving you biased recommendations if their tool cannot model something about the factory. For example, you might get a recommendation to replace or upgrade certain manufacturing equipment or processes that are working fine because the process or equipment cannot be modeled in the software. This latter point is an example of the tail wagging the dog; the tool is fine, change the factory to fit the tool. Surely, such recommendations would not be made? Occasionally they are.

The fiscal condition of the vendor and its viability is important. Any vendor hanging on by a thread is not a wise choice.

While the preference is towards a substantial vendor, it is important not to rule out a small player. A small vendor might be a fine choice if they are close to you, understand your situation, and are willing to provide the support you need. Small is not bad by itself, look at the other factors. The small vendor might also be a better choice if you need features and functions that are not available in the larger, off-the-shelf packages, and the small vendor is willing to use you as a test site. If dealing with a small vendor, protect yourself in case the vendor declares bankruptcy or cannot support you. You might need to get a copy of the software's source code held in escrow or other measures.

ROLLING IT OUT

You have licensed the technology and you are ready to rock and roll. It would be prudent to proceed cautiously and do as much in parallel as possible with any existing systems. It is important to verify that the basic operating reports will be valid before you turn the switch and go live. If you can roll out the technology in a single department, run parallel, or in a pilot mode, that is preferred. Plan to scale up in an iterative fashion. Go slow and be careful. Do not be surprised that after several weeks in pilot mode, the system has to be turned off and shipped back to the shop for an overhaul, possibly several times. Usually, there are many unforeseen requirements and data issues when the key is turned. There will be inconsistencies, ambiguities, inaccuracies, and instances of incompleteness. Count on it. Plan for it.

Do not cut over during peak load time, at the end of the fiscal month, quarter, or year. Avoid these times if you can. You will also want to avoid times associated with any other major changes to the factory, products, or processes. Failure to pick your time wisely will result in very interesting times indeed. If you have no choice, then so be it. If you do have choices, consciously pick the better option.

Expect to incur additional training costs, customization, and upgrade costs as the system is used over time. There will be ongoing costs and requirements. There might be changes in reports and functionality with changes in plant management. For example, the new president might have different ideas about what the reports should look like and how the system will be used. Any new plant manager, financial officer, quality manager, production manager, materials manager, or production control manager might have ideas. Rotating doors will keep the vendor or consultant busy. If you are unlucky, you may also get the chance to experience technology problems such as software bugs, patches, vendor-forced upgrades, viruses, security holes, vendor support issues, and other niceties.

Some companies forget a key aspect as they roll the system out — a little thing — not really important — just the scheduler. Is the scheduler ready? Is it the right scheduler? The success of the roll out will depend on the individual and the individual's training. Because of their sophistication, the use of APS tools sometimes implies the hiring of different planners and schedulers. There are several systems that require detailed cost estimates, skilled tuning of parameters, and an understanding of the mathematical underpinnings to make sense of the suggested sequences. You should always be aware of what kind of education is going to be needed to use a tool, maintain it, change or reconfigure the options, and understand it. At a minimum, extra training and support will have to be provided. Often numbers are challenged and recommended schedules must be explained. Why is something scheduled here instead of there? Why is it scheduled Tuesday instead of Wednesday? This is an issue of transparency and is important when systems are used daily. Although transparency is an important concept for the design of systems, many of the advanced scheduling tools use black-box techniques and it is almost impossible to know or understand how or why a specific sequence was generated. If you cannot look into the workings, then the level of required education and training will be reduced. This is not a good compromise, though, as transparency and understanding is preferred. Lastly, how much do you need to understand about the system in order to explain it to others or to understand its output? During the roll out, it will be very important to explain things about the output! This will be an ongoing need.

Another issue important during roll out and subsequent use is support. If you cannot modify or understand the system, for whatever reason, it will be important to have a good support contract or have trained personnel in the information technology and industrial engineering departments. The support will be critical during any special planning period, for the week, month, year. It is during these periods that more analysis and questioning will be done by management and other involved parties. It is also during these times that some well-meaning manager will suggest a few what-if scenarios that should be looked at and you will be expected to reconfigure the system and try them out. It may be hard to track down the consultant after hours, on weekends, or within the next half hour because the big boss wants the new plan for a budget meeting with bigger bosses. It is doubly hard when the big boss is standing over your shoulder, giving advice, and impatiently waiting for the new plan. You best be able to make most changes yourself.

CUSTOM SYSTEMS

Custom systems require a different strategy and approach. As noted above, they should only be considered after other options are ruled out. Some examples that might qualify for a custom system are: extremely dynamic, large job shop situations; crew-based scheduling where there are many subjective constraints, many crucial interdependencies between jobs and resources; and focused factory control where there is one person who is dispatcher, scheduler, and planner. When custom routes are taken, there should not be just one or two small gaps between problem and solutions, but gaping chasms.

If you are going to go the custom route, the choice of developer will be crucial. Try to find one who understands production control, will work in a rapid prototyping fashion, and understands enough about software to build a flexible and robust system. For a reasonably sized situation, it is possible to craft a prototype in one to two months; this will depend on tools, skill, and starting point. It will then take another two to three months to tailor and fine tune the system. This kind of performance has been achieved for tools at the detailed dispatching and scheduling level. You can also hear of implementations taking years and then being cancelled. The effort required and implementation duration is very variable for any decision support tool in production control. Supply chain systems are not any easier. They may take longer or less time depending on the level of detail and coordination desired.

It will help if the developer you choose to work with has done it before and has an existing set of tools or software components to leverage. This can reduce the time, cost, and risk substantially. Unfortunately, the nature of software development is extremely volatile. Not all programmers are created equal. Some are far more productive compared to others. There is approximately a 30:1 ratio of programmer productivity and quality out there. That means that a team of two at the top end can do the work of sixty at the lower end. It is often a crapshoot and you are lucky if you get a team or firm that is made up of individuals of medium skill. This programmer disparity has been a major problem with software project management over the decades. It is not helped by the usual programmer's ego that suggests that each and every one of them is at the top end, regardless of evidence to the contrary. If you want high programmer productivity and quality, be prepared to pay well for it.

Custom systems may or may not be cheaper than off-the-shelf tools. It is sometimes possible to negotiate a lower cost depending on who owns the technology at the end of the project, if the custom work enhances the developer's capability, and what the future business potential is. For example, some of the work can be research oriented, building new decision tools for schedulers that are radically different from current commercial offerings, and both partners can gain both financially and functionally in these arrangements. It is possible that these types of developers and opportunities exist where you are and can be sought out. Many of today's commercial systems started out as special custom packages for one factory and were later generalized and commercialized.

ESTIMATING IMPLEMENTATION DURATION

From the time you start until the time the system is live, expect at least a full year to transpire. This is our gut feel for most turnkey sites. Turnkey systems generally should take less time than the other options. Customized implementations will take a bit longer as everything is checked out and verified. And, fully custom and unique systems will take the longest and require the most effort. It is also possible for unique systems to be designed, built, and installed in a year, but these will be the exceptions and not the rule.

It does not matter if the project plan says that the system will be installed in three months and that you will be running 100 percent live a month later, do not bank on it. There are some of these installation success stories out there, but they are few. The situation has to be amazingly simple and clean for such quick implementations. The target for system implementation might be less than a year and it is good to set such targets if there is some evidence that the targets are possible, that the vendor has done it before. Just do not be surprised that after false starts and some retreating and advancing, it takes a year for the system to be stable and useful, with constant handholding by the consultant or vendor. Even if a vendor has done a quick install in the past, are your data and situation exactly the same?

If the planning and process has not been done adequately, the time can extend to several years, usually with the project being unplugged before going live. If you are not in a pilot, or are running live after a year, be worried.

ROLE OF THE INFORMATION TECHNOLOGY DEPARTMENT

Your information technology (IT) department will be vital to the success of any computer-based decision support aid, acquisition, and ongoing use, both on a management level and a personnel level. There are various levels of support needed during normal operations and there are requirements and issues related to the initial acquisition and deployment of the technology.

While it might be possible for a production control department to acquire a scheduling and planning tool by itself, most will need the help of people familiar with software and the software trade. The vendors need to be appraised, requirements determined, and the infrastructure put in place. There are the functional issues related to production control, but there are also issues about software quality, system robustness, implementation standards, migration paths, upgrade strategies, and support.

There will be upgrades and migrations over time. Different operating systems will be migrated to and the vendor will release new versions. When migrating or upgrading, it is often wise to test out the new system or configuration on a parallel machine first, instead of just converting and pressing start. This will require the assistance of the IT group. You should also enlist the help of the IT group to ensure that you can go back to the older system if warranted.

A scheduling and dispatching system is a mission critical system and must be up and running almost all of the time. It must be reliable, functional, and capable of producing useful results. This is not always the case as networks can cause problems or batch processes at a corporate service site can fail. It is also very likely that changes will be needed to the internal data model and report formats at some point. The requirements for IT skill to address these issues will vary by firm, by system, and by computer infrastructure. The possible topics to consider for support are:

- The ability to know if the system is getting the right data. For example, you get a call "This–and–that is not the right number, there is something wrong with the logic, it cannot be this–or–that, fix it."
- The ability to know if the data are being used right assuming that the data get into the decision aid. What is the source of the problem? Is it options and parameters, is it actual algorithms, or does the problem reporter misunderstand what it is supposed to be?
- The ability to make minor and major changes to the model of the factory and processes.
- The ability to make minor and major changes to the reports.
- The ability to find, fix, enhance minor functions.
- The ability to find, fix, enhance major algorithms and logic.
- The ability to explain new sequences of existing functions to address a changing need.
- The ability to explain again or retrain users in what and how the system functions.

These are all aspects of support. In some systems, many of these levels of support must be provided by the consultant or vendor. When these types of support are not time critical, waiting for a consultant or vendor might be acceptable or will depend on what can be done via remote access or local help. If you need the problem fixed in the next half hour, what are your options? The ability to sort out data flows at 6 AM is a need that cannot be delayed to the next business day, filed in a queue, or put on hold until the vendor's office opens at 9 AM on the other coast. You will need sufficient help and talent in the production control department, or local IT department, to understand sources of data, flow of data, and network issues.

In systems that are patched together, that have local and corporate servers involved, and that require batch processes, more IT skills will be required by the planners and schedulers. Unfortunately, many production control personnel do not have the training to understand the manufacturing information system and perform the problem solving. In other cases, they may know, but they may not have the computer privileges to access and trace the data.

You will need to ask yourself: What can go wrong, how long does it typically take to fix, and what happens if it cannot be fixed until later in the morning, later in the day, the next day, the next week, or the next month? Can you still function? What are the downsides? How much would the right amount of support cost you? What is your compromise position? What are your alternatives? How can you continue to plan and schedule? Can you still do some limited work if the network is down? Can you get information from previous days, recover files? All of these topics are IT related, possibly stipulated in a service contract, and you will need help from them to figure out the answers. Something may be possible, but the cost is prohibitive. With software-based decision aids, IT will become very important to production control, in an operational sense, not just supplying desktop computers and network connections.

MAKING SENSE OF SOFTWARE PROJECTS

There are also scheduling software projects that just do not make sense. Sometimes a vice president or someone gets a pet topic going regardless of match or fit and these have to be dealt with carefully. It can take a long time to kill a project; for example, showing that it is not the right solution and will never work and, if installed, will wreak havoc on the firm. Proving never is hard. It is easier to pretend that it will be OK. It took almost one year to shut down a vice president's custom project that was foolish. It was obvious to many that it was never going to work, it was not obvious to the vice president.

Sophisticated software systems really might not be necessary. Just get basic manufacturing sorted out, practice risk management, and create some spreadsheet tools. People are always pleasantly surprised when they do not need to acquire big software tools. If you are not in the top tier of execution and performance, there are many manual or simple things to do before thinking about computer-generated sequences. It is also possible to think about using a computer-based tool to help in certain areas of the plant and use other techniques elsewhere. For example, test, prototype, and complicated processes such as burn-in or heat-treat are possible candidates for scheduling aids while other areas are simply planned and controlled.

At the beginning of this chapter, we described putting the basic problem statement together. It was stated that this should be done without having a solution in mind. This means that after the problem is described, one of the possible solutions should be not to pursue the production control tool path.

SUMMARY

In conclusion, the major phases are: understanding the problem, preparing the material for quotes and development, preparing data and seeding the system, and running some form of pilot test. The phases and elapsed time will bother some people. Getting a new production control system is often triggered by the need to fix something that is broken and a new system is wanted yesterday. You can buy a new drill press and install it without bother. Why not scheduling and planning software? Hopefully this chapter shed some light on the process and explained why it takes time and cannot be rushed.

The next two chapters discuss the issues relating to the success and failure of scheduling tools.

DETERMINING
TOOL SUCCESS

PREDIGESTED THOUGHTS FOR THE BUSY PERSON

■ Success in one plant does not always mean the same type of success elsewhere. Think about a Class A MRP-II implementation versus a non-Class A one. Both can be successful, but success means something different for each. Scheduling tools have the same issues with defining success.

■ Success measures should be determined before the project starts and then tracked.

■ There are five levels of possible success. Each higher level requires greater investment and effort with a greater potential return on investment.

INTRODUCTION

You have thought about it, generated the requirements, and have a scheduling tool now installed. Or, you might be thinking about doing this. The previous chapters gave you some suggestions to think about in terms of what you should do or could have done. In either case, you need to think about success and failure.

Success, partial success, or failure, that is the return on investment. Scheduling systems cost a lot of money, although usually not as much as ERP systems. The cost to install, customize, and keep scheduling technology running is often at least double the basic purchase or licensing fee. Unfortunately, as far as we can make out, more systems are sitting and gathering dust than are used. Or, if they are used, many are being used for tracking and reporting, not for actual schedule generation that will be followed and executed. If a schedule is generated and used, many are changed so much in the manual editing phase that there is little left of the original sequence. There are also systems where the schedule can be generated and followed almost intact. These successful plants do not resemble Jake's factory. These are the top 5 to 10 percent factories — clear winners, clear successes. Most firms will be somewhere between utter failure and 100 percent dreamland; some people will be happy with the tool and others will not.

The failure of a scheduling system has three problems. First, there is the wasted money and effort in trying to get it working. Second, there are the missed returns caused by not using it. This, of course, assumes that there would be returns from using a particular piece of software in a specific situation. This assumption is a big one. Third, there is the perception that there is no value in having installed the software or in attempting to use it. There might be the perception that if magical sequences are not generated, there are no benefits.

There are many reasons why scheduling systems fail and they are discussed in Chapter 12. Before going into the negatives, we have to first consider success. The word "success" implies that there are criteria or a certain level of expectation to which the software successfully reaches. Some firms may think that they have a success. How relative is this success to another company's implementation? Some firms may think that they are a failure, but might actually be a success if the situation was viewed from another angle. Success is a matter of balancing expectations with results.

Was the implementation a success? The expectations might have been related to a savings in time taken to perform certain scheduling and planning tasks, the reduction of problems caused by miscommunication between departments, a reduction in expediting, a reduction in the necessary setups, a reduction in inventory, a reduction in overtime, a reduction in flow time through the plant, or any other number of possible desires. A goal might also have been to introduce new ideas and practices by training a new scheduler before the current scheduler retires. Were the goals and expectations well understood and documented? Were they measurable?

Unfortunately, it is rare for most of the objectives or goals for a scheduling system to be verbalized or stated explicitly when the software is acquired and the implementation started. It is also possible that different parts of the organization and different managers have contradictory or opposing objectives for the scheduling department. All of this makes it hard to determine the criteria and to know whether or not something actually succeeds. If the system was implemented and the manufacturing efficiency has not really improved, failure might be the call. Or, if the goal was to have the software system installed and functional within six to nine months, and alternative systems are still being used two years later, failure might also be the call.

Claims for lower inventory, fewer late jobs, fewer setups, or other similar objectives are very hard to prove or support. In almost any manufacturing situation, there are many ongoing improvement projects with many activities. It is very difficult to attribute clear cause and effect relationships between installing a scheduling system and having results such as lower inventory levels. Was it the inventory location system and improved tracking that lowered inventory or was it the better scheduling and sequencing? Furthermore, when a new manufacturing system or scheduling tool is being implemented, there are often activities required to document the current process, clean up the data, and in general get the house in order. These types of cleanup activities can easily yield 10 to 15 percent improvement regardless of the actual scheduling tool or technology. For example, in one factory, at least half of the customer orders were for obsolete parts and were removed from the system as part of the cleanup. These obsolete orders all had due dates in the past and accounted for much noise and garbage in the MRP system. This type of cleanup is not unique. For many factories, this 10 to 15 percent improvement probably could be derived from implementing a $5,000, $40,000, or $100,000 tool, but the $5,000 tool would never get the attention or resources dedicated to it that a $100,000 tool will. If the factory is spending $100,000 for the tool and another $100,000 in resources and support to use it, the cleanup and restructuring activities miraculously materialize.

To know if the scheduling system is making an impact, you can use anecdotal information or do a controlled study. Anecdotal information is the way it is usually done and the results are always subject to possible bias. The champion or proponent of a tool may not always make the best judge of success. In theory, a controlled study is the only real way to know if there is an impact. A controlled study has probably never been done. Consider what would be needed if you were to do it right. First, you would have to clean up the database and get two similar parts of the factory to the same state of process description and data. Second, you would need to specify and measure the performance aspects of both areas and be able to identify any changes from the previous situation. Third, you would then run both parts of the factory for several months. One area with the scheduling tool and one without. Fourth, you would put on hold any other continuous improvement activities or any other changes in these two areas. Then, and only then, could you compare the situations and possibly say that the scheduling system made a difference. Of course, in an ideal study there is yet a fifth condition: you need the same scheduler scheduling both areas and the scheduler would have to be equally comfortable with both areas and scheduling methods. After all, you want to know that it was the tool providing the true benefit and not any other factor. Not easy to do in a real factory. Impossible?

However, it is possible to get a general feeling that fewer communication mistakes are being made, that the area is running more smoothly, and that the scheduling system is making a difference. These general feelings are only feelings and are not proof. If the scheduling technology is not an expensive proposition, then feelings may be adequate. However, if the scheduling technology is expensive and will be expensive to keep going, then some kind of before-after study using a few key measures may be worthwhile to prove that the return on investment does indeed exist. You could look at inventory levels, flow time, and number of complete batches run. If the software implementation ferreted out major mistakes and forced rethinking of inventory policies and production decisions, you should see some kind of visible impact in the numbers. Did better sequences do it? Hard to say. If you can track adherence to the plan, you might be able to say so. If the factory follows the schedule reasonably closely and the schedule holds for a few days to a week, then you can perhaps either blame or credit the sequences. If the factory does not follow the schedule, if rescheduling occurs almost constantly, if the schedule from two days ago looks almost nothing like the schedule today, then there might be other causes for better performance. For example, did the better communication facilitated by the tool do it? Perhaps. If there are less miscues and a better information flow, there might be less preemptions and less errors. And, fewer errors in production control should translate into better inventory control, setups, and flow times.

If you do not look and analyze, you will definitely not be able to determine any clear cause and effect relationships, or be able to say with confidence that the system was a full or marginal success. For the sake of argument, let us assume that you can determine if the system implementation is a success. It is, after all, possible to visit sites that are publicized as an *APS Success Story*. What does that mean? In order to help ourselves, we have created a simple scheme that attempts to match what people do with APS with the potential of APS. Like there are Class A implementations of ERP, we believe that there are different classes for success and deployment of APS tools. In some ways, it depends on expectations. If you expect to get a certain class of result and you get that result, you are successful. This is different than expecting one level of performance and getting another. What are these classes?

CLASSES OF SUCCESS

To know if an APS system is successful, it is important for you to consider a few things.

First, it depends on who is viewing the situation. For example, the vendor, corporation, production control management, tool user, and factory floor executors may have different views, objectives, and perceptions.

Second, the expectations and views may include the various factors we have noted at various points in the book:

- Saving time in the task
- Improving accuracy in the task
- Improve quality in the task
- Reduce effort in doing the task
- Improve gathering of information
- Improve dissemination of information
- Reduce wastage, setups
- Reduce expediting, preemptions
- Reduce inventory levels
- Improve workflow through the plant
- Have better sequences

The various people looking at the APS implementation will have different expectations about each of these. In some cases, there will be no forethought, in others there will be an explicit objective. Depending on the situation, expectations may change to match what happens or the actual events will be misinterpreted on purpose to justify expectations. There are also expectations as to speed of implementation, cost of initial procurement, and cost and effort for support, but we will not deal with those here. Here we are interested in functional success. You can ask various people in the plant what their initial expectations were for each of the possible benefits and ask how well the expectation has been met. You can ask where the emphasis was. What was the highest priority for them? Where was the biggest benefit?

Third, there are different types of benefits that can be obtained from the introduction of the APS. These can be considered as levels or classes. The better the tool fits the situation, the higher the level of benefit can be expected. Benefits are incremental. This gives you the ability to match initial expectations with the matching level and performance achieved. You can also identify the necessary and sufficient conditions for each class. What is needed in the way of uncertainty ceilings, stability, and levels of prediction, repeatability, and process quality for each class? You can also talk about constraint dependency and environmental dependency. As you increase the level of expectation, certain of these aspects can be expected to increase, while others decrease. These issues and questions also relate to the prior state and to the current state. What was a value or metric last year or last month, what is it currently, and what do you expect it to be?

The five levels of success are:

- Class A — better, more accurate sequences, and exploiting the full potential of the APS concept and technology
- Class B — determining feasible amounts of work
- Class C — identifying resource conflicts and loading issues
- Class D — improving visibility, communication, consistency in the plant
- Class E — improving system integrity, cleaning up processes, addressing data flows

We will discuss them from the bottom up, Class E through A.

Class E: Data Tasks

Various benefits arise from cleaning up data, describing processes, re-evaluating bills of material, cleaning up physical inventory, and straightening out processes as a result of challenging part proliferation and other activities. This benefit arises from the attempt to install a new ERP or APS. Although it does not sound like a great feat, the benefits can be quite substantial just by doing a cleanup and by challenging old practices. In many cases, these benefits will match or exceed those from actually using the system.

Schedulers and planners often spend several hours a day re-entering data and manually setting up their spreadsheets. This is not value-added activity. If you are doing substantial amounts of data entry, the process needs to be reviewed and overhauled. **You should be paid to craft better sequences and make better decisions, not to re-enter or look up data.** Simple or sophisticated planning and scheduling tools can save hours each day. The key is to make sure that your time is not sucked up by other nonvalue-added tasks. Too many times, the operational improvements made at the scheduler's desk, improvements that save time, are implemented only to see the time reallocated to other tasks associated with reorganizations or downsizing. Management then wonders why things are not improving.

Class D: Organizational Benefit

This is the benefit that happens when you improve visibility, have quicker communication, establish consistency between planners and shifts, have better tracking, and have less duplication in paperwork. This benefit arises from just using a specialized information tool that can access, aggregate, and consolidate different information sources and then disperse the information throughout the plant. The benefits here are also great and should not be minimized. Miscues and similar instances of poor communication and information flow are costly! Class D and Class E activities should be done before implementing a system. You might not need a sophisticated system after you have fixed your biggest problems.

One plant we heard about had a large, custom, and very expensive scheduling system developed for it. The revenue stream of the plant was also very large. After installing the scheduling tool, the plant reported a 10 to 15 percent improvement in efficiency. This translated to over a hundred million dollars per year. Was it the advanced scheduling algorithms? Was it the user-friendly interface? No. By using the same tool for all shifts, there was no time wasted between shifts as shift supervisors figured out what should be done, why things were where they were, and what the activities should be. There was consistency and there were standard expectations. This resulted in a seamless integration of the shifts. The former organizing and start-up time per shift was about 10 to 15 percent of the plant's capacity, and it was turned into useful production time.

Class C: Resource Conflicts and Loading Awareness

MRP/ERP logic typically does not support sophisticated finite loading analysis and, hence, the first new planning aid that APS really provides is the awareness to the planner and management about finite resources, loading, and what this means. This results in earlier visibility of problems. This also makes planning quicker since with the MRP planning style, a load of 120 percent might be shown for a resource and the planner has to play games to figure out how and where the real problem is. The finite scheduling tool can provide this information far quicker. The benefit does not arise from better sequences or better loading, but from the finite loading and visibility. If what you want is finite loading and the benefits that arise from the visibility, then you are doing OK. It does not matter what the marketing hype was or what features are in the software; you got what you wanted.

This level of success is what Jake could hope for. Jake would get the visibility, fewer mistakes, and a better view of what the schedule looks like, but most of the schedule will end up being handcrafted. There is no hope that the computer-generated schedule really makes sense. It is a starting point, but that is all.

Class B: Feasible Planning

If feasible amounts of work can be loaded into a time interval or tracked to a time boundary of minutes, hours, a day, several days, or a week, the plant has new capabilities. The sequence might be a little odd, but the basic amount of work is believable. What does feasible mean in this context? Is it feasible to do these two jobs today? If you can say that the two jobs can be done today, regardless of sequence, then you have day-level feasibility. Is it feasible that one job will really start at 8:15 in the morning and finish at 1:23 in the afternoon and that the next job will start at 1:24? If you can count on the 8:15, 1:23, and 1:24, you have minute-level feasibility. Some plants will have minute-, hour-, shift-, day-, week-, or month-level feasibility. For convenience, we will say that B-1 will be at the minute-level accuracy and execution, B-2 at the hour, B-3 at the shift, B-4 at the day, B-5 at the week, and B-6 at the month.

You can think about choosing the reasonable level of time unit and the accuracy that makes sense. B-1 planning is obviously more detailed and accurate than B-5. If you are using a week unit as a loading entity, you do not care what the sequence is within the week, but you are very confident that anything planned for the week will be done within the week and not too much will spill into the next week. When going from a plant with gross month-of or week-of planning, it is best to slowly set the targets. Start at B-4, then B-3, then B-2 in iterative fashion. It is unlikely that you will succeed if you want to jump over a level. Planning within unit boundaries is significantly different from just using finite loading for capacity analysis in Class C.

Tremendous benefits can be obtained going from a Class C to a Class B. The flow and control through the plant can be better controlled and inventory levels made consistent and predictable. The rough sequences of workflow from time period to period can be improved to avoid the big problems. Many plants would call the week-of and month-of planning "bucket planning." If you think about it, even a minute or second level of granularity is a bucket of sorts, a very small bucket. The detailed logic and mathematical calculations may still use days, hours, and minutes, but the work is really released and controlled on the bucket boundary. When you get to the B-1, B-2, and possibly B-3 levels, you might hear the word bucketless. Minute-level analysis for flow, the start-duration-finish, and the synchronization of resources is the highest level of feasible planning and execution. Most factories can only dream of this level. There might be some plants that need to plan and orchestrate at the subminute level and talk about seconds, but this is not realistic for most.

The Class B level is not about seeking the best sequence of work from operation to operation with the best possible reductions in wait time or lateness. It is all about being able to predict reasonable amounts of work for a given time period and making sure that you can orchestrate your resources effectively. If each area performs its amount of work as expected, work will flow predictably through the plant or supply chain and the lead time and inventory levels reduced down to the unit level. This is satisfactory when the operations are less than a time unit in duration, or multiple units; for example, when an operation takes less than four hours to complete and you are planning work on the day boundary. Multiple-day requirements are also OK, since that uses your capacity for multiple periods. It is also likely that this approach will work best when the processing times for most work for a machine or a plant are multiples of a base value or are of similar length; for example, jobs having two-hour processing times with four jobs loaded into the time zone.

The more stable and predictable the situation, the smaller the loading interval, until you get down to the minute. The progression is usually from months to weeks to days to a single day and then to hours within the day. With scheduling technology, it is likely that your tool will be based on minutes or even seconds and you will have to think about the feasibility loading and what you will trust. How good is the model in the software? If you can trust the loading for a week, you are at B-5. If you cannot trust the loading for a week, you might be at B-6. Class B success is all about trust and faith in the amount of work that is scheduled into any zone. To summarize, the feasible planning concept can be separated into six levels:

- B-1 — minute
- B-2 — hour
- B-3 — shift
- B-4 — day
- B-5 — week
- B-6 — month

As a plant improves in its execution, you should see a progression. When you set out to acquire a tool, try to figure out your current level for feasible estimating and loading. Do not expect the software to do magic. If you are unable to do feasible loading at B-5, but can do a reasonable B-6, do not expect the software to deliver B-2. You might set a success goal of B-5 if there are other factory improvement activities being done in parallel. If you hit B-5, you can claim success as it matches your expectations. If your competition is able to do B-3, you have more work to do.

Class A: Better and More Accurate Sequences

Class A starts to exploit the full potential of the APS concept and technology and that is why it is the highest. It focuses on sequences and the ability to believe or trust in the computer-generated sequence.

How much of the computer-generated schedule remains after manual editing and how much of it happened as planned, if you look back in time? How much of yesterday matched the original computer schedule? How much of last week? How much of last month? Are the sequences better than what was done before? How much better? There are two issues: faith and accuracy.

When you can start trusting and believing in the estimated start-finish dates, you can link the use of the system to a concept called *availability to promise* (ATP). In order taking, you want to be able to quote realistic times. Times that a customer can rely on. The times might be week-of or they might even be quoted at the day level. The software may estimate a Wednesday finish, but you quote the Friday, or the following Wednesday. As you can guess, the Class A performance also has scales like the Class B.

A-1 level is being able to coordinate and believe any computer-generated start-finish estimate for the next week to about an hour accuracy. The estimates for work beyond this time horizon may degrade, but that will be true for almost any factory situation. If you can predict and execute the next week down to the hour, you are in an awesome factory. You might have good estimates for the next week to the hour, but the second and third weeks will be at the half- or full-day level. This is to be expected. One week of tightly coordinated activity is great and there will be many benefits to the plant from using the software. A possible scale would be:

- A-1 — hour accuracy for almost all of the operations within the next week
- A-2 — hour accuracy for three to four days, but not beyond that
- A-3 — hour accuracy for the next forty-eight hours, but not beyond
- A-4 — hour accuracy for the next twenty-four hours
- A-5 — hour accuracy for a day's worth of production
- A-6 — hour accuracy for a half-day's worth
- A-7 — accuracy for the next two to three hours
- A-8 — believable start/finish estimates for the next hour or two

If you are doing a great deal of rescheduling throughout the day, you will be at A-7 or A-8. Jake's factory fluctuates between A-6 and A-9. A-9 is the situation where almost nothing finishes within the next hour as estimated, the start or the finish.

You notice that we do not have an explicit scale for *better*. Better is hard to judge, but we assume that if the computer generates a schedule worse than what you would do manually, you are going to tweak it and the shop floor is going to be directed to do something different than what the computer suggested. It might be a big assumption, but we have not met too many schedulers who will issue a schedule to the workers that has obvious problems with the work sequences. This will be reflected in the A-x scale. If the system generates schedules that are truly better and believable, you will have a higher rating, approaching A-1. If the sequences are good and can be executed, they will be left alone.

A rule of thumb might be needed for thinking about the future. If you have an A-4 level of scheduling that you can trust for the next twenty-four hours, you might want to restrict delivery quotes for work in the next month to the feasible loading level; the B-5 level for week-of loading. For estimates beyond the next month, you might want to hedge on half-month or month boundaries. The scales will give you some sort of rationalization process for establishing policies and expectations.

CLASS A AND B INTERACTION

The Class A success level for better and more accurate sequences will be constrained or restricted by the Class B level for feasible loading. You will not be able to set a goal of A-2 for daily sequencing if you have trouble doing B-5 feasible loading at the week level. As you improve the feasible loading, you might be able to improve the sequencing, but not always. If you have a very flexible and capable workforce, and sufficient capacity, you might have faith in the general load, but will not be able to set precise start and finish times in advance for each operation. If there is decentralized dispatching decisions, down at the supervisor or machine operator, you might also be forced to a good Class B performance, but have trouble seeing or having visibility to the start and finish times for each operation. Studying the problem using these classes and scales may help you understand the pros and cons of decentralized decision making. If you need to improve your factory to where coordination exists between work centers at the hour or partial shift level, you need to provide good estimates for all players involved. This is hard to do with decentralized decision making. You will need a good tool and be operating at the appropriate Class A level for the processing times involved.

You go for feasibility, then better sequences if you can. Then take it up a notch, make sure you are feasible, then see if you can go for smarter sequences. Do this slowly and carefully. Once you are stable at any Class B level, you can use the system for ATP projections. As noted above, this is where you use the technology to help with the order process. Someone asks for a job to be done and you use the software tool to establish a due date. This projection takes the finite loading and feasibility into account and, in theory, gives you better dates to give your customer. This is a big topic by itself and will not be expanded on in this book. The power of using the APS technology for helping set due dates and promises to the customers is very important. The more demanding the customers are for reduced lead times and the more demanding they are for meeting the promised dates, the more the Class A and Class B issues will ratchet down. Some customers will demand good day-of estimates for the next week, the next month, or even farther out. If you can do the work far faster than the quoted lead time and can play with finished goods inventory, no problem. But if the flow and queue time is also compressed, you need to have good Class A and Class B performance.

It is wise to know both Class A and B performance, have goals for each, and monitor progress. Since Class A depends on Class B, knowing that one factory can do A-1 sequencing and execution says a great deal about the Class B capability. You might not know it precisely, but you might be able to guess the ballpark. There are issues that can mess up the guessing and these are discussed in the next section.

TOWARDS A-1

Class A and B performance, the time interval planning, and ATP consideration have several dimensions. You need to know your current abilities, what the next reasonable level is, and where you want to end up. You need to know, or guess at, what your competition is currently doing and where they are headed. How good does your scheduling have to be?

For example, how accurate does the loading sequencing need to be for the plan to be close enough? Does it have to have good quality for twenty-four or forty-eight hours, or seven or fourteen days? What information do the suppliers need to know to plan day-of deliveries? The more stable and predictable the supply and demand are, the longer the horizon can be.

The level of control will also depend on what the average run times are. For example, if the average job takes a shift or two to complete, or several days, do you really need minute-level accuracy and tuning? If all jobs and batches complete within an hour, start to finish, what level of time granularity do you need? What target should you set for tight flow and predictions? Obviously, if you are working with jobs that take shifts or days to complete, you might need to adjust the scales. For instance, if your basic time unit is a shift's amount of work, where work is started and finished on a shift boundary, A-1 performance would imply that you can predict with a high degree of accuracy what each shift is doing for the next week. Interpret the Class A and Class B scales to fit your situation.

In any factory situation, you should be able to ask what the current time unit size is and how far into the future can the time intervals be used reliably. Is this in terms of within-day or day-of shipments? How big or small did you want the time intervals to be when you first started with the APS? How small or big do you think they can get to? This is all part of the migration from a B-4 to a B-1 and A-3 to A-1. There are sublevels of expertise and achievement within each A and B class. It is hard to avoid the oscillation between the two. We are talking about improving on two dimensions and they are co-dependent. It is like lowering the water a bit with a pail and using two hands, setting down the pail, and then dealing with those rocks that appear. Then you grab the pail, lower the water again by a set amount, and deal with the new rocks that appear. On each iteration, you have full focus on lowering the water and then on the rocks. In planning and scheduling, it is also probably better to do improvements in an organized, iterative way — feasible load, then better schedules; tighter feasibility, then better sequences. Conversely, if you like excitement, you can use one hand for working the pail and constantly lowering the water, and try to deal with the rocks appearing with the other hand — there, here, over there, two at once, do not forget to keep that pail going.

The quality or success of the feasibility loading can be ascertained by looking at what moves from interval to interval with successive planning iterations, time and quantity. To us, ultimate success is when the APS tool can create a schedule that is actually followed and executed as planned! This would be 100 percent automatic schedule generation and factory execution. A factory claiming A-1 cannot be doing too much manual tweaking or tuning. If the schedule is being tweaked and tuned to any great extent, the benefit and success are really coming from the human-computer marriage, which might not be a bad thing. The human is providing the modeling and knowledge that the software is incapable of providing. Since the Class concept is meant to measure the realized potential of the technology, any inclusion of human assist will distort the claims.

The amount of human intervention must be clear to any external body! If you can create an A-1 situation with the human and computer marriage, this is great, but give the credit to both and not just the software.

Knowing how the APS interacts and complements the ERP is vital. This will affect what levels of Class A and Class B are reasonable and feasible. How much does the APS rely on the ERP for guidance? Does the APS have its own bill of material? Does it expand the bill using the demand inputs and have its own MRP logic? Does the APS do its own batch sizing? Or, does it take the ERP's MRP order list as a due date and quantity requirement? You will need to know how the analysis is done at the high level and how the scheduling tool interfaces with the ERP. If the ERP cannot model the situation accurately, but tightly guides the APS, your benefits will be limited by the ERP and not by the APS.

The future time intervals where work is loaded into can be tracked over time and the schedule changes monitored. In many firms, there is an immediate, short time period when changes are not allowed or are discouraged — the frozen zone. This time period is used to stabilize the production plans and is used to prevent schedule or plan chatter. Otherwise, requirements and work assignments may change constantly. Reducing schedule chatter is also important when you need to plan resources to reduce unnecessary costs. This is important when overtime needs to be scheduled for weekends, extra shifts are scheduled, or when preventative maintenance is planned. Unfortunately, this frozen zone can give problems depending on how well the work can be executed. If the frozen zone exceeds the reliable execution zone, then ever-increasing problems will occur with the occasional major adjustment needed in the plan. You need to know when your time intervals are too large and frozen periods too long.

SUMMARY

In this chapter, we talked about the levels of success that can be observed for scheduling tools. If you are going to claim success in the future, it is important to set the goals and criteria when you start. If you have not set your goals, how do you know if you have succeeded? A success will be if you meet or exceed your expectations. There are many kinds of successes and the right target for you will depend on where you are and what you can achieve realistically.

The five levels of success are:

- Class A — better, more accurate sequences, and exploiting the full potential of the APS concept and technology
- Class B — determining feasible amounts of work

- Class C — identifying resource conflicts and loading issues
- Class D — improving visibility, communication, consistency in the plant
- Class E — improving system integrity, cleaning up processes, addressing data flows

The next chapter discusses why some firms fail when they try to implement and use production planning tools. Combined with this chapter about identifying targets and levels of implementation success, the reasons for failure in Chapter 12 can help explain why you might have failed in your implementation attempt or came up a bit short. They might help you understand why the attempt was successful. The two chapters might also help you look forward to the future.

12

SCHEDULING
TOOL FAILURES

PREDIGESTED THOUGHTS FOR THE BUSY PERSON

- It is easy to point fingers. Understand the causes before assessing blame.

- There are as many nontechnical reasons for failure as there are technical ones.

- The scheduling tool may be adequate, but the failure was caused by the way the project was executed.

- If the tool is not used, the project is a failure.

INTRODUCTION

Chapter 11 described five classes of APS success. Why does everyone not easily get these benefits? Why is it so hard to succeed with these tools?

There are thousands of scheduling systems in use with varying degrees of success. There are implementations that are everything that the factory ever dreamed of. There are other implementations that have not worked out so well. We suspect that many more thousands of implementations have been attempted and have failed. If you consider the number of vendors and the length of time scheduling systems have been marketed, there should be many more successful implementations — many, many more. Compare the installed base of factory planning systems with the installed base of project planning tools. Is there a factory planning tool equivalent to Microsoft Project? There are hundreds of thousands of factories, but the number of factories using advanced planning tools is relatively small. In this chapter, we will discuss various reasons why scheduling systems fail and why they are so hard to install and use.

POINTING FINGERS

If the system is not being used or the implementation is not considered a total success, the blame will start to circulate, trying to stick to someone or something. Is it a technical reason or is it something to do with the user or other nontechnical aspects? The scheduling software vendor justly may point to problems within the factory and the plant's manufacturing systems. The plant might point at the vendor. Both might point at you, the user. You might point back at the scheduling software and corporate MRP/ERP tools. Probably, when a scheduling implementation is considered less than a success, there is more than one reason and there is more than one guilty party.

At the extreme level, there is complete failure and the system is never used in a live situation after the pilot. Major mistakes must have been made by the people specifying, acquiring, supplying, and deploying the tool. The situation was misread on many dimensions. The factory is responsible for understanding what it needs and conveying that in an understandable way to the potential vendors. This does not have to be 100 percent, but it should be close enough. The factory may do this with help from corporate officers or with a consultant, but it is the factory's responsibility. It is not up to the vendor to do a complete and thorough requirements study before quoting on the job. If the reasons for failure include problems with specifying what was needed and the needs changed during the implementation, the vendor cannot be blamed totally.

The vendor should be responsible for doing a basic fit analysis to ensure that they can come close to modeling your situation, handling your data, and generating your desired reports in the quantities and time that you want. If the vendor is trying to push into a new manufacturing area, extra analysis is warranted and the risks identified at the beginning. The vendor might have specialized in electronics and you are the first automotive sector client. You need to know this and be prepared. Generally, if the factory's requirements are stated clearly and the vendor claims that they can do the job, then the blame drifts towards the vendor. This implies that the modeling and basic functionality in the tool may be at fault.

It is possible that the factory did not assess its data readiness accurately and did not know that the routings, processing times, setups, and bills of material structures were a mess. If the data are a mess, they can extend the implementation to the point where it fails. The vendor should be responsible for documenting what state the information needs to be in, what information is needed, and what the implementation plan looks like depending on the starting state. In the final analysis, the data integrity and quality should be the responsibility of the client. You can have this covered by contractual terms with the software vendor, but it is the plant's personnel who will be supplying the information, checking it, and maintaining it.

The vendor should be held accountable for delivering a software tool that is functional and will run. Software is rarely bug free. It does not rust or develop mildew, but the internals are very complicated. Functions that are used irregularly or are considered to be very complex are possible sources for bugs. Some problems are reasonable with the complex stuff or the stuff that does not get much usage. Functions that you expect to use hourly, daily, weekly, or monthly should be robust and functional. Through the requirements analysis, the vendor should know what these functions will be and the vendor should be blamed if the frequently needed functions do not work. Scheduling software should not crash daily, weekly, or multiple times each month! It is too critical for that. Scheduling software should not generate standard reports with calculation errors either. Special reports with special formulas will take a while to sort out, but the basic reports should be bulletproof. The vendor should be accountable for installing, or trying to install, immature software. They should have not agreed to the sale. If you are knowingly a test user for a new version or a new product, this is different. In this case, blame cannot be laid and everyone has to chill out and be patient. If you are using custom or heavily customized software, then you should be reasonable and expect a normal maturing period for the software. This is part of the cost of going the customized route. The road is not smooth.

The implementation process can be delayed and extended by both parties, and this can result in the project not succeeding. Are enough resources dedicated to the project by the plant? Are there enough installers and implementers from the vendor? Is enough of the key users' time freed up for creating the specifications, reviewing proposals, participating in the vendor review and vetting, helping with the prototypes and pilots, and receiving training? Does the vendor put the right people on the job? Personnel that understand the type of factory you have? Sufficient senior or experienced personnel who have done similar installations in the past? It is easy to share blame here.

The scheduling software might fail because people just do not use it. Certain functions take too long. They work, but they are laborious and not user friendly. Certain functions are confusing, not easy to find, not easy to use correctly. They work, but not in a nice way. Who is to blame here? The vendor has supplied functional software, but you are not using it. Are you not using it because you do not know how to use it better or is it because it is truly unfriendly and your job is easier to do the old way? One factory had installed an APS and was not happy. They were not getting the expected value from it. The users complained that certain functions were laborious, that they could not find other functions easily, and they did not know how to use others. The planner complained that it took a long time to add a new product and find all of the necessary tables. He had a hard time finding the table for the processing times. The software's help system did not help. It did not work. Hindsight is always wonderful. Perhaps the client did not do sufficient due diligence when the package was purchased. They should have gone through the process of adding work, new resources, new products, changing products, and deleting products as part of the demos and vetting process. The unfriendly nature of the software should not have been a surprise. A few functions might be overlooked during a demo, but they should not be sufficient to kill a tool, and the problems should have been known during the early stages of training in any event. The vendor can be criticized for having a poor design and a clumsy interface, but this is not a crime unless they promised that a specific amount of effort was needed for such functions and then failed to deliver. When a scheduler is not using a tool, careful analysis is needed. The scheduler might not use the system because of the software, but they might also not be using the software because of their training, their skills, or their attitude.

The following sections go into the technical and nontechnical reasons for failure. No one forces a company to select a certain vendor and to select a certain tool. The decision might have been made at a corporate level, but that was still an internal decision. If greater care is taken up front and due diligence undertaken, the laws of natural selection might work to everyone's benefit and the weaker software vendors will become extinct. The vendors can help themselves by ensuring better fits and by developing deployment methods that will detect and highlight problems early in the process. No one forces them to sell to a specific client. It will never be possible to specify everything, have everything ready, have all functions exactly as the client wishes, and mechanisms are needed to provide visibility on these issues. Realizing the problems one or two years into a botched implementation is bad. Implementations with a few issues and some minor problems should be considered a resounding success. In assessing blame and thinking about who to point the finger at, consider who said what, who specified what, who promised what, and how each party carried out their obligations, legal and otherwise. Some failures will be definitely the fault of the vendor, some will be largely the fault of the client, and many failures should be shared.

TECHNICAL REASONS FOR FAILURE

What are the technical problems? Potentially, there are many. The technical problems can include:

- The totally wrong program was purchased, e.g., a *process* type product for a *discrete part* environment.
- The software keeps crashing or is not robust enough for an industrial situation.
- The parameters were set incorrectly in the beginning.
- The ability of the system to model the problem is insufficient. It is not possible to model the essential aspects of the resources, work, routing, and interrelationships. The inability results in schedules that are infeasible or unrealistic.
- The system cannot represent the units or the degree of accuracy needed.
- The length of time it takes to initialize the system and to run it in the morning is too long.
- The system does not support streamlined start-of-day or other routine activities that are done under severe time pressures and require a reduced number of keystrokes, fewer window manipulations, or data entries.
- The number of jobs and operations that the system can handle is too few.
- It is not possible to obtain information in a timely fashion from the MRP, ERP, or MES system.
- The number of windows and the number of screens the operator has to access to get to data is too many.
- It is not possible to modify the schedule enough manually to create the schedule that needs to be created.
- It is not possible to create or format the appropriate reports and control what is found on a report; for planning, management, and the shop floor.
- The system does not support the terminology or phrases needed to communicate with the workforce.
- It is not possible to understand why some sequencing decisions have been made; there is insufficient transparency to trust the recommended sequence.
- The data in the tool are not kept up to date, are inaccurate, or are incomplete.
- The necessary supporting software or systems are not in place for feeding the scheduling tool. The scheduling tool cannot obtain the right types of data at the right time.

■ An untested, new advanced algorithm with a promise for great results is brought in for implementation and fails to deliver.

Of course, some of these technical problems are also partially related to people or organizational issues.

NONTECHNICAL PROBLEMS

The major personnel or nontechnical issues can be with the vendor, the consulting firm installing the software, or your own production staff. The problems can be related to skill levels in the domain, such as knowledge of factory scheduling procedures, or to the tool itself that is being deployed. It is also possible that someone knows what to do, but is simply sloppy. There can be other problems as well with personality conflicts, the ability of the vendor to communicate with you, or the other people who will be using the software.

The skill level of all involved is important. The inadequate skill level of the initial problem assessors can lead to the wrong tool being chosen. Any unskilled people installing the software can lead to the wrong configuration options being set. The possible ineptitude of the deployment team can affect the quality of training that you actually receive. You may not know what you are doing.

The suitability of the people using the scheduling technology also has to be thought about and assessed. After all, the people who are using the software on a daily basis will dictate to a large degree if the software will be successful or not. As we have said elsewhere, not everyone can be a scheduler or a planner. Not all planners and schedulers will be able to use APS technology effectively. There are probably two dimensions to consider: knowledge and skill.

It is obvious that you must know the factory and must know the process within the factory as a bare minimum. But is this sufficient? For example, to use a given APS tool, do you need to know the theory of inventory as it is implemented in the manufacturing system to be able to use the system? Do you need to know the terminology and mathematical formulations? Do you need to understand probability, statistics, and how to calculate averages and variances? Do you need to know the costs of every operation, what a minute of lateness costs when a job is late? Do you need to know the monetary aspects of the work in addition to the straight processing aspects? There might be many new factors that you, as a scheduler, will need to understand and be able to play around with.

The education or knowledge base of a planner or scheduler is important to think about. Do you have to take special courses in order to use the software? Should you have an industrial engineering undergraduate degree, or even a graduate degree, to use the tool? There have been some industries where the schedulers have always been highly educated; for example, chemical firms, process industries, aerospace, and other high-tech firms. In other industries, the education of the schedulers and planners has not been as high and in many cases it did not have to be high. In the latter cases, the real requirement was probably high, but was not perceived as being high. With the introduction of sophisticated software systems such as MRP-II and ERP, the requirements have changed and many firms require the CPIM (certified in production and inventory management) designation from APICS or an APICS equivalent. Adding an APS or FCS system further increases the educational requirements. Either you should have the education and training as part of your normal development or correcting steps should be taken prior to the system's introduction.

You may view the tool as a threat to your job security. You may think that the tool increases your workload and will create problems for you. There are many reasons why systems are acquired, many differences between systems in the way they help or can help, and many differences in how the systems are used. You might be right about your fears or you might not be. Do not assume initially that the systems will hurt you, nor assume that the systems will help you. Look at what the tools can do, how they will be used, and think about the possible impacts. Then, think about your fears. Some fears will be real. In one factory, the system provided more information to management than management had before. The management started to ask more questions and expected different results. Management suddenly expected the schedulers to understand inventory theory and how to control the dynamics of the MRP logic. Implementing a tool suddenly increased the job requirements, job expectations, and job stress. This is OK if you will get the training and proper support, but not OK if you are just expected to do this through the touch of a magical wand.

There are more problems if the added value to you is not clear. Even if the company would benefit from the system, it might mean more hassle for you, as you have to sell the plan or explain it and deal with one part of the organization playing games with the others. It is easy to forget that the user of the software needs to see personal added value in using the tool, not just firm-level benefits. What is in it for you? If it takes more work and is a pain in the butt to use, it is unlikely that the software will see sustained or successful use. This is a *big* issue.

The time available for training and education about the system is another critical aspect. It is unlikely that you will have enough dedicated time to actually learn enough about the system. You will not have enough time to learn how to use it easily and without difficulty. You will have to do most of the learning in the heat of the moment as you try to plan and schedule the real factory. How friendly is the software if you have to learn on the fly?

There are aspects of the system that will be used infrequently. These will cause difficulty for you when you have to use the features. For example, there may be actions or functions that are only done at the end of the month or once a year. It will be difficult for you to be able to remember the functions and to be able to use them correctly. This in itself may not be a problem, but on the other hand, usually the monthly or yearly functions are done under stressful situations, sometimes with little or no warning, and with management waiting impatiently for the results. Can you quickly find them? Can you use them intuitively?

Scheduling tools have failed in the long term for other interesting reasons as well. For example, if the schedulers or planners change, the tool might not be adopted by the new planner. They might not understand it and hence not use it correctly. The new person might want to use the bunch of custom spreadsheets that had been used on their old job. Whenever the planners or schedulers change, there is a chance of tool abuse, misuse, and nonuse. Another example is when there is a senior management change. The senior manager might not understand or appreciate what the tool does and mandates that a different tool or solution be acquired and used. The new manager might not use the tool's output or capability properly. There are many scenarios that result in partial tool usage or termination.

Partial tool usage is interesting. If you are using an ERP or APS, how many extra spreadsheets do you use? Do you use the spreadsheets each day or are they for the weekly, monthly, or yearly tasks you do? Is there a separate spreadsheet for the long-range planning? If the ERP or APS is really doing its job, why do you have any extra spreadsheets? What would happen if, all of a sudden, all of your spreadsheets disappeared? Think about it. If you rely on the spreadsheets more than the ERP/APS output, then you do not have a great fit. Success is partial. You might be getting benefits from the ERP/APS tool, but the total performance of production control cannot be attributed to it. In some cases, these spreadsheets are totally warranted and are the only way to get the job done. If the spreadsheets exist because you do not know how to use the APS correctly as a result of inadequate training, then get the training and get rid of the spreadsheets. Looking for extra spreadsheets is a little test for factories claiming that they are one of those APS success stories hitting A-1 or A-2. Few if any secondary tools, great. They are true A-1 or A-2 successes. If they have many additional spreadsheet tools wrapped around the APS, not so great. A claim of a A-1 or A-2 implementation should be based on the ERP/APS' own capability and not based on additional crutches, bandages, or fixes.

Perhaps the single, most important key performance indicator on scheduling system implementations is nontechnical:

If you use the system, the project succeeds.
If you do not use the system, the project fails.

That might be all that you need to remember. Of course, by *use* we mean that you actually use it as an aid and not as a momentary activity during the day or week just to satisfy a reporting or process requirement. By use, we mean actively using the tool to create better sequences and allocations, helping you to foresee problems and discount them.

Related to the above is another important reason for failure or extended implementations: lack of basic system and computer literacy. In addition to the extra training needed to learn the new scheduling software and its concepts, some schedulers need training and help with the existing systems. More than one scheduler has not known how to use the mainframe or corporate MRP/ERP system beyond the minimum sign-on and knowing how to print a report. One scheduler did not know how to use the e-mail system. He actually deleted all of the e-mail each morning and did not read it. Of course, the deleted e-mails included the ones about how to use the scheduling tool. In addition, he did not know how to turn the computer off at night. Other schedulers have overtyped blanks into a field to erase data instead of using the backspace or delete keys. If you cannot see it, nothing is there! Unfortunately, to get any real benefit from MRP/ERP and scheduling tools, you need to have good computer skills and you need to know how to use the corporate information systems. The lack of knowledge is not usually your fault. Management might have overlooked you for serious training or assumed that you knew or could do the task. Serious training is more than that one- or two-hour session on the basics. You need more than a few hours to understand the systems and the other tools on your computer. If the key knowledge and adequate skills do not exist before the scheduling system is introduced, you are learning multiple systems at once and this is not good. These implementations will be rough and bumpy.

SUPPLY CHAIN MANAGEMENT PROJECTS

Supply chain management projects can be of two types. One type is focused on the driver plant and looks at the plant's immediate supply chain and inventory; one level up and one level down. These projects typically focus on the inventory involved in shipping and receiving, and really do not involve explicit, coordinated planning between the players. The driver plant really does not model the plants up or down in the chain. Policies and strategies might be modeled, but that is it. There are some project-related issues that can result in problems, but they are relatively minor.

Another type is actually closer to the intent of supply chain management, the active coordination of multiple plants and multiple levels in the chain. This type involves the modeling, at some level, of each plant. In extreme cases, supply chain management involves build and ship instructions for the majority of the chain. Detailed modeling of each plant or major processes might also be attempted. When you have multiple plants involved in a coordinated venture, some high-level problems can arise:

- The type of functionality may not be appropriate for each part of the chain. The main driver plant, or corporate head office, might make a decision about what software is to be used. Then this decision is imposed on the local organizations throughout the chain. The driving corporation has a standard for all plants to use and the fit is secondary. A factory with a simple problem is forced to implement a sophisticated tool. In other cases, a factory with a unique or complex situation is forced to make many serious compromises. Sometimes you can fight the mandate, but in most cases you will likely have to accept the inevitable. The software requirement may be specified by the big customer driving the chain, regardless of corporate boundaries.

- The software does not fit the management requirements of each of the corporations involved in the supply chain. The choice of one piece of software may imply certain reporting, objectives, metrics, tracking, policies, methods, terminology, data standards, and other fun stuff, applicable to one and all. This may or may not work when you cross corporate boundaries. In an extreme case, multiple or different software systems may be needed for different parts of the chain and integrated.

- The planners are not trained adequately in the changed way of working in the firm and between firms. They might have training on the tool, but do they understand the bigger picture? If there is more than one planner or scheduler involved, the issues become important. Are the various planners and schedulers allowed to meet and sort out the polices and methods or are they told what to do? How will the planners and schedulers communicate with each other?

- There will be many cultural and political barriers to solve. When companies need to cooperate, there are shared objectives and conflicting objectives. To embed the software in each company, you may need to change the production control structures in each piece of the puzzle. You might have to make changes in the staffing of departments as well.

SUMMARY

In the above paragraphs, we talked about technical and nontechnical reasons why scheduling systems fail. There are many organizational and cultural problems that could cause a system to fail. For example, departments can just ignore the schedule and do what they want to do in any event. Another problem can be with the manufacturing enterprise as a whole. It might just be the case that nothing — no scheduler, no scheduling system — could help or do anything for the firm. As we have pointed out, if the production system is not predictable and if you do not know what is where, nothing will help. Another point worthy of repetition is data accuracy. It is important for scheduling and planning to have reasonably good expectations for setups, processing time, and yield. This has not changed in one hundred years. It is equally important to know with reasonable accuracy what was built and where it can be found. Inventory tracking and accuracy is important for successful production control, always has been, always will be. There are factories where these basic manufacturing processes remain the first challenge. Do not blame the software for bad schedules if the situation is bad to start with.

The focus of this and the past few chapters has been on the commercial or full-solution approaches to decision support tools. When you are analyzing a situation, it is always good to challenge assumptions and ask some basic questions. How big of a solution do you need? How much of the factory or situation do you really have to plan and control? If you fixed things up manually and with some simple spreadsheet tools, would you still be looking for an APS tool? For those with some in-house programming skill or reasonably priced consulting help, it is sometimes possible to craft decision aids in spreadsheet tools such as Excel. The following chapter gives some brief ideas and suggestions if you are thinking about this route or if you want to create a slightly functional prototype as part of the APS acquisition process.

13

EXCEL AND VISUAL BASIC TOOLS

PREDIGESTED THOUGHTS FOR THE BUSY PERSON

- Prototypes may be necessary to understand what is really needed.

- Spreadsheet tools can be used for prototypes and for fully functional purposes.

- Prototypes need not be too expensive, but fully operational tools will not be cheap.

INTRODUCTION

In earlier chapters, we discussed the issues associated with custom systems and how one idea to help make the APS acquisition easier is to use a prototype. A spreadsheet tool like Excel can be used for this purpose. We also talked about various ways to improve production control and occasionally noted the possible application of spreadsheet tools.

There are five types of things that you can use spreadsheet tools for:

1. You can use them for the simple purpose of gathering data, the inputs and outputs, and creating mock-ups of reports. This is one level of prototyping and shows vendors what is available and what is needed. We will not discuss this use as it is pretty obvious what you can and should do.

2. You can use spreadsheet tools as secondary data repositories, calculators, and report generators. You can usually export or copy data from ERP and APS tools in spreadsheet format or as text files and then use them in other spreadsheets. There are many unique and special reports that you are asked to generate, and most planners and schedulers have a whole bunch of spreadsheets lying around. You probably have at least a half dozen that you use each day, even if you have an APS. These spreadsheet tools are often controlled by formulas in the cells and the logic is pretty straightforward. There may be several workbooks hooked together via lookup functions, but the various spreadsheets do not really work together as a system or a fully functional tool for planning and scheduling. We are not going to discuss this type of use either. The ability to use a spreadsheet, use basic formulas, and be able to import/export data should be considered a basic literacy requirement for all planners or schedulers.

3. You can use spreadsheet tools for generating slightly functional prototypes to explore any sophisticated relationships and to make sure that requirements and issues are better understood before a full APS tool is acquired or built. If you are worried about a few functions or concepts, it is probable that you can build a spreadsheet tool using formulas and simple spreadsheet functions. You will not be doing menus, pop-up data forms, and complicated tasks, but you might want to create some machine data, a few orders, and generate a tabular schedule. This is a good exercise. Can you create a schedule for the next twenty-four hours using simple data and simple formulas? You might need a little bit of Visual Basic programming, but you should be able to get a pretty good prototype without going that far. This level of prototyping will not result in an operational tool that can be used.

4. You can create a prototype that has quite a bit of functionality in it and one that you could actually try to use on a limited scale in the factory. This will require programming and more effort. If you are going into an area that commercial tools have not tread or an area that you think has subtle and poorly understood requirements, this is a good idea. A decent prototype capable of actually taking ERP data, scheduling, and generating reports will cost, but it will be substantially less than acquiring a full commercial version and then discovering that you cannot get to where you want to go.

5. You can create a fully functional planning and scheduling tool for finite loading and feasible assignment of work. The tool can have almost all of the capability of the commercial offerings. For this type of tool, you

will be best to avoid any formulas and have the tool programmed in Visual Basic. The tool will be reasonably expensive, likely less than a big APS, but still expensive. The major benefit will be the custom fitting of terminology, tasks, screens, functions, and reports. The spreadsheet tool can also be very flexible, and in some cases, partially maintained by the actual planners and schedulers.

In this chapter, we will be concentrating on the fourth and fifth types of spreadsheet tools. These are the categories providing nontrivial functionality and possibly requiring a software development strategy and programming. Our focus will be production planning and control software that uses Excel or a similar spreadsheet program as the base and a programming environment behind the scenes, such as VBA (Visual Basic for Applications).

You can also get to the nontrivial category from the first and second categories. For simple reports and calculations, formulas in spreadsheets work well. The first and second types of tools may remain at the formula level for a long time. The formula approach starts to fall apart, however, when extensive logic has to be imbedded — *if* X *then* Y *else* Z. If you need a lot of if-then-else formulas, then reconsider your use of spreadsheets based on formulas. Think programming.

NONTRIVIAL SPREADSHEET TOOLS

Are you tempted by a custom, unique planning and scheduling spreadsheet tool? Your own APS? Do not go the custom or unique code route unless you are sure that you must go this way. Can you live with compromises, can you change the corporate culture and process to accept the off-the-shelf package? Can you accept certain limitations in reports and modeling capability? Is it good enough? In many cases, an 80 percent compromise is good enough. Do not go for 100 percent. There are commercial packages that are good enough for many factories. The commercial tools are not cheap, and it will take six months to a year to get them up and running, but it is the path of reduced risk.

But what happens when it comes down to the final analysis and commercial tools just do not cut it? This can be due to modeling or operational issues. If you have a third to a half of your processes with unique process quirks that cannot be modeled in MRP or a commercial APS, what do you do? If you have operational requirements for certain information processing at 6 AM, 6:30 AM, 7 AM, and special reports that must be generated? What if you are in a factory that is out of control?

178 Practical Production Control

Thank goodness not every factory is this difficult and troublesome, but there are many factories that are dynamic and unique and cannot use off-the-shelf systems. Thus, one is forced to either take a system and perform heavy customization or create a system from scratch. Excel and VBA are possible ways to deal with these messy situations.

A spreadsheet tool or system can be created by someone within the production control department, by someone in the information technology department, or by a consultant. In any case, ensure that an in-house system is really needed before you make the decision. There are some individuals who want to develop their *own* system, regardless of a suitable one being available.

Be careful of dozens of separate spreadsheet programs scattered around an ERP or MRP-II implementation, the type-two tool. Too often people, management and staff, see the spreadsheets as quick and dirty solutions for putting decision tools together. The maintenance problems can be extremely large and the effort to keep the tools running enormous. This is true for either individual spreadsheet tools or those that are linked together.

Ad hoc creation of type-two spreadsheet tools can be OK in the beginning, but over time the situation often becomes messy and unmanageable. It is better to have a limited number of tools that function as true systems and programs. These are the level-five types, even if they are implemented in a spreadsheet. There is one danger of type-five spreadsheet tools. If a system is built based on a spreadsheet, management and users must understand that it is indeed a hybrid system with compromises and with limitations. For example, in our type-five systems there are no formulas and everything is controlled by software. The users must contain their desires and tendencies to hack together quick little formulas and insert them into cells. This hacking does not work when a programming or system view is taken. The software makes assumptions about what is where; the software might be expecting to manipulate a text string and finding a formula is not a good thing.

Note: It is important to remember that spreadsheet solutions may only be temporary solutions for the first steps of improving production control and once the situation is under control, a commercial system might be considered. If the effort is taken to create the spreadsheet tool in a professional fashion and have reasonable functionality, the tool might have life as an operational tool. This will move the tool from a type four to a type five. However, if there are many holes and workarounds and constant messing around with the formulas and logic, the spreadsheet tool should be considered a temporary solution. The spreadsheet approach may also be useful to clean up data, processes, and understand what a system should do. Then a suitable commercial system may be sourced. If a commercial system is close enough, buy it. It might require compromises and some muttering, but it is the better way to go unless you have local support for building and maintaining the spreadsheet tool.

It is possible to develop and use commercial systems written in different computer languages and using various database programs. Excel and VBA are not the only choices. There are times when one strategy makes sense and times when the other approach makes sense. Do not blindly advocate one over the other! It depends on the problem and what might be called the reasonable solution.

RATIONALE FOR SPREADSHEETS

Why use a spreadsheet system as a base for production control? Surely it is slow, unreliable, and incapable of really doing the job? To build an operational planning and scheduling system in VBA must be impossible? Too much data, too big of a problem? Sometimes the answer to these questions is yes, but there are times that Excel and VBA can provide an adequate solution.

There are several reasons for choosing Excel and VBA:

- There are many factory situations that are within the scope of a spreadsheet tool. For example, handling less than a hundred resources, several hundred part types, and less than a thousand work orders on the time horizon is doable. It would be hard to handle hundreds of resources and thousands of part types, but even large plants can be decomposed into smaller areas for decentralized control. For example, the prototype area in a large plant is not necessarily a large problem. The job shop area of a large plant may be reasonable. The assembly area might also be reasonable by itself. Not every manufacturing problem is huge if it is decomposed to where the decisions are made.

- It is possible to build large, robust tools in Excel and VBA. You just need to know what you are doing. It is a matter of software engineering and software architecture. We have done it. If we can, others can too. It is not impossible, but it requires thinking like a programmer and a software developer, and not a cell-formula spreadsheet user.

- Excel and VBA offer a very quick prototyping environment and the features of Excel can be exploited without duplicating code and functions. For example, Excel has many features for importing and exporting files, formatting cells, printing, and data entry. Once you master the basics, you are able to build prototypes of many planning tools in days, one or two weeks, or less than a month of effort. It is also easy to reuse or recycle existing subroutines for many of the mechanical or routine software functions from tool to tool.

■ A tool in Excel is nonthreatening to the average planner, scheduler, and dispatcher. It is likely that they already use Excel and a scheduler's information system based on Excel is accepted readily. They do not put the "Not another system to learn!" barriers up immediately. Our tools have been viewed as another extension to Excel and they will operate and function like Excel. We could have used Access or another database tool with GUI support, but we think Excel is the better choice because of this acceptance issue.

■ It is a fundamental requirement of planning tools that the user can intercept and change reports before they are printed. This is not simply the formatting of columns, rows, and the inclusion of data. This is the insertion of special comments, altering of data, and altering of instructions. The computer database will never be perfect and up to date. Our systems cut paperwork for the factory floor and for the machine operators. The paperwork must be perfect and you do not want machine operators guessing and interpreting. You need the paperwork to reflect what machines, material, and timings are to be used; not possibly out-of-date industrial engineering values in the ERP. Using Excel allows the software to prepare initial reports and paperwork as worksheets and then allows the scheduler and dispatcher to edit whatever they want before the final paperwork is printed or distributed. One scheduler uses about two-thirds of our reports as generated. The scheduler then spends from five minutes to half an hour editing several other reports before they are printed.

■ It can be relatively easy for the scheduler to maintain the system and to perform guided maintenance by phone when needed. The code is in the tool and VBA is simple enough for someone who is not a trained programmer to understand. A scheduler can make simple changes to the code and understand the structure of the system. This reduces the problem of programming support and the need for trained programmers for all functions. This self-reliance and the ability to do problem solving is important at 6 AM when downloads do not work or network problems arise. You need to debug and sort it out before the information technology folk arrive. The tools built with Excel and VBA have proven themselves in this regard.

There are two main outcomes of a serious spreadsheet exercise. First, the spreadsheet might be a prototype. Second, the spreadsheet might end up as a permanent decision aid in the production control department.

TYPE FOUR: PROTOTYPES

Prototypes are a good use for a spreadsheet tool. The tool does not have to be industrial grade, robust, or fully functional. This limited use assumes that ultimately it will be possible to find a commercial tool that does the job.

The prototype is a great way to force the planners and schedulers to think about what they do, what information they use, and how the information is used. The clarification of requirements can be of tremendous value. In one factory, the prototype started off with a shift definition of eight hours. This was fine and the prototype work proceeded for a bit. Then, it turned out that weekend shifts were not the same as the Monday through Friday shifts. A little later, it turned out that Saturday shifts were not really the same as Sunday shifts. Finally, it turned out that Friday evening shifts were different too. Actually, it turned out that shifts during shutdowns, vacations, and long weekends were also possibly different. Without the prototype, these issues might have been buried until the full implementation was tried. This prototype was based on formulas and did not take a long time to build. It was not pretty. The effort did not waste time on things that did not matter. The pretty stuff was not needed to check out definitions and the basic rules for scheduling.

A prototype is also useful if computerized decision aids have not been used before. You may have a problem, but no idea of what a solution might look like or what might be possible. The prototype allows you to visualize what might be possible and this process can unlock other ideas. This might involve some of the cosmetic stuff if special or unique visualizations are needed.

Once a prototype or mock-up is built, it can be talked to and it can become the focus of a discussion. Every piece of data has to come from somewhere. Does it exist? Where? What is the quality of the data? If it does not exist, how will it be obtained? It helps you think about how each field will be maintained. You can ask how often will the data change, who will do the changes, and how will the requirement for the changes become known? Is every value a constant or is it a derived value based on other information? You want a certain value on a report. What data are used to generate the value? What might be valid or invalid values for the information?

By using the prototype, the issues and ideas surface early and are not hidden for later discovery. The discovery process is not only for the benefit of the actual planners and schedulers. In some cases, management can make a discovery about current practices as well. One factory found this out. The design of the APS was almost finished and a discussion was held with a senior manager and the topic of capacity calculation arose. The manager was told how the capacity calculation was done. She was surprised. It was very rough and imprecise. The manager thought the planners did not do it that way and that the current practice was more precise. The planner was checked with. The software did what the planner did. The manager was further shocked and surprised. Unfortunately, the APS design was almost finished and this type of discovery should have been found earlier. Perhaps a prototype would have helped.

TYPE FIVE: PRODUCTION TOOLS

Production quality tools can be built with Excel and VBA. We have built two big ones that have been in use now for many years: one that does job shop scheduling in a hierarchical fashion for scheduling and dispatching, and a second tool that does planning, scheduling, and dispatching for a focused factory area that is repetitive and a flow shop. We have also built smaller tools for things like stabilizing upstream material pulling from the job shop. All in Excel, and all in VBA and with no formulas. They have been designed and built as software systems, and Excel is simply the host.

The job shop and repetitive flow shop tools are in the megabyte size and each tool has thirty thousand to forty thousand lines of VBA. The workbooks for logic are separated from the workbooks with data and all tools are integrated with a large ERP system. The ERP does the basic demand processing and bill of material explosion for the repetitive area, but is not used for the detailed planning, scheduling, or dispatching. The tools have been shown to be very robust. There are things to avoid in Excel and simple is always best. You have to be careful, but it is possible to run a large factory with such a tool base.

The job shop tool looks and functions like an interactive Gantt chart system with electronic magnets representing jobs associated with machines. Jobs that are OK are blue, jobs that are risky are yellow, and jobs that are late are red. The jobs are synchronized with the ERP and the user can move the magnets around like they would on a wallboard. The other tool is more tabular and is a planning board that is focused on finished goods inventory, on-hand positions, and building certain quantities per day of certain parts on dedicated lines.

TYPE FIVE: DEVELOPMENT APPROACH

This section summarizes a strategy for developing large spreadsheet tools for planning and scheduling and talks about how spreadsheet tools are actually developed. We assume a reasonable level of programming knowledge and experience. You can skip this section if you are not actually going to design or program such a tool. It is also assumed that you have done a good requirements study, know generally what the problem is, and what you think the solution should be. You have done your homework and ruled out all other reasonable options. Nothing is close enough.

How do you do it? First, you need to make sure that you can get the data you need. This is no different from implementing any APS system; data drive everything. In many cases, it is enough to get information extracted out of the MRP/ERP system several times each day, such as inventory positions and demand. Depending on the system, once a day is sufficient. In other cases, you might need more frequent uploads and downloads. Almost every MRP/ERP system has the ability to extract data and generate text or spreadsheet files via interactive or batch means. This is very convenient. There are very simple ways in VBA to access files and manipulate downloaded files. In one case, we download about two dozen files each morning to a number of different tools. This brings information together from multiple systems and presents it in a way that the users find friendly and useful. You can figure out the information needed to bring together by monitoring and observing the actual planning and decision processes. For example, what pieces of data are often referred to, what data are needed to make a decision about a job, what current status information is accessed, what special information is frequently referred to? The data downloads will likely involve the information technology and corporate people to create the extracts, test them, and support them. Start early, this stuff takes time.

Next, you need to have a decent software structure. In our approach, we have three types of workbooks — yes, types of workbooks, plural. We use multiple workbooks to create an interlocked and integrated system. One workbook has logic; no data, nothing else except the VBA code and forms. This is all of the logic. There is no other logic scattered about. This is critical for maintenance and robustness.

There is a second workbook that is the current schedule or plan. The scheduling and dispatching system works on one view as the job shop is pulled by the flow shop. The scheduling and dispatching system is refreshed daily based on the MRP/ERP explosion. The flow shop system supports multiple plans and views of the world. It is a complete planning system and deals with customer demand, manpower planning, and the repetitive area. The plan or schedule files do not have logic or parameters per se. They can be considered a database file, the current schedule, and reports. The repetitive area tool also tracks month-to-date performance against a baseline plan and has historical data.

The third type of workbook is that of data repository and parameters. As much of the system as possible is table driven from the data repository files. The job shop tool uses two background files, while the flow shop tool uses a dozen. All of the files can be easily opened and closed automatically and be kept in synch by using VBA functions. Having a whole bunch of workbooks open and orchestrated is not difficult. The key point is to decompose and isolate:

logic, plan or schedule entity, and parameters or data that define what is what. This makes it easier to maintain and to use.

The next part of the design is to separate the internal representation of the plan or schedule from the visual representation. The external view or representation is likely to change dozens or hundreds of times over the life of the system. A conscious decoupling done with consistency will allow the smooth evolution without jeopardizing robustness. The job shop tool has changed dramatically since the mid 1990s, but the internal scheduling engine and the basic scheduling parameters have not changed. The reports, extra functions driven off the schedule, and the visuals have changed. The part that knows about shifts, setups, processing times, routings, and calendars has not. We have gone from a first prototype tool of approximately six thousand lines of code to thirty thousand lines of code.

Another key aspect is to use object-oriented thinking. This style helps to ensure that the code is isolated and packaged so that physical versus logical aspects are hidden and that an object's characteristics are only known to the object. We use a specific style when building our tools. The scheduling engines and all detailed logic work on the concept of currency. There are concepts like the current resource, the current job, the current planning time, the current parameter set to use, and the current row of report generation. The methods and logic do not need to access and hunt for things, they simply refer to the current entity and the background toolkit and object structures resolve this to the current item or value. This approach allows any method or detailed piece of logic to be used quickly; set up the current items and then invoke the desired method. The methods do not care or know where the items came from, they just work on the current instance. If the whole system is built on this philosophy, the toolkit functions and building blocks can be constructed easily and quickly. You take a little bit of time in the beginning to set up the structures and mechanics, but then everything goes quickly. The flow shop system takes the concept of currency further and all data records for the various parameter files have effectiveness dates. This allows every aspect of the planning problem to be controlled for the time horizon and have values such as part numbers, weights, processing times, shift parameters, and planning options change with time. The currency logic resolves the current planning time to the appropriate data record and retrieves the appropriate value.

If you get into this area, think about tool smithing and tool design. After you have created a few of these tools and discover what is needed and how to master the Excel/VBA platform, you can consider creating a reusable tool kit.

Although a prototype can be used as an operational system, it is more likely that the prototype will be used to show vendors and consultants what is required or what the problem is. Prototypes are very useful as they address the legendary exclamation, "Oh, is that what you meant?"

SUMMARY

This chapter is not intended to be a complete do-it-yourself guide for building decision support tools, but does show the basic approach and concepts we have used. We also use a specific style for the user interface, menus, and functions, but that is beyond the scope of this book. The key is to understand what the planner or scheduler needs, what they do, and then support it. Encourage the good things and try to minimize the bad. Try to eliminate all of the nonvalued tasks and try to create a consistent and robust tool. Always remember that tools have to provide personal value to the planner and not just better sequences for the factory if you want them to be used.

14

CONSULTANTS

PREDIGESTED THOUGHTS FOR THE BUSY PERSON

- Not all consultants are created equal and not all are well skilled in production control.

- Size does matter. Sometimes smaller is best. Sometimes bigger is best. It depends on who is actually working with you.

- You should be making the critical decisions about your business, not the consultant.

INTRODUCTION

Many firms need to use external skills at some point to solve problems, carry out projects, or implement systems. It is not possible for many firms to have specialists or experts in all aspects of their business, especially production control. Each year, a lot of money is spent on consultants and since consultants are generally not cheap, you need to make sure that you get value. Many, if not most, consultants are worth their fees, but like all things in life, some are not. However, it is hard to judge from self-reported claims of success if value will be derived. In the following pages, we will share some of our thoughts on consultants, groups of consultants, and some aspects of consulting that it might be wise to think about.

LARGE FIRMS

There are small local firms, small national or international firms, and larger firms. Each type has strengths and weaknesses. There might even be corporate-level specialists or agencies that behave and act like consultants.

You might know the large consultancy firms. A number of them are consultancies that have emerged from the big accountancy firms. Some others are information technology firms that have upgraded to include management consultancy in their portfolio. These large firms work on an international scale. In a production control capacity, you might have seen them involved with ERP implementations, plant- or firm-level reviews of production flow and inventory management, or involved with the infamous re-engineering exercises.

These large firms will sometimes contact the highest levels in your organization and establish a relationship, with the objective of being granted corporate-wide consultancy. They will fly in the most experienced consultants in the area to achieve this and talk about the synergy effects that the company gets when all consultants come from the same source.

What happens when such a deal is struck? Often, but not always, most of the experienced consultants leave to go establish another corporate relationship and relatively junior-level consultants arrive to continue to work with the client. The amount of business is thus maximized and this is good for a senior consultant's career. Depending on the study, the consultants easily can recommend large changes in your organization, usually combined with large information technology projects. There might even be consultants to the consultants.

If the consultants are inexperienced, they may explain to you that you have always planned and scheduled in the wrong way and that blah blah and blah is the one and only solution. They know this because they were taught *advanced* manufacturing in school! They make their recommendation after a short walk through the factory or a discussion over coffee. They have learned the one tool or technique, and one way or another, your problem will fit their solution. Many junior consultants have never run a production control department, been in the factory at 6 AM, launched a product, or actually negotiated with customers or suppliers. This experience is not necessary to make good recommendations or to think of solutions, but they should be smart enough to figure out the problem first before throwing solutions around. If they take the time to think, the juniors can be amazing.

There are some of these good junior consultants around and there have been many successful projects. You should be aware of the experience and skills possessed by the consultants you are working with. Junior consultants are learning and can make mistakes on your project unintentionally. Use appropriate caution and do due diligence when senior consultants leave and others take their place. If possible, try to know in advance what the personnel plans are for the consultants. For example, how much access and guidance you are being allocated from the senior consultants, middle-career types, and the juniors. If you are getting a good balance, you should do OK.

STRATEGIC CONSULTANCIES

Another type of consultancy are the strategic firms. The business model of these companies is somewhat different from the large consultancies. While the large companies go for volume by using a few seniors to sell a lot of juniors, the strategic consultancies use a few very expensive consultants. Supply chain studies often come up with the same themes: standardization, centralization, consolidation. It is possible that the strategic consultancy does understand your industry, your plant, and your issues. In these cases, a strategic thrust may be very valuable.

Typical for the strategic consultancies is that the customer needs to implement the recommendations themselves or hire other consultants to help implement the ideas. Hence, the strategic approach may be valuable if your firm or plant has the resources to carry the suggestions out and just needs the direction and motivation. It can also work if you can bring in secondary consultants to help out.

However, the strategic consultants may be out of their area of specialization and might rely on suggestions that fit situations they have worked with in the past, but not yours. They may not understand some of the key relationships in the situation or how to make them operational. It is like talking about football or soccer. There are many experts who know how to make the local team successful. They must attack more, make less errors in defense, work together better. OK, but how to do that? As you look deeper into the problem, you will find out why inventories simply cannot be reduced, push cannot be converted into pull, and products simply cannot be transferred from one factory to another. You might not have a say in it, but you would be wise to make sure that someone checked out the track record of the strategic consultants and made sure that they have experience with your situation.

SMALL FIRMS

There are the small firms, where there is a large variety in quality. Niche players can have a definite advantage in that they will speak your language better, and because they are small, they will not send in the team of fresh graduates.

Moreover, the grapevine works quite well within a specific industry and if they do not perform, they are out of business quite fast. When the consultancy firm is small, you will be relatively important to them, which means they are more likely to work harder for you. It takes more time on your side to select the right niche player, but if you succeed, you will likely get the best value for money.

However, the small firms may not have the breadth and depth that a large consultancy might have. The large firm will be able to call in specialists and sufficient manpower if it becomes necessary. The larger firm may also have a better relationship with the vendor. There are trade-offs in all of these decisions.

THE CONSULTANT

Consulting is a very difficult job, especially for the experienced ones. Because a senior consultant will have seen so many production control situations, it is tempting to classify a problem all too soon based on a first impression. Consultants should keep repeating to themselves: "You may not know the business as well as somebody who has worked here for years." The better consultants try to understand how the factory currently runs before determining solutions. This is not a quick process. It can take from several weeks to several months to get a handle on a plant. The consultant should want to know what practices are really good and should be encouraged and extended, and what practices need to be changed. They should really want to understand the difference between symptoms and the underlying problem. Not everything a scheduler is doing might be right, but neither is everything they are doing likely to be wrong!

One challenge for any consultant is knowledge about the long-term facets of your plant or business. Consultants have a temporary relationship with you, they will move on.

You want to find a consultant that believes in understanding what the workforce knows and knows how to work with the workers to exploit and leverage that knowledge. Often the ideas suggested by the consultants are not new and variants might have been tried in the past. It is important to understand why the previous attempts failed and if the reasons for failure still exist. It is likely that personnel exist that can provide these insights and their knowledge should be respected and help solicited.

Attitude is crucial for any consultant to be effective. A consultant should:

- Listen, not only hear what you have to say.
- Have a will to understand and learn from you.
- Be willing to spend sufficient time with you from the crack of dawn and understand what you do, when you do it, what information you use,

what questions you need to answer, and understand how this varies by the day, week, month, and season of the year.

■ Approach the world with common sense, knowing that concepts are a toolbox of rose-colored glasses. Knowing how to put ideas into practice is a key skill.

■ Be flexible and willing to deviate from the original approach when that does not work. You do not need a dogmatic and one-size-fits-all consultant.

■ Be sincere and give honest feedback.

■ Have a passion to be the best consultant in the world, not the highest paid one.

■ Try to set up a situation where they help you once on the topic and should not be needed again to help with the same problem. A goal should be to make you self-sufficient.

■ Be willing to tell you what consulting is not needed and when projects should not be done.

SUMMARY

A foundryman once came at me with – 'If you white-collared gentry would once get out here in the thick of things, you would soon cease your ranting about how a foundry should be run. I'm doing all of the jumping around I can, but the result seems to be a slam at this and a kick at that performance.' I replied that his criticism was a fair one; that knowing how he was hampered because of the conditions under which he was working, there was certainly little use of kicking without offering at the same time some workable suggestions aimed to boost things along.

Knoeppel was a very active consultant in the early part of the twentieth century and he was not adverse to sharing his own experiences as this quote from 1911 shows. Now, as then, we should be cautious of consultants or experts who only know the inside of an office cubicle; who do not take the time to see, observe, and talk to you; and who only criticize without offering help.

This chapter completes the scheduling tool section of the book. We talked about what the tools are, what types of benefits you might expect to get, how to acquire them, and a little bit about the people you can expect to interact with: the vendors and consultants. For those so inclined, we included some ideas on how to create your own partial prototypes or fully functional spreadsheet tools. The next set of chapters, 15 through 19, focuses more on the *how* of production control.

15

UNCERTAINTY IN PRODUCTION CONTROL

PREDIGESTED THOUGHTS FOR THE BUSY PERSON

■ You can be a victim and a specialist in reacting or you can become part of the solution.

■ Not everything surprising in manufacturing is truly surprising in all regards. It is the job of production control to understand this and foresee many of the surprises.

■ Even if you can catch one or two things per month, that will save you unnecessary setups, wasted material, expediting, and possible overtime. If you are really good, you can catch quite a few things before they bite you.

■ There are a number of things you can do to anticipate and control for the risk and impacts associated with uncertainty.

INTRODUCTION

Chapters 15 through 19 form the third section of the book and focus on *how*; what you might want to do or avoid while actually planning and scheduling. This chapter starts the discussion by addressing uncertainty and concepts for how to deal with it in a proactive fashion.

Why do things hurt? It is because you do not wear protective clothing, take preventive measures, or do not duck. Right between the eyes. Full force of the blow. A full-force hit hurts more than a glancing blow. It also hurts because what is affected can hurt. Your forehead can feel the hurt, while a block of steel will not feel the hurt unless you are a philosopher. This chapter explores strategies and concepts for minimizing, or avoiding, the hurt associated with production. Just like protecting yourself while doing tasks, it is possible to protect yourself against many of the harms that can befall you in manufacturing.

THE STUFF THAT HURTS

There are two types of nasties that can occur in the future. First, something bad happens and then second, something else bad happens that is associated with the first bad thing. For example, a wave solder machine goes down for a few hours in a printed circuit board shop. This is the first bad thing. You just lost a few hours of production. The technician has been up all night and does not get the repair just right. The next few hours, perhaps one or two shifts, are lively as the machine is brought back to the control point. The problems during the one or two shifts, after the machine is supposedly fixed, are the second type of nasties.

The first kind of nasty can impact inventory positions and delivery dates negatively and represents lost capacity of one form or another. The machine is down. We will call this the first-order effect. There are many types of first-order nasties. For example, material arrives that is faulty and this is not discovered until it is on a machine. You just lost time, perhaps a setup, and will need to expedite replacement material. You might lose additional time sorting out the problem before the next job starts on the machine. This is the immediate problem that people see.

The second kind of nasty also loses capacity and affects productivity, inventory, and the plan. This type of side-effect nasty will be called a second-order effect. This is the other stuff sometimes associated with a first-order nasty. Stuff that is not immediate. The second-order effects are sometimes subtle, not turning up for days or weeks, perhaps in another part of the plant. Consider the above example. What might have happened if the bad material was actually in the machine and the operation was attempted before the bad material was discovered? This might negatively have affected other good material that is now scrap, the machine might have been broken, and the tools and fixtures damaged. These are the side effects associated with the primary problem.

Unfortunately, second-order nasties are not restricted to the direct side effects associated with first-order events. A purposeful action intended to benefit the firm can also trigger an indirect second-order effect. For example, one factory had four parallel lines, seemingly independent, each with their own product, operators, and schedule. One line was being upgraded and new processes installed. Did the scheduler plan the other three lines as if everything was normal? No. The scheduler realized that during the upgrade, supervision's attention would be split, supporting trades focused on the new line, and a certain amount of time consumed by talking and chatting about the new line. This would result in reduced capacity by about 10 percent. If the scheduler did not plan for the loss and take proactive measures in advance, there would have been hell to pay as the second-order effect kicked in.

In summary, there are bad things that can happen and there can be side effects. There are also side effects possible with any change in the status quo. While it is possible that the side effects are positive, it is more likely that the side effects will affect capacity and production negatively for a period of time.

WHY WORRY?

The truly random bad events and unpredicted changes in status quo cannot be dealt with directly. You never can predict that a die will be smashed at exactly 1:34 PM next Tuesday. You may never be able to predict that the Chairman of the Board will arrive for a surprise plant tour next Wednesday at 9 AM. The truly random stuff supposedly is handled by the planned utilization of the resources. For example, most resources are not assumed to be running for a full eight hours of an eight-hour shift. Something like six or seven hours of available time will be used instead. This one to two hour gap is assumed sufficient to mask, or deal, with the vast assortment of things that cause capacity to vaporize: small repairs, lunch breaks, small interruptions of material flow, small work stoppages.

The problem is when the downtime exceeds the expected daily average by any substantial amount. In scheduling and planning, we cannot bank time or capacity, and each day the future is rescheduled based on current status, demands, and capability. If we had a great day yesterday, this has already been taken into account when replanning was done in the morning and any benefits utilized. Any progress we made was applied to the order backlog, reducing the number of late jobs or the amount of expediting needed, and lowering the amount of projected overtime. If the shop is not working at capacity and all orders were on time anyway, and if no overtime was planned, the gains yesterday really did not help anything since the increase in capacity is not being used. If there will be a significant loss of capacity at a resource, or a sustained decrease in capability over a period of time, it should worry someone. There should be specific actions taken to minimize the effects. If the interruption affects a bottleneck resource, the loss of capacity is definitely worthy of note.

Management and production control should monitor any losses or reductions in output. For example, if the target of three hundred was not made yesterday, a valid question the next morning is "How do you plan to make today's three hundred and yesterday's shortfall?" If the shortfall is not addressed, the variance in production will cascade into other side effects. Overproduction is also bad. If you built more yesterday than the plan called for, then you need to think about what you could do wisely with the time saved. Does it make sense to keep building today and pull the demand in from tomorrow? Or, does it make sense to use the few hours gained today for cleaning, training, maintenance, or other special demands that have been sitting off-line waiting for a chance to be filled? Blindly building ahead without considering options and the consequences is as bad as not catching up when you fall behind.

THE PREDICTABLE AND UNPREDICTABLE

The future will not be known until it reveals itself. This is true. Only in hindsight can you know with certainty when something happened and what the impact was. Have you ever heard phrases like "No one could have seen that coming," "Always happens at the worst time," "We did as well as anyone could have done, given it happened unexpectedly," and "Shit happens"? Is there anything that can be done for the first- and second-order nasties in advance? Can you only react after the fact?

Some people operate in reaction mode because they consciously or subconsciously want to or are forced to. For example, some people seem to like firefighting and the thrill that comes from it. The adrenaline is pumping and **you** are the one saving the day. The white horse is rearing and the guns are blazing. "Hero rushes in at 10:23 AM and saves the plant." Or some organizations reward firefighting and give **no** recognition to proactive avoidance of problems. Hence, reactive management is good for career management in some firms and proactive management is bad. Think about it, if you think about the future, you might just become accountable for what actually transpires and we cannot have that now, can we? If you reward firefighting, remember to increase the match budget.

Luckily, not everyone operates in a purely reactive mode. The key is in the sentence: "The future will not be known until it reveals itself." Revelation is the key. The easy things to work with are any planned changes in the status quo. Anything, and we do mean **anything**, that changes the status quo has the potential for first- and second-order effects. Due diligence suggests that the change or event should be at least thought about and possible effects reflected on. We still find many people are sloppy about change and most really do not understand change management. They assume that a change can be made without any impact on capacity directly or indirectly. They assume that a process or procedural change can be introduced with no one getting confused, no one proceeding more slowly than planned, no one still using the old process, and no one making a mistake with the new process. They assume that it should not matter when the change is introduced. One factory has the usual shutdown over the January–December holiday season. They may or may not do some preventative maintenance during this period. Every year they plan as if production will start up immediately after the break without any problems or losses in productivity. Every year there are problems. By planning for the higher production, they artificially load the factory and then have to expedite and react. Each year the same story. Another factory was involved in electronics. They switched over from central heating to air conditioning each May. Each May they lost about 10 percent productivity as the humidity and other environmental factors sorted themselves out. The humidity caused problems with the paste and other process materials. The factory loading ignored the 10 percent drop and assumed that May was no different from April or June. The scheduler was aware of the productivity problem in past years and discreetly moved 10 percent of the forecasted demand from May to April and had built himself a little stash of parts. Sure enough, May had lower productivity, but the final targets were still met.

Ralph, the best proactive scheduler we have met, thought about this type of stuff. He anticipated and knew that any planned change or event that altered the day's production rhythm revealed potential losses in capacity. He was not worried about the small contributors to downtime, he was worried about additional losses that really hurt. One November and December, he anticipated that January was going to be a real problem. Many of the management team and industrial engineers disagreed with him. Ralph had seen clues, read the signs, and smelled trouble in the air. Before January, he predicted what was going to happen. We were tracking his actions and predictions during this period and it was an interesting time to be an observer. He pulled 33 percent of the demand from January into December. He also did a bunch of other things that changed his capacity and capability options. He got some overtime approved and some of the other actions authorized, but there were other things he manipulated that management did not see. By the end of January, his predictions had been shown to be accurate, and he hit the plant's production target within 1 or 2 percent. What would have happened if he did not pull the demand ahead by so much and activated a number of other backup plans in advance? Ralph was not perfect and did make the occasional mistake. There were several times where he caused himself some pain. But during the study, he showed an amazing ability to foresee trouble and act in advance to discount it.

Now, it is true that not all changes to the status quo can be anticipated. The machine breakdowns and surprise tours are two examples of the unpredictable. However, there are four aspects related to the unpredictable that can be predicted.

1. It is likely that you can predict the side effect and use this information immediately when the event does occur. For example, you cannot predict when the lathe will break and for how long the lathe will be down, but you can predict that for the next shift or two after the break is repaired, there may be reduced productivity and possible other problems as the lathe is checked out.

2. It is likely that something bad will happen at the worst possible time. The system is under extreme pressure when peak load is being experienced and when extra effort is being applied to get product made and out the door. People are often working overtime, rushing about, pushing the envelope, and it is highly likely that mistakes will occur or equipment pushed to their limit and beyond. The precise problem cannot be predicted, but it is likely that something, somewhere, will go wrong.

3. There are events in the future that are expected to occur, but the timing and/or location are not known precisely. For example, it is known that a certain machine is getting old and the bearings are likely to go sometime in the next three months. It is not known when, but you can count on it; that machine will be down for a major repair soon. Direct capacity will be lost and there will be side effects.

4. If you know something different is going to happen in the immediate to near future (e.g., within the next two months), you can think about possible side effects. You can anticipate some issues and have backup plans or strategies in place. If you do not think about the possible side effects, they will be a surprise. You know when a new line is being introduced, or a product change is to be phased in, or if a vendor is planning a plant upgrade, or a different material is going to be used. These types of things may or may not go smoothly.

The best planners and schedulers think about these aspects. It is all part of the game. What can be anticipated and planned for? What backup plans exist and can be activated if things go awry as expected? Schedulers have been observed to request machines upgraded and engineering changes made in advance of anticipated problems and then be used effectively when the smelly stuff hits the fan. This is what effective production control is all about. If you do not believe that things can be anticipated, then you will not see them.

TAKING CONTROL

There are a number of strategies and methods that you can use to deal with future uncertainty. The precise implementation will differ from site to site, but the basic ideas should be applicable. Some will be hard to sell to management as they first appear counterintuitive and suboptimal. All we can say in our defense is that we have seen them used, we have used them, and they work.

Detect It Early

The earlier you can find out about some nasty happening, the more options you may have to mitigate its impact. For physical types of issues, there might be things you can do for early detection. For example, you may be able to put extra sensors on your critical machines and pick up unusual vibrations, temperature values, or adjustments. You could perhaps communicate any special status information to the planning office. If you cannot provide direct communication back to the office, at least put a flashing red light on the machine so that, as strange things start to happen, you get an early warning, not after the fact. You can do this type of analysis by looking at every key piece of equipment and determining the normal operating profile. This is like a profile for a healthy person. What are the key operating characteristics for the machine? See if you can measure them. You want to know that something is heating up before it sizzles. For nonphysical types of issues, you need to pick up the signals of impending risk as soon as possible. This will depend on your information network. It might be the way work is piled, the body language of the operator, the frequency of communication traffic on the radio, or the number of e-mails. Be aware of the signals and you can pick up early warnings of potential risk.

If you have studied statistical process control and learned about control charts and run tests, you can use these ideas to pick up variances and problems before they become headaches. In many cases, the run tests are more important than the actual limits on the control charts. The run tests pick up nonrandom patterns of numbers and can be used for any time series of data. The tests will give you good indicators of possible problems as the problem is developing, if it is related to something going out of specification or if there is a pattern to the problem. It is possible that the run tests will give a false signal to you, but they are one of the most useful things you can do with your data. A nonrandom pattern should be investigated further. If a process is in control, there should little bits of random noise in the data and recognizable patterns should be rare. If there are underlying factors or influences, it is probable that nonrandom patterns will be detectable. What causes these nonrandom patterns should be your concern!

Scanning the Horizon

Once a week, or thereabouts, have a specific meeting with key departments and discuss any changes to the status quo planned for the next two, four, six, eight weeks. You might also want to consider changes further out, but that depends on the process and firm. This discussion should note the change, direct impact, possible impacts, and the timing. Is the change scheduled for a peak or hectic period? Can it be moved? The purpose of the meeting is also good for getting various departments to start thinking about how their actions affect the system. If you cannot have a meeting with others, do it yourself, a meeting of one. If it is not a formal part of your process, you might want to make this probing and thinking a conscious part of your socializing. As you talk to the various people in different departments, get into the habit of asking them what is happening in the next month or two, then write it down. You do not want to forget anything that might affect you.

Spread the Impact

If something has not been made for a while, or is about to be made via a new process or new equipment, schedule a small batch several weeks or at least a few days in advance of the main production. If there have been many changes since last production, allow time for several small batches. These small batches will absorb any instability and unknowns in the system. It is better to take 100 percent variability in time and materials on a small batch than 100 percent on the whole batch! It is better to damage a few parts and not the whole lot. It is better to waste a setup and a short run, than to blow the delivery to a key customer. Why is this type of detection and spreading so useful? Have you had any changes to the machine since the last time the part was made? How many changes? Is the crew or operator the same as before? Any changes to the material, tooling, fixtures, or methods? Any changes to upstream, or feeding machines, or processes? Is the vendor supplying the material the same? The longer you have not made it, the more chance there is of these types of things happening. Can any of these things mess up your production in an unexpected way? Are you insulated from these types of effects?

Stress It If You Can

If you have the technician or support on site, and you have the time available, stress the machine or process as soon as possible. If the technician is looking for a part to check the machine out on, find a problem child. If you can, pick the part that takes the resources to the extreme. This is the part that is the most complicated or has the highest tolerance requirements. After a change, it is likely that the basic, simple stuff will work, but the most extreme aspects will be untested. If the process is not at a peak load condition, let rip and force the ugly job into the system to see if there will be problems. Get it out of the way. Better to do it when you have time to fix it, then later when every second counts. This is not making a whole batch or using an existing production order; just pick the test piece carefully.

In a similar theme, if you can, try to make bad parts so that you and the actual production personnel know how they are made, how to recognize them, and how to deal with them in advance. Consciously trying to create bad parts, and the subsequent analysis, can also help you improve the process and reduce your wastage.

Baby It If You Cannot Stress It

If you do not have the time, and you are in a peak load right after a change or repair, do the contrary. Use an easy part for testing. Continue this philosophy for the production orders. Find and run easy work that will take some of the backlog off the machine. Avoid the complicated and ugly work. You cannot afford to have the machine stressed and further messed up if you are going flat out and every minute counts. You need to make wise choices if the resource is critical. If you know that a part or process stands a chance of causing additional problems, try to avoid it.

Burn the Cheap and Plentiful First

Once the machine has been turned back over to production, you have another opportunity to make a risk minimization decision. If the machine does a process that potentially can damage parts, pick parts with the least amount of potential hurt associated with them. For example, if a machine has just been fixed or a process changed, pick the cheapest and easiest part to replace in case things go wrong. This is when you have a choice and all else is equal. You might be forced to pick a part with scarce material next, but if you have a choice, do not do it. It is better to burn something that you have a lot of, does not have a lot of value added, and is not critical than something that will cause additional expediting and panic.

Do It Early

Pull ahead and bank it. If you suspect a problem in the middle of next week, then you can look at the schedule and may be able to pull some of the critical work ahead. Try to get it done before the anticipated problem. It is better to have extra inventory than possibly damage the critical job or a key delivery date.

Planning Utilization

Whenever possible, schedule and load up the least flexible and powerful resources first and keep any spare time on the most expensive and powerful resources you have. These are the machines or people that can do multiple tasks, solve problems for you, parachute in, and take over multiple operations. Your best resources for dealing with uncertainty are not the machines that can do one and only one thing. They are not the people who have single skill sets. If a problem occurs, spare capacity on a multiskilled resource is better for firefighting and prevents the side effects from rippling far and wide. Planning underutilization on scarce and expensive resources, likely your most useful, may cause eyebrows to raise, but at the end of the day, they will be used and the overall utilization and productivity increased. If your most useful machines are loaded to the gills initially, there will be more jobs preempted, moved around, and changes made to the schedule. It is better to keep 90 percent of the shop or plant stable and running smoothly and use 10 percent of the resources as flying squadrons or SWAT teams.

The Backup Plan

If something is supercritical, or is a unique process or resource, it is reasonable that you should have identified it in advance. You should have some sort of option or alternative already thought through. The contingency planning must identify the key liabilities and the crucial characteristics or requirements associated with the risk. If something breaks, what is the option? If the part has to be shipped from another continent, what alternative exists? An alternative to a core process, the essence of the firm, should not only be thought about, but should be tested on a regular basis, once a year or more often. You should know and be prepared for the tasks to be done to activate the backup plan and have run the fire drill. The fire drill will cost time and money, but what will it cost if you have to invent the option in a panic situation where things will be overlooked and the situation not go as desired?

SUMMARY

In this chapter, we tried to introduce and discuss various sources of uncertainty. There are certain types of uncertainty that you just have to accept and there are other types that you can take a proactive role in controlling and mitigating. The various ideas may sound radical and nontraditional; however, there are things you can do that will help or hinder the impact of uncertainty and it is your choice whether or not you want to do it.

Bottlenecks are resources that you need to focus on specifically, during periods of high uncertainty and during periods of normal production. Chapter 16 summarizes a number of concepts for bottleneck control.

16

MANAGING BOTTLENECKS

PREDIGESTED THOUGHTS FOR THE BUSY PERSON

- Read *The Goal* and *Critical Chain* by Goldratt, but with several grains of salt. Most of the stuff is good, common sense. It must be interpreted, assumptions understood, and compromises appreciated. Few things are as black and white, or as extreme, as described.

- Focus on the bottlenecks. Think about how you are using them and what the wasted aspects are. Invest in them and the supporting departments that are associated with them. Do not focus on areas that do not help the bottleneck!!!

- Watch for the moving bottlenecks and the critical resources that feed bottlenecks. What you think is the bottleneck today might not be the bottleneck tomorrow. A nonbottleneck resource can starve a bottleneck if production is disrupted and insufficient inventory exists.

- There are a number of things you need to think about when considering bottlenecks, and often issues at bottlenecks consist of interdependencies. You will need to fix many things before an improvement will be seen.

INTRODUCTION

Whole books can be, and have been, written on bottleneck management. For example, in *The Goal,* Goldratt refocused manufacturing in the mid-1980s on bottleneck resources. He addressed similar issues in *Critical Chain* for project management. These two books should be read. Whether or not you agree with everything stated, or all of the claims, he forces you to re-evaluate your thinking. At the time, manufacturing had lost sight of bottleneck management and Goldratt helped people realize that bottlenecks gated the whole process and needed to be managed. Always remember, a minute gained or lost on a bottleneck means that the whole firm gains or loses the minute. There will always be a resource, or a group of resources, that will function as the bottleneck; the slowest part of the process. The bottleneck will be stationary or it will float. Stationary bottlenecks are the easiest to deal with and usually occur in automated systems, flow, or assembly situations. The floating bottleneck situation occurs in job shops or where the processing is highly variable and depends on mix, types of setups, and crews. In this chapter, we will briefly visit bottleneck management concepts that should be known by everyone in a production control department. The production control personnel should always be watching for and actively managing bottleneck resources!

BOTTLENECK ANALYSIS

How do you know where the bottleneck is? It might be at the start, middle, or end of the process. In a small or simple situation, the simplest way is to look where the largest pile of inventory is. This will be in front of the slowest process that is controlling the output of the whole system. Any operation downstream must be faster since they have less inventory. Any upstream operation is also faster. There are, of course, some caveats; for example, what was the work release pattern or what machines have broken down? All of these issues can influence where inventory will pile up. In complex situations with mix-dependent processes and flows, quick managerial walkabouts are apt to miss the real issues. Unfortunately, these problems do not seem to matter to many managers who, even in the largest and most complex of situations, rely on irregular fly-bys to know where all of the problems are and to know what the best solutions are. Some of the junior suits from large consultancies are also prone to this technique. However, one logistics manager and planner took the walkabouts up a notch and they walked the factory together twice a day. They would stop and chat with the workers and discuss their work and personal matters of interest. This was not a quick fly-by. The manager knew that the information he wanted was on the factory floor and he was prepared to make a twice-daily investment to know what was happening. He and his planner probably had a good idea about where the bottlenecks were and what the issues were.

The second easiest way in a simple situation is to look at the processing steps and identify the slowest based on setups and processing times. This is a little bit more work than just taking a tour through the factory, but is likely to be a bit more accurate. However, if there are multiple resources or processes possible for each step, or if there are substantially different product flows, this simple analysis may not work. Another underlying assumption is that the variability in the process is not too bad and that the rough estimates are good enough.

A third way to look for bottlenecks is to do a resource requirement analysis and see what you need to get the work done by the scheduled receipt date. In this approach, we assume that work is not released until it is supposed to be and that no delays are introduced because of resource conflict. You pretend that each job can flow from the starting gate to the finish line without impediment. As each job is processed, a running tally is made for each machine, or group of resources, that the process routing encounters. The level of analysis can be varied and can show the required number of processing hours per hour, shift, day, week, month, quarter, or year. This is the loading table approach that some people use. The machine or resource with the highest demand for processing hours will be your problem.

If the required processing hours in a period are greater than the available number of hours, you have a bigger problem than a simple bottleneck. You do not have enough capacity, even in an ideal world. Something has to be done: overtime, weekends, a third shift, alternate processes, or subcontracting. Whenever an overloading is noted, attention should be paid immediately, especially since this analysis does not include delays caused by resource conflicts. For example, only a total of eight hours of machine ABC's time is needed during the forty-hour week. Sounds OK, but the problem is that two competing jobs want four hours each in the same morning. A capacity analysis by the shift might show this conflict, but an infinite load analysis at any higher level of aggregation would mask it.

PROCESS BOTTLENECKS

If a resource is a bottleneck for a specific job or process, but is not at peak capacity yet, there might be an opportunity to resequence work on the machine to allow the one job or process to flow through like an express train and bypass other jobs. Let us look a bit closer at this idea of process bottlenecks.

The first operation that delays a job from its ideal trajectory through the plant is the job's bottleneck. What is the ideal trajectory? Working from the release or due dates, you can determine the earliest or latest any specific operation must start or finish in order that the due date will not be jeopardized. You can either use the job's complete slack all at once or spread the slack through the job's routing. As long as an operation starts within a time period and finishes in time for the next operation to start by its latest start time, all is well. The first operation that misses its latest finish time is the immediate problem. This is the starting point; where to look backwards from. You want to challenge each earlier operation in the job's process, and on the resource itself, to know if there is some way that the problem operation can be started earlier.

Let us pretend for a minute that you are using one of those electronic Gantt chart systems with finite scheduling capability and you have hit the schedule button. The software may or may not have special bottleneck capability. Assume it does. If the current bottleneck operation for each process or job is highlighted, different patterns can be seen. For example, if one machine is indeed the bottleneck for all products, then the delaying operations will be concentrated on this machine. If the bottleneck problems float based on product specifications, then the bottleneck operations will be scattered throughout the schedule. The easiest situation to deal with will be the case where there are one or two clear bottlenecks. You know where to concentrate your efforts and you can keep the focus there. When the problems shift with time and mix, it is hard to identify the problem, figure out solutions, and keep focus.

NINE ASPECTS OF BOTTLENECK MANAGEMENT

There are at least nine aspects that need consideration for bottleneck management. There are five that are outside of the direct influence of production control, but dramatically affect it, and four that are within the production control domain.

Strategic and Tactical Issues

We will first mention the five decisions usually outside of production control's domain, but that production control should know about. These decisions are usually associated with managers and industrial or manufacturing engineering:

- All supporting departments and management should know what the bottleneck or key resource is and ensure that the appropriate staff and other resources are available when needed, without delay.
- Any activities should be anticipated, parallel or concurrent actions done in advance, and everything primed. Bottlenecks have been delayed

because a cleaner could not be found, an electrician was busy elsewhere, or a QA inspector was on break. These types of delays are unnecessary and costly.

- More capacity at the bottleneck should be created through parallel resources or upgrading the machine itself.
- Operation elimination or reduction should be investigated.
- Placement of buffer space fore and aft of the bottleneck should be considered.

You need to make sure that things are ready for the bottleneck operations — that you perform as many actions or activities in parallel or in advance of bottleneck operations; that you put more capacity on the problem, if possible; that you reduce or move the problem requirements, if possible; that you have space for work ahead of the bottleneck and an empty area behind the bottleneck for finished work.

These decisions are more tactical, perhaps strategic (depending on the cost of capital), and usually are not operational. They become operational if you have extra equipment or a flexible system that can be manipulated on the fly. You should understand these points and challenge the status quo whenever you constantly find yourself dealing with a bottleneck. There might not be much that can be done, but it should always be challenged and questioned.

Operational Issues

The four aspects that are almost always operational and in the control of production are the *starvation*, *blockage*, *dispatching* at the bottleneck, and *effective loading* of the bottleneck. The bottleneck should always be working when the plant is operating and it should be working in a way that gives the plant the most benefit in a global sense.

Starvation and Blockage

The bottleneck should not be starved for work and forced to sit idle. Neither should it be forced to sit idle because it cannot unload finished work. Therefore, the trick is to make sure that it has a steady stream of work to do whenever it can work and to make sure that downstream operations do not back up and cause blockage. Unlimited inventory is not the solution and we assume that you want the minimum amount of inventory possible.

In simple situations, it should be relatively straightforward to plan work in such a way that batches are split, sized correctly, and moved appropriately. This often requires challenging assumptions about part movement and job sizes. If the bottleneck can work in a transfer-in-batch or pipeline fashion, that is the way it should be fed. Any assumptions about what can be done in a concurrent fashion should also be challenged. For example, can you schedule the tool and fixture prep for the next job before the current job is finished? Sequence-dependent setups should also be reviewed to determine lost time due to changeovers and nonvalue-added activities. If it costs you a $1,000 per minute that the bottleneck machine is not running when it should, what kinds of reasonable investment or actions can you consider to avoid this cost?

The bottleneck resource should operate through breaks, lunch, and across shift boundaries if it can and needs to. Caretaker operators or special scheduling of the operators should be considered. This could keep the bottleneck going for more scheduled hours of operation. We are not suggesting that the machine be run when it should not or that preventative maintenance be ignored. You know the amount of work you need to get through the bottleneck to make your production plans, meet delivery dates, and make your target revenue streams. Run it accordingly and do not waste any capacity that you need. Industrial and manufacturing engineering might have made your job easier or harder to do this. It is easy if the bottleneck can be run independent of the resources ahead of and behind it, and it has an inventory bank fore and aft. It is hard if the bottleneck is hardwired into the system, cannot be decoupled, and there are no inventory banks around it. This latter situation is not good.

When the bottlenecks float in a job shop, or float due to a variable mix in a flow shop, the task of creating suitable flows to each bottleneck is extremely hard. This is further complicated if the shop has any significant levels of uncertainty or instability. If the shop is reasonably stable, mathematical algorithms can be employed to synchronize production, determine batch sizes, and orchestrate the flow to ensure that when a resource becomes a bottleneck, it has the work necessary to run. This type of solution is definitely leading edge and is only suitable for best-in-class situations.

It is possible to starve a bottleneck by not having focused on nonbottleneck resources sufficiently. While it is true that the majority of attention should be paid to the bottleneck, some of the lesser machines and resources must also be paid attention to. They must be able to feed the bottleneck as desired. If they are not maintained correctly and end up with highly variable production cycles and repair profiles, they will not be able to keep the bottleneck functioning. If a nonbottleneck machine can go down hard and is vital to the flow, it warrants your attention.

In cases where there is high variability, the mathematical approach is unlikely to work. Any carefully crafted plan to have one job finish and flow to the bottleneck in a JIT fashion would probably be considered foolhardy. Trying to have levels of pending work in front of potential bottlenecks is also not the answer. It is the work that will appear Tuesday morning that will make it the bottleneck resource for Tuesday's work. You do not want extra work that has slack in its schedule sitting at the bottleneck; you want nothing else at the bottleneck when Tuesday's morning work appears and must flow through.

Dispatching for a Bottleneck Resource

What can you do with a bottleneck? It might be possible to release the work a little bit earlier to hit a slack period on the resource, just before the current assignment. Or it might be possible to change the routing and flow the work to a different resource that is not busy. Or it might be possible to change another job or operation so that the key resource is less busy at the desired time. Whatever the solution, you want the key resource working on the job that gives you the highest return.

This leads us to Morton's concept of Bottleneck Dynamics. While the idea was introduced as a mathematical modeling concept and illustrated with a dispatching heuristic, the concept is relatively simple and straightforward. If there are jobs currently scheduled on the machine that will be late or incur a penalty, you want to pick the job from these potential candidates that gives you the most marginal utility. You determine what the penalty is for delaying the start of each job by another minute and then pick the job that gives the most return. You do this by knowing the remaining slack and current sequence; you then determine what job should be processed next. If all of the jobs are within their time thresholds and are not in danger of being late, then the resource is not a critical bottleneck for any of them. The Bottleneck Dynamics process is not a static approach and the future is reviewed each time a job finishes; what job from the list of available jobs should be started next.

It is possible to view process bottlenecks in an iterative way. Whenever an operation is completed, the remaining operations in the job can then be analyzed. Of the remaining operations, there undoubtedly will be another slowest operation. You have just cleared a bottleneck, but if the job is late, you want to look ahead and see if there are any options for batch splitting or starting work earlier for the remaining operations. Can you recover lost time? If the remaining operations will sit in a queue for any period of time, the answer will be yes. It might be that several late jobs end up competing for the downstream resource and create a conflict. This can be sorted out by determining what job has the highest marginal return. The first thing to look for is wait time in a queue. Once this is dealt with, additional resources may be an option. You might be able to run two machines at the same time instead of one. Or it might be possible to transfer-in-batch and flow parts from operation to operation in a continuous fashion.

Effective Loading

Since bottleneck resources are so key to the success of the firm, you must take extra care with each decision. You want every decision to be the best possible and avoid any potential for damaging capacity. The bottleneck cannot be effective if capacity is wasted. Parts that are high risk for destabilizing the bottleneck or that might place additional stress on the bottleneck must be carefully considered. Any process or procedural change that directly or indirectly affects the bottleneck may also lower the system's effectiveness. An innocent procedural change can upset the factory's rhythm and lower productivity by 20 percent instead of raising it by 20 percent. If the resource or area is not a full-time bottleneck, one of our floaters, the slack time away from peak loads should be considered for any change or high-risk activity. If the resource is always a bottleneck, then all you can do is identify the period of time that has the least amount of critical work scheduled and cross your fingers. Depending on the factory, Mondays, Fridays, and the end of any reporting period should be avoided at all costs since they often imply recovery from the weekend, trying to hit the weekly targets, and other pressure activities. For these activities, you want your bottleneck resource to be fully functional and want to avoid anything that could possibly reduce this functionality.

The bottleneck warrants extra monitoring and reporting. It also warrants increased supervisory attention to make sure that everything happens when it should and everything is ready when needed. A minute lost looking for a gauge appears innocent at the resource, but that minute just delayed the final shipping by a minute too. If all work goes through the machine, all orders just got delayed by a minute.

The trade-off between inventory levels and setups should be analyzed consciously for bottleneck resources. If setups take a substantial time to perform, it is important to understand if fewer setups and higher inventory levels are warranted. The bottleneck aspect of the machine must be considered and not just the normal setup cost. Every minute that the bottleneck is in setup, the factory suffers a full minute loss in productivity. What is this cost compared to the inventory costs?

When a bottleneck process is placed under a microscope or extra pressure is applied by asking for more operations to be done, it is likely that more mistakes or problems will develop. People become nervous and will begin to lose concentration during the peak time, which is why it is even more important to consider each decision that affects the bottleneck. Any monitoring or control at a bottleneck should be part of the normal process and institutionalized and, if possible, automated. At a bottleneck, special requests or activities only add to the capacity problem; they do not help. Is the tour that will delay the bottleneck by five minutes part of the planned dead time on the machine or is it part of the needed capacity? If the latter, the tour just cost the whole plant five minutes of output. What is the value of one minute to your plant? If you plan work for twenty hours a day, 220 days a year, and have sales of $300,000,000, a minute is about $1,110 in gross revenue. If you now have to work overtime to recover the five minutes, your profit margin just got nailed. Do not be sloppy with bottlenecks.

SUMMARY

Bottleneck management is not a simple case of keeping it working. You have to think about what it is working on and when this is happening. You need to think about the physical and logical flows ahead of and behind the bottleneck process. This becomes a problem when the bottlenecks float about the factory like fireflies. However, it is a key point. A minute lost at a bottleneck is a minute lost for the plant, so how do you value the time and contribution made at the bottleneck? Do you just use the direct labor and capital issues, or do you look at the system cost? If you do not look at the system effect, you are likely to misuse the bottleneck and make it worse than before. All decisions about the bottleneck need to be considered, such as the choice of operator, material handling, concurrent setups, or redesigning the process to move some operations before or after. A bottleneck review should be a regular activity in the plant.

The following two chapters explore other aspects of how production control functions or is affected by others. Chapter 17 itemizes a number of problems caused by others and Chapter 18 looks at problems created by production control itself.

17

NAUGHTY THINGS OTHERS DO

PREDIGESTED THOUGHTS FOR THE BUSY PERSON

■ Managers, supporting departments, and the direct labor unintentionally can cause available capacity to be misused and lost.

■ Inappropriate or misused information systems can result in reduced capacity.

■ You should know what the source of your problems is. If you are losing capacity, what are the causes, what can be done?

INTRODUCTION

There are the people in production control and there are the *others*. At the plant where Ralph worked, most of the *others* actually helped production control and were positive forces. There are many plants where this is true. Everyone knows what people should do to help and be a positive force. In this chapter, we will talk about the types of things that are less than satisfactory.

First, who are these others? Well, they can be management, peers, and/or people doing the work on the factory floor. Each of these groups can do things to lose capacity or to damage the manufacturing capability. We will take each in turn and discuss the naughty things that these people do. Unfortunately, all we can do is identify the naughty action or practice. Most actions are accidental and are not intentional. The perpetrators just do not know the damage that they are causing. Other damaging actions, however, are conscious. These are policies or decisions made for short-term gain and that will incur long-term pain. These actions are not healthy for a plant.

The source of the damage is often outside of the authority or control of production control itself and must be lived with. It is possible to escalate the situation discussion to higher levels within the firm, but in some firms it is unlikely something will be done. If you have to live with them, all you can do is to create countermeasures and safety zones to contain the damage, if possible. The naughty list is:

- Management
  1. Believing in the improbable
  2. Helping only themselves
  3. Autocratic behavior
  4. Knee-jerk reactions
  5. Planning interruptus
  6. Indecision
  7. Failing to know and understand
  8. Overloading the task
  9. Management by buzzword
  10. Irrational outsourcing
- Supporting actors
  11. Failure to communicate
  12. Ignoring risks
  13. Independent action
- The doers
  14. Lack of consistency
  15. Misplacing parts
  16. Recording errors
  17. Not following the sequence
- The system
- Out of control situations

MANAGEMENT

There are many managers in a factory. Each and every one of them influences something that a planner or scheduler relies on or has expectations about. The managers participate in the tactical and operational levels of decision making at a minimum, and the inner circle participates at the strategic levels. At the tactical level, they may decide about personnel levels, policies for inventory levels, daily-weekly-monthly targets for production, what is outsourced, and many other aspects of the production process. They may have the best of intentions and they may be trying to do the right thing from their perspective, but not everything is helpful. In this section, a number of naughty management practices are documented.

Naughty Practice #1: Believing in the Improbable

Occasionally, management acts like the past is no indicator of the future. There are many situations where production has never hit 60 percent utilization, but during the planning meetings, management insists that 70 percent will be hit this month. Why? Because they say it will happen this month. Has never happened before. Has not come close. But, it will this month. Trust us. We will make it happen. We will make it so. Asked how this will happen, no precise plans are given for the miracle and there is no justification for the claim. It is nice in a meeting to be gung ho and show other management that you have the "make it happen" attitude, but it might just be a kiss-butt or protect-butt strategy. Unfortunately, this overoptimistic estimate is put into the planning process and this overspecifies production ability. The optimistic estimate will bring in inventory early, create false expectations for due dates, create congestion in the plant, and result in unplanned overtime in expediting. It can also frustrate you when management forces plans that you know are not feasible. In a large MRP system, the optimistic view of capability also forces rescheduling and constant monitoring of exceptions since nothing will go as planned. In production control, you rarely set rates, production targets, design the actual manufacturing process, or supervise the direct labor. You have to work with what others have done and use what others say the machines and operators will do. This is fine when realism exists in the standards and targets, but it can make your job very hard when the reverse is true. Depending on the factory, you might be asked constantly to fit a square peg in a round hole.

Naughty Practice #2: Helping Only Themselves

Production planning usually takes the system view of dock to dock and this view crosses many departments and managers. If your organizational structure does not have system-level performance metrics and objectives, then the individual departments and managers will not want any compromises made in their department. They will want to protect their department and have any problems or lower performance found elsewhere. This creates a challenge when negotiating and when the system has to be bent to achieve the global goals. This myopic and selfish attitude is often not the managers' fault per se, but the fault of upper management to set appropriate goals and objectives for the departmental managers.

When managers fail to bend and accept lower performance in their department to help another department, overall capacity and production capability is damaged. As we know, not all resources and all machines have to have high utilization. Only the bottlenecks and resources feeding the bottlenecks need to be managed tightly. Downstream departments and processes need to be measured against the flow coming to them, not what they might do. Upstream departments should be measured on their ability to feed the bottleneck. Unless the performance metrics recognize this, the different departments are likely to fight between themselves and resist any decisions that reduce their own utilization.

In 1910, Gantt had some interesting thoughts on this problem. In *Work, Wages, and Profits*, he described some of his consulting work on how he got people to help each other. Within a department or area, he had bonuses and incentives in layers so that you got something for your own performance and something for how well the whole area did. It got people working together in the department. This was good, but not his best idea. He set up the department's management bonus based on how well the downstream departments used the generating department's products. A person's performance incentive was based on how well the next department performed using their stuff. He noted an increase of communication between the departments and a continuous improvement in quality. 1910! Sounds like a good idea for today's factories.

Naughty Practice #3: Autocratic Behavior

Have you ever heard the phrase "Do it his way or the highway"? These are the managers who believe in only two rules. Rule No. 1: the boss is always right. Rule No. 2: when you think the boss is wrong see rule No. 1. They never want to hear the **no** word. They always want to hear yes. To these managers, any constructive criticism is just being negative and any statement that something cannot be done is pure obstructionism. When the manager has a thought, the thought must be right and must be included in the plan. You might even be told that your job is not to think, but just to do what you are told. This autocratic approach can result in silly plans at the best of times and plans that damage the firm in the worst of times. Rational suggestions for production timing and sequences based on sound knowledge of processes, products, and production theory are rarely in evidence. The manager has a suggestion for a better plan and that will be the plan. This type of egotistical mismanagement has damaged many a firm. They may not know they are autocratic or that their actions are not positive influences, but the damage is being done nonetheless.

Naughty Practice #4: Knee-Jerk Reactions

"Do this now!" Often from the same gene pool as the autocrat, this type of manager is not an asset, but a liability in many firms. He or she might be known as a knee-jerk sort. Without thinking through the situation, identifying alternatives, considering the short-, mid-, and long-term ramifications, the knee-jerk manager decides on the spot the best solution chosen from the large set of one. Are the necessary parts somewhere in the plant? Not the issue. Pull another job and start the setup for the missing parts. Bunch of workers standing around, looking bored? Start a job, any job, to keep them busy. Tour going through the plant? Hold that job and machine until the tour is over. Customer yelling for the product? Other customer not yelling yet? Pull the quiet one and start on the noisy one. Trouble with some material? Use another material. Affects tomorrow's production? Not a problem today. Are these decisions made in the production office? Usually not. They are often made on the fly, out on the factory floor. Direct intervention!

Often you are notified of the new dispatching decisions after the fact, not before. It is not too often that you are asked for your opinion or blessing. You get to live with the result and the necessary rescheduling around the scene of the crime. These types of shortsighted decisions can create other resource conflicts, screw up bottleneck sequencing, and otherwise result in all kinds of grief. But that is tomorrow, and today we are heroes, the fire is put out, and the day is saved. Whew! Tomorrow is another day and we are indeed confident that tomorrow's fires will be put out too. Unwittingly, these types of managers often set more fires than they put out. Ask any scheduler or planner. Amnesia seems to be a genetic trait with these types of managers. They forget that they made the decisions and set the fires and blame others. They rarely look in their own pockets for the matches.

Naughty Practice #5: Planning Interruptus

Good planning requires thinking; good uninterrupted thinking in a quiet surrounding. Too many managers fail to provide a suitable environment for the production planners and schedulers. If you do not have enough contiguous time to start and finish a thought, what kind of planning quality can you expect? Do you have an office with a door on it that can be closed with a do-not-disturb sign? Phones can be ignored and the calls every three to five minutes assigned to the bottomless pit of voice-mail, but people standing over or around the desk and yelling are hard to ignore. Someone who is in your face asking for advice does not have a mute button. Pity.

Managers expect you to think about the options and come up with smart sequences. You are often blamed when something is overlooked and time, capacity, or materials are wasted. Planning and scheduling is like playing chess. When was the last time you saw chess champions playing a tournament in the middle of a crowded expressway or in a lunch room? Schedulers are often assigned such work places. When was the last time you saw a golf champion interrupted by someone in the middle of a putt and asked what club they should choose on another hole? Obviously, these tasks are done in hushed and quiet situations where the individual is allowed to concentrate on the task at hand without annoyances, interruptions, and noise. Home team fans are noisy and unruly when the opponents are trying to think and work, but are often well behaved when their players are trying to do the same task. But management usually fails to recognize the contribution that good plans and schedules make to the firm and rarely provide you with the tools and work environment to really plan and schedule. There might be some superficial recognition made with partitions or an extra-long phone cord, but these do not replace a nice quiet office with a door that can be shut and locked.

Naughty Practice #6: Indecision

The inability to provide clear, concise, unchanging, and consistent objectives and rules to the production control department is a major problem. Objectives and rules can change hourly on a whim:

- We are not doing any overtime this month. We are allowing overtime. No, do not use overtime. OK, use overtime on cell #2 on the weekend. What? You scheduled overtime? What did I say? No overtime.
- You must use industrial engineering's recommended preferred equipment. Use any equipment that comes close.
- Treat every customer the same. Except, of course, these customers and any other customer I tell you about.
- Minimize inventory levels except when I decide today that we needed more inventory ordered last week.
- Do a better job scheduling! Whatever that means.
- Do whatever is needed to be done. Oh, you cannot do that.

How can you decide what trade-offs are to be made in the schedule if you do not know the goals or the rules? If the goals and rules constantly change or are kept secret, then the production control department cannot be held accountable and responsible for the quality of any plan or schedule.

Naughty Practice #7: Failing to Know and Understand

How many managers actually know how the plant is scheduled and what you actually do? Many managers think they know. They "taught the scheduler everything he/she knows." They know how you spend your days, the information you use, the logic used, and the options explored. They know who you talk to and why. Some of the managers know this, many do not.

Unless the manager has been promoted from the planner's desk or has actually spent one to two weeks sitting with you from the time you arrive at the plant, it is doubtful that the manager really knows too much about the production planning process.

A scheduler usually works with at least four plans. There is the political schedule and plan that is prepared for political reasons and for getting people off your back. It is the schedule that says what the bosses want to hear. The second is the verbal schedule or sequence that is communicated to the supervisors and floor personnel that may bear some resemblance to the political schedule, but is usually different. The third is what you actually think is going to happen. You normally might not believe any schedule you issue or what you are asking the shop floor to execute. The fourth schedule is the blue sky one. If you could produce the work in any way you wanted — not jeopardizing quality, costs, and due dates — how would you get the work done? Do most schedulers want their managers to know what they really do in all cases? Probably not. But, the manager should have a general idea.

The unknowing manager can be a problem in several ways. First, by not understanding what you really do, the manager can undermine and unknowingly mess up the carefully made plans crafted by you. Second, by not understanding all of the tasks and activities being performed, more work can be added to the pile. Third, the manager does not give you the environment or support you need to get the job done. Since the managers do not see all of the activities, information flows, and individual tasks, the necessary investment is not made.

Naughty Practice #8: Overloading the Task

Management is responsible for having enough people in production control and for allocating the tasks so that the job gets done. You can be given a very myopic task and you cannot see anything coming or going. This is bad. On the other hand, you can be given way too much work and responsibility. You might be expected to know where hundreds of jobs are currently, what hundreds of resources are doing, what they have done and will do, what is happening in receiving, at dozens of suppliers, and multiple vendors. This is too much for any single individual. There is information overload and it is impossible to keep an eye on all of this. It is sometimes possible for you to watch the whole process, but this better be a focused factory with few parts, flow lines, and a reasonably low number of vendors and customers.

It seems that few managers figure out how long it takes per part, per vendor, per machine, per cell, per area, and per operator to control each day, and they just keep adding and adding more to the pile. Management, along with you, should try to estimate what each incremental change in the production control task translates into. Management should use this in estimating the number of planners and determining the scope of control and responsibility.

Naughty Practice #9: Management by Buzzword

A leading magazine or guru book talks about how one firm's success was based on so-and-so's theory of whatever or was based on them implementing so-and-so's method. The light goes on and a message is sent far and wide:

> We will now do blah or implement blah! Blah everywhere. Now!
> Hoist it high on the flag pole – Blah!!!! Add blah to all of the
> managers' objectives for the year!!!!

Immediate success can be found in quality circles, TQM, Six Sigma, JIT, TOC, lean manufacturing, concurrent engineering, supply chain management, relationship building, ad infinitum. No? Possibly, but success is not likely unless all other elements are also present and aligned. In the history of manufacturing, there has not been a single silver bullet that slays the werewolf. There have always been a number of factors at play when one firm excels over the rest. Why then do managers and others seek out and subscribe to one attribute theory? They keep doing it. In the late 1980s, one automotive concern thought they could catch Toyota in one to two years just by mimicking the pull production process with kanban cards. Surprise, surprise, it did not quite work. The Toyota production system is multifaceted and is a chain of interrelated and interdependent traits. Doing just one thing will not cure all of your ills, and missing just one of the key links can possibly nullify some or all of the other activities, even if they are done to perfection. To achieve the total benefit requires the total package. You might get some benefit from single buzzwords, but you will not get the total benefit.

Buzzwords are like the book-of-the-month club. If you do not send them back, you own them. Dangerous activities instigated by management include, but are not limited to: attempting Six Sigma when the factory cannot do basic manufacturing, implementing JIT in a dynamic job shop, setting lean inventory levels in unstable situations, outsourcing troublesome processes that are core to the business just because they are troublesome, and trying continuous improvement when major surgery is required. In some cases, the solution is for a problem that does not exist. The result of doing something half-assed or doing the wrong thing is clear and sinful damage to the firm's capacity and ability to function. Care must be taken to understand the assumptions and necessary conditions for a method or concept to work. Management must also be aware of others who have tried and failed. There is nothing wrong with trying a concept or method in a new situation as long as the risk is acknowledged and managed.

If you think that this practice is relatively new, think again. In 1913, Emerson discussed people going to visit state-of-the-art factories and returning with the artifacts that would hopefully yield the same results. He made the analogy to someone buying a library of law books, sitting in the middle of the room, and imagining themselves as being a lawyer. Some things never change.

Naughty Practice #10: Irrational Outsourcing

Outsourcing can be a very effective tool for a manufacturer. There are all kinds of things that can be rationalized and placed in the right hands. However, it is a naughty thing when the wrong kind of thing is outsourced or the wrong time is chosen.

Management sometimes outsources work that is problematic or cannot be made reliably or consistently in house. By outsourcing the crappy work, the internal metrics improve, and the affected departments look better for utilization, quality, and efficiency. From a system viewpoint, this is probably the worst stuff to outsource, especially when the plant is struggling. Think about it. If you cannot make it, why do you think a vendor can do any better? They are likely to do worse until they learn the quirks. They do not have the history, they do not know what has been tried, what worked, what failed, and what to expect. They might not carry enough safety stock or have enough lead time built in. If the crappy parts are in house, at least you can rally the troops you have control over and get the job going. If the parts are at a vendor, you lose control and will suffer the consequences. When problems start, they will likely affect all of your production and require your personnel to go help out at the vendor. This is a double whammy. Instead of saving time and resources, it will likely cost.

Think about it — work outsourced in a panic during peak loads and when deliveries are in jeopardy. People could sell tickets for the show that results. Vendors must be qualified, processes transferred, material rerouted, extra transportation laid in, and processes stabilized. The opportunity for little things to be overlooked is tremendous. Anything and everything you can think of could go wrong. To compound the problem, the key people that should be running the plant are involved in the outsourcing and might overlook other issues.

Backup suppliers and processes need to be in place and qualified before the panic situation. In software project management, Brooks noted that adding people to a late project makes the project later. A similar rule works in manufacturing too. Creating solutions and working in uncharted water during critical times is too little, too late. Henry Ford realized this and had backup plans for materials, suppliers, and processes. Approximately 66 percent of the Model-T and Model-A production was outsourced, but Ford was able to make something of everything. He had working processes that could be scaled up or transferred when needed. He got burned, learned, and then institutionalized the process.

SUPPORTING ACTORS

Here we are referring to the nondirect labor force: the tool and die room, electricians, industrial engineering, mechanics, plant facility personnel, cleaners, product engineering, training, traffic, purchasing, human resources, executive office, information technology, and accounting. Did we miss anyone? These people do not have the higher authority of management and direct influence on the production flow, but they can impact it, positively and negatively.

There are three key naughty things that we see committed by this varied crowd.

Naughty Practice #11: Failure to Communicate

The information flow to and from production control is critical. If the planners and schedulers do not know what is going to happen that will change the status quo, it will be impossible to take this into account. The production control department needs to know about anything in the present or future that will affect capacity or capability. This is the who, what, where, when, and why aspects of production. For any upcoming event or change, you might have to schedule certain production before, orchestrate the change to ensure that everything comes together correctly, schedule differently immediately after the event, and then institute a learning curve or maturity process.

Naughty Practice #12: Ignoring Risks

Not doing diligence in thinking about the timing of the event is another no-no. Being a dumb bugger in the woods is no excuse for overlooking the impact of doing prototype work, changing production equipment during the last week of the fiscal quarter, or changing methods and processes for receiving and trucking during a new product launch for the most important customer. It is wise to institute policies and guidelines for when changes can be made. Supporting groups can assume that any day is as good as another for a change or event and schedule their actions in the dark. This assumption does not make sense to any scheduler. You can restrict changes to the first three weeks of a month and on Tuesdays through Thursdays, day shift only. The goal is to schedule any change to the manufacturing system to avoid key times when problems usually arise and when full concentration is needed on normal production. Changes can often be timed to allow full concentration on the change and when the appropriate staff is around.

Naughty Practice #13: Independent Action

The third naughty practice of the supporting teams is failing to orchestrate their own resources for a change. When a major change occurs to the manufacturing process, all hands are needed to be on deck. It was noted in 1885 by Sweet that when dealing with new inventions in manufacturing, people should not be surprised by the unexpected. Business is not as usual and there are likely to be ramifications in many areas, not just where the change is. Other activities that you consider to be cosmetic surgery should be rescheduled to another time and capacity created to help out if needed. The supporting groups should look at their resources and their least skilled workers should be loaded up. Slack should be created on the most skilled and talented individuals. The heavy hitters can be assigned fill-in work so time is not wasted, but the work should be of the nature that it can be dropped and personnel reassigned. How many times have you seen activities and projects stumble because the right people are not available to help out? They are traveling, on vacation, or assigned to another hot topic.

THE DOERS

The *doers* are the actual production folk. The people that do the heaving, the toting, the turning of knobs, the throwing of switches, and the running of equipment. Now, some of the following issues are not necessarily in their own control, but at the end of the day, they are part of the problem.

Naughty Practice #14: Lack of Consistency

Planning and scheduling requires a few things to be successful. One of the most important is repeatability and predictability. There are usually four phases of a job: setup, getting the first quality part and production approved, running the quantity, and then teardown and cleanup. If you cannot use a reliable estimate, how on earth can you be expected to coordinate multiple resources and synchronize production? You do not need the estimate to be down to the minute, but rough execution to expectation would be nice. Setups can be estimated at four hours, but take several days. Processing times can be so variable that the average is equivalent to the standard deviation, and this is not good. A four-hour setup should be accurate to within plus or minus one-half hour, if not less. Processing time for a batch or job should also be predictable within limits. It should be the accountability and duty of the actual production department to meet the expectations, assuming that they have been agreed to in advance.

Naughty Practice #15: Misplacing Parts

It is funny when you think about it. Production control does not actually move, make, or handle product, but if something cannot be found, it is your fault. The product was made or so it is believed, but material handling and stores cannot find it. If it cannot be found, it could not have been made since material handling would never lose it. Everything would be in its place and there is a place for everything. If the missing product is important, it is most likely that another special run will be requested. This will bump other work out of the way and will use material that might have been allocated to another job. When the parts are found, as they most often are, either partway through the run or just as the run finishes, an excess of inventory is created. This disrupts the future build cycles and screws up any interim planning. It is a bad thing if material handling cannot store and locate inventory. Inventory accuracy is a mandatory requirement for good production control.

Naughty Practice #16: Recording Errors

Ten parts. Not eight or nine, and not eleven. If production tracking is not accurate on the part identifiers, quantities, and yields, then production control is working with a house built of playing cards. In some factories, the wrong part types are reported, the wrong number of parts recorded, the number of times the machine cycled reported for the number of parts made although the machine made multiple parts per cycle, the weight of the job entered as the number of parts made, the wrong order reported against, fictitious orders reported against, sister plant's part numbers used, to name just a few. There are many different types of errors possible from receiving, purchasing, through shipping. It is also possible to accidentally add zeros to a final stock item requirement and have this expanded through the MRP logic. One forecast had three zeros added to a fifteen thousand item order. This error was accepted as accurate by the ERP system, and the fifteen million demand rippled through the MRP netting logic. A human might have noticed something was not right, but the software merrily generated all kinds of orders and material requirements to meet the increased demand. In the ERP, this error generated big problems. Almost all reports and transactions before the problem was found and fixed were garbage. This affected preventative maintenance, purchasing, suppliers, finance, and almost every other part of the plant. The plant's division was also affected as the numbers were rolled up into reports. Recording errors in ERP are more troublesome than the old-fashioned, batch-oriented MRP systems. ERPs are real time, integrated, and when a mistake is made, the error immediately affects anything and everything related to it.

All of these types of mistakes drive into the planning department and create havoc. If the problem is big enough and at the right place in the system, almost all of the information is suspect until the problem is detected, found, and corrected. Attention must be paid to the details and accuracy of floor tracking, especially with today's integrated systems such as ERP/MES/APS combinations. Production control will have to use yesterday's data and manual records of what was built, shipped, what might be in inventory, and what might be hot listed. This just creates more errors and problems.

Naughty Practice #17: Not Following the Sequence

There is many a worker who has decided to work on one part or job instead of the one next on the dispatch list. The last one was tough or heavy, so is the next one, so we will just pick a lighter or easier one. What is the difference anyway? The worker might be working on piece work and one item might be chosen over another because of processing speed. Creative dispatching by the worker is prevalent in incentive shops or where simple metrics are used to measure productivity. Let us find that job that increases our metric! In some cases, it does not matter. But in other cases where sequencing is down to the minute or hour, the decision can affect the bottleneck resource and the whole plant is at the mercy of one worker who decided to work on job ABC instead of DEF.

THE SYSTEM ITSELF

The manufacturing system and supporting information systems, including the ERP/MRP, MES, APS, and other information systems, may or may not be helpful. On a good day, they can be positive contributors to efficiency and effectiveness. It would be nice for this to be the case every day. The next best case is when the system is neutral compared to legacy or manual systems. It is not any better, but it is not any worse. You should not be happy about this, but it is a reality you have to face. You spend the money, do the process, and at the end of the day, have no major gain.

The bad news is that some systems will cost you production and costs, directly and indirectly:

- First, there are the buggy or wrongly configured systems that cannot give reliable netting or requirements and force you to misuse resources.
- Second, there are systems that cannot model or capture key aspects and they rely on human memory and manual monitoring each day to catch any issues. These are like walking blindfolded in a mine field.
- Third, there are systems that seem to promote or encourage bad data entry and mistakes in terms of the user interface. The little errors going into the material master or inventory records then ripple throughout the plant.
- Fourth, there are systems that are not friendly to use in terms of information presentation and work flow. Their use takes more time and effort than legacy systems or other approaches. If a system takes more time to use, this eats into decision time, and this translates into decision quality, and this translates into misuse of capacity.

One factory had implemented an ERP, but was not using it because of unreliable data. They were using historical records and simply adding percentages when they wanted to determine things like selling price. This was not a good situation and it was obvious that the ERP was not helping the factory. The ERP might help in the future, but not then.

It is possible that if you encounter a system exhibiting any of these problems, you will either avoid the system; minimize its use; rely on other tools like spreadsheets, pen, and paper; or just revert to old practices and ignore the system until yelled at.

OUT-OF-CONTROL SITUATIONS

There are times that production control cannot control. If the overall manufacturing system gets itself into a state of poor inventory control, it might not know what is where or how much. Poor production tracking might result in not knowing accurately what is actually made. Sporadic manufacturing execution makes the standard deviation equal to or exceeding the mean. There might be systems problems. The workers might not have the discipline to follow processes and methods. The workers might not get the right training or ignore it if provided. There can be a lot of problems. In these out-of-control situations, production control cannot control. If you cannot fix these problems manually, what makes anyone think you can do it with special software or with schedules? These problems are bigger than production control.

You may or may not have contributed to the situation. Production control is not perfect and things can be missed and overlooked. However, if the machines have not been maintained, proper tooling acquired, workers trained, or the setups and processing times end up varying widely, how can you estimate when something will start or finish in order to coordinate resources? If the physical shop-floor tracking methods do not provide accurate counts and if the forklift truck drivers lose or damage goods, how are you to know when something is running out? If you have one of these symptoms, you might still be OK, but if you have all three symptoms of being out of control, production control will be a hot spot. Production control will be found at fault for almost all mistakes and any resource utilization problems, unfairly and unjustly in many cases.

In these situations, better sequencing and similar objectives should not be the major part of production control's mandate. Production control should be looking at improving the tracking and information flows. You should be trying to pick up clues and information in the system that indicate problems are arising. The use of APS tools is foolish at best. So is any consideration of personnel reduction. Production control will need more people to keep hot lists, cycle count, track missing inventory, reconcile errors in reporting, and fight fires.

Develop simple scheduler and planner information systems, reduce or eliminate all manual data entry or redundant information processing, and give the thinkers more time for firefighting. Make sure that you have the information you need, when you need it. This is the best you can do. You can probably focus on the next forty-eight hours, but do not waste your time smoothing and optimizing the work load four to eight weeks in the future.

SUMMARY

Production control personnel are not perfect, never will be. We are not perfect. You are not perfect. But neither are the people above, beside, or below production control in the decision chain. In some cases, education and policies can be instituted to minimize or avoid some of the blatant causes. For many factories, over half of the problems facing production can be considered to be created by the plant itself. In some of the more challenged shops, the number is higher.

About half of these problems are probably caused by management, some by the supporting actors, about a third by the floor, and the remainder by production control. However, you are caught in the middle and are likely to be initially blamed for almost *all* of the mistakes when the wrong parts are made, parts are not ready in time, or the wrong number of parts are made.

Chapter 18 looks at the problems caused by production control. The problems that can be created by you.

18

SELF-INFLICTED WOUNDS

PREDIGESTED THOUGHTS FOR THE BUSY PERSON

- If you repeatedly play with a loaded gun and leave it around, do not be surprised by repeated trips to the Emergency Room. You should assess what problems are controllable or avoidable and what problems are truly out of your control.

- There are good and bad times for considering when to schedule special, problematic, prototype, or changed parts. A conscious review and sequencing should be done for these parts.

- If you tell lies, they will eventually come back! Planning and scheduling needs to work with realistic estimates and not make-believe dreams.

- You have to talk to people and communicate. It is a two-way process.

- Rarely are processes and situations identical and interchangeable, You need to understand the implications of choosing one resource over another, one operator over another.

- For every action, there better be a reaction! If you pull short or make an adjustment, at least one other change in the production sequence will be needed to keep the larger plan stable.

INTRODUCTION

The last chapter talked about the naughty things other people do to mess your lovely plans and schedules; how they unintentionally reduce your capacity or create surprises for you to fix. Is everything their fault? It has to be. Production control never, ever does anything that will cost capacity, create late work, or increase costs. To some people, everything is peachy keen in planning and everything is production's or management's fault. Unfortunately, production control can make mistakes too and no one or no system is perfect.

What are the classic mistakes you might make unknowingly, and how can you avoid them? In this chapter, we will share some obvious, and some not so obvious, mistakes that you can make.

SINNING

This is a chapter of sin. Unlike certain other sins, there are no pleasures associated with these. Why do these sins occur? Sometimes it is through honest naivete and not knowing that a better decision can be made. In other cases, you know that you are dancing with the devil, are doing something that will possibly and likely backfire, but are forced for various reasons to proceed. You can overlook, forget, ignore, communicate erroneous instructions, miscalculate, and generally screw up. If these are sporadic and relatively rare, they cannot be considered sins per se. You are doing OK. However, if they are habitual and happen almost every day, then you are sinning. There are other reasons why some less-then-optimal decisions are made. For example, when nothing is going right and rabbits have to be pulled out of the hat, it is often necessary to jump knowingly out of the frying pan and into the fire to grab the elusive bunny and suffer some burns and scarring along the way. Hard to call this a sin. In other cases, it is *do it now* and *beg forgiveness* later. Whether or not this last point is a sin is debatable and we will not turn that stone over.

The sins discussed here affect the capacity and ability of the manufacturing enterprise. It is possible for you to make decisions that end up shooting the firm in the feet. These are self-inflicted gunshot wounds. It is bad enough when capacity is lost through no fault of your own; it is very bad when you cause your own problems. In this chapter, we are concerned with problems attributed to you. We have not attempted to document every type of mistake or problem that can be made. The summary list is composed of our classic "You should have known better!" mistakes:

1. Starting before all is ready
2. Ignoring time-sensitive jobs
3. Assuming all operators are equal
4. Pulling jobs short
5. Failing to know

6. Ignoring the risk
7. Misusing a critical resource
8. Failing to tell
9. Failing to remember
10. Ignoring side effects

Sin #1: Starting Before All Is Ready

It is not uncommon to see machines start to change over, material moved in, and personnel reallocated while something is still allocated elsewhere or tied up. The missing piece of the puzzle is scheduled to be available and ready at a certain time — the truck is arriving at 2 PM, for sure; the job at its upstream operation will finish by 1:30 PM, guaranteed; the incoming material will be transported directly to the machine by 2:05 PM and the batch of parts moved in at the same time.

There are times the parts or material will arrive and there are other times they will not. You have to assess the various issues in a realistic fashion and plan accordingly. If outside transportation is involved and it is Tuesday morning rush hour after a long weekend, you are in for possible delays. If the upstream operation has not been performed recently, it is likely that processing times will take the high side of any estimate and not the average or below average. This is not the same as truly parallel setups and hot changeovers. In a concurrent setup situation, the majority of the setup is done off-line and the machine keeps running if it is supposed to, and then the changeover is conducted with minimal time delay. What we are talking about is perhaps the bottleneck machine sitting idle waiting for something to arrive or be done. If a machine is not a bottleneck, or will not starve a bottleneck, or will not cause a job to be late, then sitting idle and waiting for the material to arrive is not a sin. There are times, of course, when even a bottleneck or otherwise critical process must be launched on the chance that all pieces of the puzzle will come together at the same time. Such is life and the risk must be taken. Situations such as these need careful analysis and the risks brought to the table. Someone should be accountable for authorizing these types of decisions, and it is not the scheduler.

Sin #2: Ignoring Time-Sensitive Jobs

Many tasks and operations are insensitive to time. They can be scheduled without discrimination on any shift, on any day, and at any time. However, there usually are some operations in a factory that are sensitive to when they are scheduled. If they are scheduled at nonpreferred times, the setup will likely take longer, or the job will take longer to get a first-off quality part accepted, or the yield during the job will be lower, or the processing time will be longer. If the job is scheduled when suboptimal performance will occur and if there was a way to hit a preferred time, this is a sin. Systems that run on tight JIT or low inventory levels with carefully calculated stock-out expectations typically do not take this type of information into account and innocently schedule work to be done at a nonpreferred time. Computerized systems also do this. When the nonpreferred time is selected, there are the added costs associated with the job itself and the effects ripple through the schedule when the problems occur. If the impact is taken into account and the schedule generated with any extended times, the ripple effect is minimized. The worst situation is during peak load and the preferred estimates are used in a nonpreferred situation. During peak load, the schedule is packed tightly and any unexpected result such as longer times, lower yields, and breakdowns will ripple quickly throughout the system.

Sin #3: Assuming All Operators Are Equal

In today's politically correct environment, all operators within a classification are considered equal. Jack, Jill, and Jim can do the job equally, just as well as the other thirty or forty welders. It does not matter which operator is assigned as long as they have the basic skill set, attended training, and have the right checkbox in the skill matrix. If life was only so simple!

For the majority of work in a plant, it might be that any classified operator can do the job as well as the next. However, we think that this is a rare state, a factory where all classified operators can do all jobs equally all of the time in all situations. Think about it. If you have new work or prototype work, do you funnel it towards a new hand or one of the experienced workers who can get anything working? If the crews have just finished training, do you send critical work to a crew who was noted as barely paying attention and bored or to a crew that was gung-ho and keen? Both crews passed the technical aspect in a pass/fail criteria. If work is critical, would you send it to a crew or operator that got 51 percent and barely passed or to personnel who aced it and got over 90 percent? Both are technically qualified and have the little x's in the right training matrix square. To add complexity to the problem, Bob or Jane might normally be the operators of choice, but both were known to attend a social event last night with their spouses and they are definitely not the best choice this morning.

A new scheduler might not know these nuances or know enough to track them. Hopefully, an experienced scheduler is aware of the differences between operators and crews, and exploits this knowledge intelligently. If an experienced scheduler blindly assigns critical or high-risk work to any machine, resource, or personnel without considering the quality and state of the operators, it is a sin. There is high risk in assigning work to the least-preferred person or crew. This decision can affect time, material, and generate many other side effects. It is a sin if you can avoid a dumb mistake or high-risk situation and do not.

Sin #4: Pulling Jobs Short

Sometimes it makes sense, sometimes not. Consider it a momentary lapse when it occurs with unwanted side effects. In the heat of the moment, the current job on a machine or cell is pulled or stopped ahead of time. The full order is not made. The decision was made because another hot job must be run. If a job is pulled short, consider the impacts. First, there may be an unnecessary setup when the job is restarted. This can cost time, resources, and materials in the direct and indirect departments associated with production. Second, the pre-empted job was scheduled to be completed and moved on; the subsequent schedule and sequencing is messed up. The sequencing can be maintained if the partial batch can be moved and the batch finished on the first machine before the second machine finishes the partial work. If the job being inserted creates a longer delay, the sequence is damaged. Third, personnel associated with the preempted setup are now doing something that was unscheduled and it is likely that other jobs are being delayed, rescheduled, or idled as the hot job is set. Fourth, if the shop has high standards for tracking and paperwork (e.g., medical, military), the split batch adds to the paperwork and involve possibly different operators, inspectors, or material tracking.

If a job is to be pulled short, you should consider the full system cost versus the full system benefit. What is the impact today or tomorrow? If the job does not have to be pulled short, that is a sin. If the proper steps are not followed to minimize the impact, that too is a sin. For example, in a repetitive build situation, a pulled job should imply a manual tweaking or tuning of the future orders to put the part back in cycle. What was not built should be added to the next order as a minimum consideration. The next order for the part will move up, but subsequent orders will stay as planned. This will stabilize the inventory flow and keep the future cycles relatively stable. If the proper steps are not taken, not only will the next order be moved up, but later orders will also be disrupted. At a minimum, the next order for the part should be a full batch size to prevent two out-of-cycle orders from occurring. A partial batch size may result from the MRP settings and should be watched for. In this case, you made less then the desired batch size so MRP inserts a partial order making up the difference while keeping the order for the next full batch size on the schedule.

Too often, pulling a job short is a knee-jerk reaction. The immediate stock-out situation is handled and the hot job can be accommodated. Other options have not been explored thoroughly and the impacts of the job disruption have not been analyzed. The lack of thinking is a sin and it costs time and resources. Do you know the true, full cost of running a job through the plant? This has to include paperwork, counting, storing, setups, setup crews, and the cleaners. What does each extra setup imply in terms of effort? What happens to the future plan and sequence when a job is pulled short?

Sin #5: Failing to Know

A lack of communication, an oversight, or something else causes it, whatever. A job is scheduled for a machine, cell, or line that cannot make it and the mistake is not discovered until the work is in the queue and about to be run. Sounds like a stupid mistake? Yep. Does it happen? Yep. Does it happen often? Hope not.

If you have information that the machine or resource is not capable, then it is clearly your fault. It is a sin to plan something you know cannot be done or if you are hoping and praying that it will work this time although it never has in the past. The costs and impacts of making a wrong decision in production control can be immense. If someone knew at one point of potentially bad decisions and failed to document them, then that is obviously their fault.

Unfortunately, if you do not know that the machine or resource is not capable, you are still partially at fault. Why? You are responsible for creating the information network that will feed you with all of the information you need to know. You need to know when machines are modified, what can be done where, and whenever a status quo changes. If you do not know, then your communication system is faulty. Sounds tough. It is. The refrains "I was not told" or "I did not know that" are unacceptable. Part of your job and allocated tasks must be to create the necessary information flows, passive and active, that will keep you up to date. No one else will be worried about this. No one else will have it as a yearly objective. Time to seek and cull information should be recognized as part of the work day. Management should be required to provide support and the appropriate tools to help you get and track information. If management does not permit you time to seek and cull, and does not provide support and tools, the blame is at higher levels. In our world, crap can flow upstream as well as down.

Sin #6: Ignoring the Risk

You know the feeling. You were under pressure, peak load times. A problem part had to be made and sure enough at the worst of possible moments, things went bad. Scheduling a problem part or job that is known to have high variability in its production during a peak period when other choices exist is a sin. Problem parts should be made before or after peak periods, or when the maximum skill and support level is present. Extra care should also be planned and executed in getting things ready for the part. To blindly schedule a problem product with the normal industrial engineering standards, with no special handling, and expect it to happen is very sinful. A problem part is one that often wastes time, resources, or damages processes and equipment and forces them out of a stable state. A problem part may be a prototype, a special engineering change, or a special test of a new material or process. In some cases, the source of the problem is not on your desk. For some reason, manufacturing and product engineering just love to schedule new things during peak times. Your peak time is usually not theirs. In one factory, management instituted a rule as to when industrial engineering could make changes to avoid this problem being caused by outside forces.

You do not need this sin in a peak load situation. Have you ever noticed that more mistakes are made under pressure? Guess what happens to your problem part during a peak load? The problems are worse. Far worse. People are cutting more corners, pushing the envelope, rushing around, not dotting the Is or crossing the Ts. The impacts associated with problems get amplified and small problems become big problems. Some of the impact amplification is very problematic; with peak loading, there is little spare capacity and almost no elasticity in the system. If one job has a problem, it is likely that many other jobs will have problems shortly too.

Sin #7: Misusing a Critical Resource

If you know that low yields will result or that not all of the parts will be made, and you do this on a critical resource or during peak loads, you have committed another sin. It is double trouble. An unnecessary setup likely would be incurred on a key resource, critical material wasted, and a great deal of frustration and stress generated. How much does this cost you? How many unnecessary setups and changeovers do you do? If you have to make the product, at least schedule it and have sufficient support present that you do not lose capacity. It is better to make nothing than to make the wrong part or a part that is not needed and just waste capacity. The machine could have been cleaned and tuned in the idle time. For some reason, many schedulers do not look far enough out on the time horizon to craft sequences that avoid wasting capacity. It is hard for a computer system to do this type of reasoning since none of the systems we know of can detect risk problems or reason at this level. They will just schedule anything on anything anytime and expect normal results. This is fine for about 90 percent of the decisions, but terrible for the 10 percent that are critical.

Without looking at the complete system cost issue, it is hard to reason with management and workers on this topic. What do you mean? Not run the job? What will the operators do? Who cares if we are not making the standard rates? At least we are making something and something is better than nothing! This is rarely true and is usually not a smart thing to do. If you are making something that will be used in the immediate future and are just moving up the build by a day, then the extra inventory costs and possible risks can be weighed against the costs of not keeping the machine busy. It is unwise to keep pulling the schedule ahead by many days or weeks just because the machines are running great and the operators are standing there. It is also unwise to keep running one part way beyond its demand just because the batch is going well. What are the ripple effects? What are the risks?

Sin #8: Failing to Tell

A cardinal sin is forgetting or failing to communicate. You did not say something. You were quiet. Assuming that malicious obedience is not present, you must have simply forgot. Perhaps you had a senior moment, forgot to remind tooling to do something, forgot to tell purchasing about a change in timing.

Forgetting and failing to communicate what is needed when is perhaps the biggest mistake that you can make. It is not enough to assume that people will read reports and pick it out for themselves. You must be proactive and ensure that all vested parties are kept informed and aware of what is going to happen. You are like a ring leader in a circus and it is your job to synchronize the performers. You should have adequate and thorough means with which to track, communicate, and remind. You can have these types of functions more commonly in custom systems and sometimes in commercial offerings. For example, you may need special communication hooks between yourself and supporting groups, and special pop-ups to remind you to do things for certain jobs.

The failure to communicate can waste many resources and lose capacity. It is the old saying: How does a project become a year late? One day at a time. How is capacity lost? One minute at a time. Poor communication implies that departments and resources will not be ready when they are supposed to be. The tools may not be ready, material present, workers trained, and trucks at the dock. During the peak and crisis periods, communication is probably the most vital task and the one task that is reduced and shortchanged.

Sin #9: Failing to Remember

A good memory is hard to find — so many things, so little space to put everything in. One planner held back a complete order of electronic parts because the associated remotes had not been ordered. He forgot to order the remotes and there was a six-week lead time. The planner did not realize this until the order had to be shipped. A partial order was shipped, but the rest was backordered. The backordered customer was not very happy. The customer was in the midst of a large roll out and had been assured when the order was placed that the quantity of parts and the associated pieces were not a problem. To recite "to err is human" is not really a good idea in these types of situations. You are responsible for keeping track of things and are expected to have an orderly house. You should have adequate manual and computerized tools that help you keep track of what is needed, when it is needed, when special things are expected to happen, and when you need to remind or contact others. You should have prewarning or detection points in place to check things before the last minute. And, you should have the processes in place to track and follow activities you have launched. It is also not good to say "I told them when it was needed" or that "I called and left a message" when the shipment fails to turn up.

Sin #10: Ignoring Side Effects

On the surface, many decisions make sense. You operate a food factory and one of the products involves a lot of onions. You should be able to schedule onion production on any day of the week. Not always. We heard of one factory where onion production had to be avoided on Fridays. If onions were scheduled on Friday, the production output would decrease by one-third. Why? The onions were dusty and the area around the line would be dusty when onions were processed. At the time, the afternoon shift was largely composed of women who would go out to the pub after work on Fridays. The hairstyle of the day required large amounts of hair spray to fix it and hold it up. Big hair was the rage. The dust of the onions would stick to their hair and spoil it. By the ladies decreasing the speed of their machines, this problem was avoided.

Another friend shared a story about a meat packing plant and its truck routes. Nice, optimal truck routes had been designed, but the drivers were not following the instructions. Why? The truck drivers continued to get together in the same village at the same time of day to have coffee. Regardless of the official routes, the truckers still had their coffee meeting. This had to be taken into account by the truck routing.

There are many such issues. If the scheduling creates side effects, the impact might be significant enough to take into account. The issues may be personal as the two stories imply, but the side effects may also relate to less arbitrary aspects. For example, scheduling can create sequences of work that cannot be performed easily because of physical characteristics such as weight or volume. Part A or part B might be OK, but try to make part A and part B at the same time, the aisle is just too small, and the parts cannot be moved without difficulty. The physical space needed for the production is a form of secondary issue or side effect. Facets like this should be considered, but they are sometimes too easy to ignore or forget. If these factors are not found in the official ISO 9000 specifications or in the MRP/ERP records, it is almost certain that they will be overlooked.

SUMMARY

Of course, there will be times you just have to be a sinner. Sometimes sinning is the only way to stay alive. Unfortunately, you can be caught in a downward spiral as one sin leads to another and then another. Sins can become institutionalized and the accepted way to solve problems. That is a sin in itself; consider it Sin #11. If you have to sin, then do it knowingly, above board, and discuss ways of minimizing or avoiding the negative impacts. Whenever a sin is planned, management should expect and ask for a reason why the sin is going to happen and what is going to be done about the downside. Follow-up should be expected and measures taken to avoid repeating the mistake in the future. Any planned sin should be approved by management and normally should be beyond the scheduler's level of authority. We like and trust most schedulers, do not get us wrong here, but anything that consciously and purposely loses capacity should be given some management attention.

Once capacity is lost, it cannot be recovered. It is like time. You cannot bank time. You cannot bank capacity. If you waste it and fritter it away, you have flushed it down the toilet. Usually, there are not one or two big reasons or causes of lost capacity; it is all kinds of small little mistakes that eat up an hour here, an hour there, and now and again a partial shift. A really bad mistake can eat up multiple shifts and days, and if the job damaged a resource, weeks.

Institutionalized sins are bad for production control and for others. Just because it has always been done or is being done, does not mean that it is right or wrong. Periodically, it is important to challenge all processes, methods, and assumptions in production control to make sure that problems are being addressed and symptoms are not accepted as being cast in stone. Things that add value to the production control process and results should be encouraged, reinforced, and extended. Things that resemble sacred cows and have little or no merit should be put out to pasture. When you are doing a review or are part of a review, challenge, challenge, challenge and ask the classic five levels of why. Act like a three-year old: Why? Why? Why? Why? Why?

The appropriate style of production control is not the same at each point of time in a firm's existence. Chapter 19 looks at four phases of production control that a firm might expect to go through.

19

PRODUCTION CONTROL AT DIFFERENT POINTS IN A FIRM'S CYCLE

PREDIGESTED THOUGHTS FOR THE BUSY PERSON

- Industries, firms, and plants have different personalities and profiles, and this suggests different tools and methods. There is a manufacturing evolution as the industry and factory matures.

- You cannot naively copy another plant's methods without first understanding why they are doing what they are doing, what the interdependent factors are, and how the methods are actually used.

- Mechanical or automatic scheduling and dispatching is the ideal and it can be achieved in certain factories.

- If you use methods appropriate for one stage of evolution in another, you might achieve effective production control with a bulldozer when a shovel would work, or you might be laying the foundation for ineffective production control that will fail and might cause your plant to close.

INTRODUCTION

Firms go through a number of phases or eras as they, and the industry in which they exist, evolve. The firms go from a start-up or Wild West phase, to one of systemization, to a focus on quality and proliferation of features, followed by periods of internal and external efficiency efforts. This affects how you plan and schedule. It affects what you should do.

Obviously, there are different styles and approaches to production control suitable for each of the situations, and discrete manufacturing will be different than process industries. There is no one production control approach that is appropriate for any firm in all situations. You must review your production control practices periodically and reflect on their suitability. A set of processes, methods, policies, and tools used a year ago, two years ago, or many years ago might, or might not, be appropriate. The business situations change and it is not wise to assume that the great system you had working in the past is the best system for today. It is very hard to change areas like production control and evolve them; there is a great deal of history and critical mass associated with production control systems. If you do not evolve and have the appropriate solution for the problem at hand, it is possible that you will become vulnerable and lose any competitive edge you once had.

EVOLUTION

There seems to be a set of natural and predictable phases that a firm is likely to go through. A firm can start off with an entrepreneurial opportunity, do well enough that it has to start mass production on a reasonable scale, competes with other domestic firms on quality and cost, slowly introduces multiple models with different features, and ends up competing on the world market. This can happen for whole industries, firms, or parts of an existing firm.

While it is true that not every firm will go through the phases — some firms might have a tortured path through the phases and some firms might have renewal phases that cause some previous phases to repeat — the basic phases make sense, have been repeated by many firms and industries, and are likely to be valid for the foreseeable future. The four main phases described in this chapter can be found in many industries from the 1880s through the 1930s. The phases can also be observed starting in the 1950s through today. If you look closely, you can even see the phases in the 1700s when the industrial revolution was just developing. The phases have repeated in the same sequence and the manufacturing practices or management methods have also followed the same order.

Large triggers or big changes in the situation will cause many firms and industries to shift and evolve at almost the same time. For example, the application of water power, steam engines, and hydroelectricity have all been big disruptions and have caused rapid development of new products, processes, and the exploitation of new markets. Other events such as world wars have also caused the cycles or phases to be reoriented as new materials, new processes, and new advances in manufacturing were explored.

It is possible for some firms to enter partway through the normal evolution process; for example, when foreign firms enter an existing market by cherry picking the high-volume, low-variety parts, and creating lean, efficient systems for their production. The newcomers are not burdened by existing customers, conversion or compatibility issues, service parts, or the high variety of parts that are needed for the existing customer base. This cherry picking has happened for centuries and is sometimes innocently helped by the players being picked. It has happened that older equipment has been sold to foreign companies when the new equipment upgrades are being done. The foreign companies have then often used this equipment to target the sweet spot in the existing catalog. This is the 20 percent of the parts that make 80 percent of the profit. Outsourcing of the old models or service parts while a firm concentrates on the new generation can also create this situation. The firms that start off making the older-generation parts and servicing the existing customer base are in a great position to learn and enter into future competition. It does not have to be foreign manufacturers either. Some firms have created their future competition accidentally by supplying another domestic firm with the underlying knowledge and technology.

Small evolutionary changes in processes, materials, and products will not cause firms to suddenly leap from one cycle to another, or to restart in an earlier cycle. It will require a substantial event or trigger such as a radically different material or whole product design. For example, when Ford phased out the Model-T, which was being manufactured with a beautifully orchestrated system of resources and processes, and moved to the Model-A, the firm regressed in manufacturing systems and it took two years before the same volumes were achieved. A change from vacuum tubes to transistors and solid state electronics was a major shock to the industrial situation. Plastics and composites have also caused discontinuities in the evolutionary path.

There are two aspects to the manufacturing evolution. First, there is the situation that makes sense given the market demand, competition, volumes, technology, product variety, and other manufacturing parameters. You can reflect on what is happening in the general manufacturing milieu and make some observations about what manufacturing system makes sense or does not make sense. Second, there is the situation for a specific plant, firm, or industry. If the physical reality of manufacturing makes sense for what is needed, all is good. The firms and plants might change their processes, methods, and systems just at the right time and be positioned to exploit the next evolutionary phase. The firms might change or do things before they should and this can result in unnecessary costs and problems. The firms might not realize that they need to change, do not recognize the changing characteristics in the manufacturing problem, and keep on doing what they were doing. Then all of a sudden, the sleepy heads wake up and realize that what they are doing does not make sense, that others are zooming by, and that something needs to be changed. It is easy to miss some of the evolutionary changes. For example, when is variety OK for a mass production line and when do you switch over to focused factories or start to use flexible cells? Some firms try to keep handling more and more variety with the existing paradigms and strategies when they should have invested in a new way of doing business.

Firms that match the manufacturing system to the manufacturing problem will be more successful in the bigger picture. Firms that can anticipate that a change is coming and do some preliminary work in advance will be the leaders that others will chase. If no one picks up on the changing problem, someone from outside might and then they are the ones being chased. If no one recognizes the situation for what it is, the first one to wake up and do the right thing will be the leader. It is easy to think everything is OK. Everyone has the same high inventory, same lead times, and everyone thinks this is fine, but the inventory is really unnecessary, quality could be improved, and lead times could be shorter.

What does all of this evolution stuff have to do with production control? If you do not use the right methods for the situation, the production control problem is harder than it needs to be. That is the first thing. You need to adjust and adapt to fit the problem you face. In production control, you need to be sensitive to changes in the manufacturing problem and to be proactive. You should be able to recognize when the manufacturing situation is awry and that a new paradigm should be investigated. Whether or not someone will listen is a different issue. Assuming that you are interested in your pension and a future career within the same company, you should have a vested interest in making sure that the plant is using the right methods at the right time and is poised to evolve when it needs to.

The four main phases you might find yourself in are depicted in Figure 19-1. In the remainder of this chapter, we will discuss these various situations. For the most part, we will describe practices that seem to make sense for discrete manufacturing. Similar concepts and ideas can be interpreted for process or continuous flow situations. There are still the issues of starting up, trying to systemize the flow and control of materials and goods through the larger system, and dealing with variety.

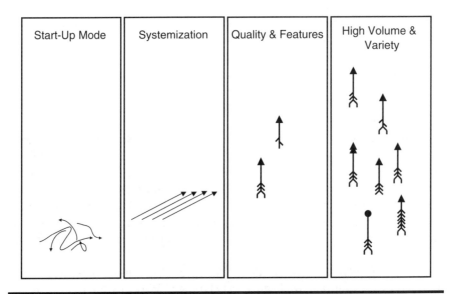

Figure 19-1. Four Phases of Production Control.

START-UP MODE

In this stage, we are considering the true start-up firms, the totally new product or offering. We are not considering those players who are setting up a firm to cherry pick or enter a field after the industry has been established. Late entrants have the benefit of the original start-ups and enter at a later stage, usually when there can be mass production of the limited number of products that make up the majority of the profit-generating items.

When a firm is in a true start-up mode, waste elimination and systemization are usually the farthest thing from an entrepreneur's mind. The market is usually willing to buy the product at prices that gives the start-up nice margins and waste is almost economical. The firm is likely to subcontract many of the normal manufacturing activities and will concentrate on the unique or special operations that make the start-up a reality. If no special physical processes are needed, it is possible that the complete manufacturing process is outsourced. We are not worried about these extreme cases of complete outsourcing, we are discussing those start-ups that have some in-house capability.

The production profile is likely to be that of small batches or almost continuous flow from one machine to the next as there is the need to get the product out the door. The mix is probably low and the products will have few features.

The key will be subcontractor or supplier coordination and getting the stuff to and from the line. Production might be relatively unstable as new processes are tried and changes are made to machines and products in real time. As long as the product basically works, it will be bought. Without competition, the features are not important and there might be no one to turn to for an alternative. Since the price is set based on costs and a target profit margin, the efficiency of the system is not the key.

You do not need large-scale systems such as ERP. Simple bill of material structures and planning tools are satisfactory. Many firms go with no formal production control and the engineers and line designers are also ordering parts, receiving, and shipping. Since the profit margins are high, it is hard to argue with this strategy. It would take time to put systems in, reduce the focus on the initial product development, and add costs to the process. Trying to formalize the system too early also locks the firm into standards and processes before these are really understood.

To reduce the chaos, all but the critical processes can be outsourced for a while. Why do your own packaging and shipping? Why buy the drill press and the lathe, or deal with the operators, if you can have certain parts made or processed outside? We suspect that many start-ups do not consider the make or buy decision carefully and get carried away with creating the complete picture when it is not needed. A key component of production control in a start-up will be to know what to make in house, when to make it out of house, when to move it out, and when to bring it back. Production control will be more of a tactical role trying to set up policies, negotiating with vendors, and orchestrating the bigger issues with the supporting departments.

The higher margins and minimal competition allow you to buy more raw material and have higher work in process without concern. Volumes will be relatively low, you will not be into mass production scale yet, and planning work is reasonably easy. Without conflicts and tight constraints, work scheduling is easy. Just make sure that there is a lot of material in the factory and that the machines can work whenever they can.

Eventually all good things come to an end, and either suddenly or gradually, the peace and tranquility of the start-up is shattered. Someone else is on the scene and has started to compete with you. In addition, volumes possibly have increased.

FOCUS ON SYSTEMIZATION

When the threat of a competitor becomes real and things are not as easy as they once were, you get the first wake-up call. The factory management looks for the big and obvious ways to decrease costs and possibly increase production. The more you make, the less each unit should cost. That means that you can lower your prices relative to your competitors while keeping the margins high. If you can reduce some of your other internal costs, the price can also be adjusted while you retain the nice margins.

Confusion in the manufacturing process is no longer acceptable and this is the start of the professional manager, formal organization, standards, and processes. Investors and backers can see and feel the chaotic waste throughout the plant. They want it straightened out before scaling up. The plant may have expanded in an ad hoc fashion in the past and is capable of hitting the production targets, but it is just flailing, or a major new expansion may be justified if the economies of scale could be reaped. In any case, to protect or increase market share or profit margins, some housekeeping needs to be done.

There are two ways new companies can be structured in terms of manufacturing: the functional or product views. There is no one magic or ideal answer. The best fit will depend on market demands, availability of skilled work force, and specific technology requirements. Out of chaos, the usual transformation that first occurs is the functional grouping.

The *functional grouping structure* is where you organize by characteristics such as drilling or grinding. There are a few reasons why functional grouping makes sense. To get things consistent and working to the same drummer, it is easier if they are all in the same area and under the command of a supervisor or manager who can specialize and focus on the operations. If you are scaling up, there is possibly a shortage of skilled workers and that is another reason for putting all similar pieces of equipment together. Another reason for the functional grouping is if certain of the machine types have extreme requirements: clean rooms, high ceilings, or vibration-free bases. It might not be feasible to build ten clean rooms, but you might be able to build one clean room big enough to put ten identical machines in. Functional groupings also make sense if you are concerned about making sure that you can route work through the plant regardless of machine uptime or repairs. If you have the similar machines grouped, you can develop greater team knowledge and be able to select from many resources when needed.

However, functional groupings are not always the best for low inventory and quick dock-to-dock flow times. Historically, the functional groupings ended up with the infamous buckets of work — week-of and month-of. This made it easy for planning. Each operation was planned on a week or month boundary. For example, a ten-operation job was allowed ten weeks. The factories used inventory banks to isolate the work and work would go to and from inventory stores between each operation. The flow and manufacturing process was controlled through inventory and this was easier than controlling people. If the markets were good, inventory cheap, and sufficient profit could be made, the week-of or month-of model was OK. The problems came when inventory started to cost a lot and costs had to be trimmed.

You can flow work through quickly and keep inventory low in a functional situation, but it will require a high effort from production control and the workforce to do it. You will need to expedite, monitor, and replan almost constantly. You will also need a great deal of process duplication, routing flexibility, and cross-training on the factory floor so that alternatives and options exist.

The functional arrangement has its time and place, and helps to sort out the chaos. It also creates the common base and consistency for a future process flow.

The *process* or *product flow structure* implies that instead of having all of the drills in one department and in one area, you have the drills placed where needed. This might require replication of equipment if you take it to the extreme, or you might just have a drill placed in close proximity to the middle of the line and have some material movement to and fro. The logical move to process or product occurs when you start to have enough demand for one product or family of products that justifies dedicated equipment. In some firms, this is a swing of the pendulum. The firm starts out in a process flow with very low volumes, moves to functional groupings, and then as the mix sorts itself out, puts in some process flows. The resulting profile may be hybrid with some functional areas dealing with the low-volume items, the cats and dogs as they are sometimes called, and the process areas handling the high runners.

Process or functional, production control is instrumental in the systemization of production. Production control is involved in the design of the bill of material, determining what will be inventoried, thinking about what will be tracked, collaborating on where measurements will be taken, and specifying the wide assortment of reports and forms that will be used to plan, track, and otherwise control production. In this phase, the wide sweeping reforms are considered and fine tuning is not a requirement. Taking lead time from years and many months down to several months is usually sufficient to deal with competition and stay ahead of the game. Taking inventory down from many months to one or two months is also usually sufficient to better the competition. Any extreme reductions or changes will be challenged since there is a danger of having too small of an inventory or quoting too short of a lead time. It is likely that most of the work will be planned as batches with ample safety stock or time between batches.

It is at this stage of production control that MRP/ERP systems are considered and introduced. The demand needs to be expanded back through the bill of material taking into account on-hand and scheduled receipt of goods to determine when activities should be started or when resource conflicts will arise. Simple loading tools can be used to visualize or present the load per work center. This is the minimum amount of production control that you need. If the situation is relatively stable and predictable, advanced planning tools may be considered for finite loading and sequencing the work, but these need to be carefully considered. They should probably be delayed until the system is more mature and in a steady state. Any of the computer-based tools cost quite a bit and they require a substantial effort to install. This would take away from activities on the direct process and the process of creating a system.

In the beginning, with few features and little variety, the problem is manageable. It is likely that after the initial commissioning of the high-volume equipment, there will be a honeymoon period during which time things happen largely as planned and adequate cushioning exists with inventory to deal with almost all problems.

Depending on the actual size of the factory and the various process methods, there may be separate planners, schedulers, and dispatchers, or varying combinations of job tasks. As noted, a common historic technique in this phase of manufacturer is to use buckets of time and buckets of work. The planners and schedulers do not worry about precise sequencing at the machine and you can let the worker or supervisor make the decision. This bucket approach can create problems when the work is really needed at the beginning of the next period, is delayed towards the end of the asking period, and problems occur. For example, work needed on Monday started on Friday, then problems occurred on Friday at the last minute, and the job will now be finished on Tuesday. If the system is reasonably decoupled with excess inventory as safety stock, these small boundary problems are buried.

FOCUS ON QUALITY AND FEATURES

It is sometimes hard to identify what comes first: the claims of quality or the claims of variety. In order to compete against a few competitors who are all using the same basic technology, material, and processes, the only options available to the firm are features and claims of quality. A few firms are in the mass production mode, each carving out a chunk of the market. They are likely to be using the same types of machines, at the same level of refinement, and there is nothing really different between the two firms if they are looked at closely. Both might be using batch modes of production, factories may be of the same size, and the personnel of similar backgrounds. The fixed and variable costs of the product itself will be similar between the competitors. They can set the selling price within reason and everyone is playing the same game. If you can capture more of the marketplace with less internal changes, that is good for you. Hence, the focus on features, customization, options, and quality.

While both impact production control to some degree, quality impacts it less than variety. Depending on the style of quality control, the impacts associated with enhancing quality are restricted to topics related to:

- Ordering lead times to give time for raw material inspection
- Increased setup and processing times to allow for in-line inspection and rework
- Potential backflow or reflow for rework
- Increased queue times for in-batch inspections
- Final inspections

There might also be new or renewed requirements for tracking material or who did what. Quality adds work and makes the problem a little bit more complex, but the basic flows are going to remain intact, for the most part.

Improving quality will not impact the bill of material structure, part numbers, ordering, or storage. Variety and the proliferation of features impacts almost everything. Quality will not impact the number of routings, the routing detail, or the work center loading. Variety does. To improve the process quality in many cases, you do not have to alter the design of the product, involve the customers, or ask for the advice of marketers. It might affect the quantity you expect to sell, but it does not increase the number of items being forecast, serviced, documented, or maintained. Variety will. Quality does not affect the combination of parts or sequence of operations. When is the customization and combination done? This is what variety is all about. As soon as one option is added, the fabric is ripped apart. It might not look too bad in the beginning and can be managed on the back of a match box, but in time the situation mushrooms and takes on a life of its own.

For a period of time, the mix and variability will be a matter of guesswork. Until the market reveals itself, the popular items may remain obscured. Traditionally, firms avoid going to the process model immediately for the high runners and, instead, ramp up and scale up the functional areas. This is a conservative and least-risk approach. It is not the easiest entity to manage or the easiest in which to lower costs, but it does have redundancy and reduces the risk. This is not a bad thing in all cases. However, it does increase the need for version control, enhanced inventory management, and a greater reliance on the bookkeeping capabilities of MRP-type systems. Until the work is sorted out, the production control system will likely use inventory and batch theory to decouple the departments. More inventory will be needed and longer lead times will result, as more routings meander their way through the factory creating floating bottlenecks and resource conflicts.

The key for this phase is to recognize the developing situation and, before it gets out of hand, address the situation and move to the next phase. The batching and functional approach for the early varieties cannot be avoided in many cases, but the practice should be stopped when the inventories and lead times approach foolish levels.

FOCUS ON HIGH VOLUME AND VARIETY

As production increases and the volumes rise, it is usually possible to identify the 20 percent of production parts that represent 80 percent of total production output. These are the high runners. There will be old service parts and oddities that will require production capacity and these should be separated from the high runners. You can sometimes split the factory into a job shop for the low-volume items and a flow shop for the high runners. If 80 percent of the revenue and profit does not come from the same 20 percent of the production, then this is a bigger problem and must be addressed. In this latter case, it might be wise for the firm to do some serious rationalization exercises. We will focus on the 20 percent of the parts that represent the 80 percent of the physical production.

Whenever you do any operation you do not do regularly, there is a chance for introducing uncertainty and variability. For example, the documentation may be slightly out of date, the machine has been upgraded since the last run, there are different operators, or the material is coming from a different source. If your livelihood depends on the high runners, separate them, baby them, line resources up like a dedicated process, and just flow work from dock to dock. You do not need to do detailed scheduling on a continuous flow process. You do not have resource conflicts and you have fewer destabilizing factors being introduced.

The parts that are made infrequently or in low volume require additional production control monitoring and tracking. They can also create little piles of inventory and stock throughout the process. You might actually want to schedule your most skilled workers in the low-volume area and rely on automation, JIT practices, and system checks for the high runner. You definitely do not want to intermix the high- and low-volume parts. We can hear it now. Of course, if everyone does their job perfectly, there should not be any problems if you intermix work. How lucky do you feel? It is not likely that everything will be perfect and there is more chance of less perfection with the periodic or irregularly produced parts than with something that is made frequently. One factory had ten flexible manufacturing cells, very big and flashy, much money, and they were being used for high-precision work: milling, grinding, drilling, and boring large metal castings. When the cells were installed, the factory had grand plans. The cells could be used for all kinds of parts: prototype, production, and one-offs. After a while, they discovered that running prototypes and one-offs created problems on the cells and discontinued the practice. A special prototype area was set up and used for the limited production processes. The prototypes upset the rhythm, tool magazine balancing, palette usage, and routine settings for the machines.

For the high-volume parts, you can consider the ultimate, the focused factory with automated or semi-automated lines with material handling conveyance between the resources or a kanban system with controlled inventory flow. It is important in the high-volume situations to control the entry of raw material and thus control the flow within the system. The focused factory with complete support and dedicated primary and secondary resources will be the best bet for dock-to-dock flow. However, focused factories may not be needed initially and a few dedicated lines may be sufficient to maintain market growth or position. Again, it is always important to consider how much control and structure you need and less is better. If you are competing against small, dedicated upstarts who are cherry picking your business, then focused factories or new small green-field plants are about the only way to beat the streamlined production of the competitors. If you are competing against a bunch of job shops, the first dedicated line will win out. Robb wrote one of the first books on business organizations in 1910 and noted the idea of having dedicated resources and infrastructure. He suggested this organization for companies that needed to focus on speed.

It is important to manage and monitor the product mix and situation as high-volume production is undertaken. It is possible that options and features will continue to be introduced and the high-volume situation needs to be designed accordingly. Being able to postpone customization and features will be a gain, as will standardization and modular designs, but these are not in the realm of production control influence in many cases and production control must often take what is given in terms of manufacturing systems and structure.

If possible, it is best to give the high runners to one production control person to plan, schedule, and dispatch. Let them have it dock to dock for planning and monitoring. They will see the impact of their decisions and have knowledge of the complete chain. This is much better than splitting the control problem into several pieces with hand-off between individuals. The hand-off or hierarchical control model may be fine for job shops or batch production, but it is not the best situation for flow control with a focus on speed and minimum inventory.

SUMMARY

Production control cannot be static and must adapt to the problem at hand. It is wrong and dangerous, possibly career terminating, to assume that a department structure, role definitions, and tools will continue to be relevant, effective, and efficient as the firm's production profile changes. It is also wrong to assume that you need the same level of production control in all factories and situations.

For people trying to find new or improved ways to improve production control, it can be very dangerous to look at another factory casually, via a visit or benchmark, observe their production control methods, assume that you can lift them, and use them to the same level of success. Many a firm has been surprised by failure when doing so. They did not do sufficient due diligence to understand what all of the factors were and what was needed based on their own manufacturing profile.

20

FINALE

PREDIGESTED THOUGHTS FOR THE BUSY PERSON

- Excellent execution in production control results in a boring job.

- Get the basics down first. Before doing advanced manufacturing or production control you need to know, and be able to describe, what you want to control and be able to deal with things manually, repeatedly, and in a predictable fashion.

- Production control is the heart of the plant and requires monitoring and control for blood flow, heart rate, and cholesterol. If you ignore it, your firm will have frequent heart attacks and strokes.

FINAL THOUGHTS

This book has been largely about the bad and the ugly. It is a survival guide for schedulers who find themselves in a challenging situation. Although we have not talked too much about the good life planners and schedulers have in factories that do not resemble Jake's, we have tried to give suggestions and strategies for how to improve your planning and scheduling.

Does your current production control situation sound like the reverse of Jake's? Is your day nice and relaxing? Do you consider your job to be a walk in the park? If you answered yes to these questions, you are in the good category and do not need many tips on survival. Especially if the firm is making money. You probably do not need to apply too much of this book. You are surviving. We know of factories and situations where very few of the Jake issues we describe exist. They are considered crown jewels in the firm's portfolio. They do many of the proactive processes we have tried to describe implicitly or explicitly. They have their act together. It is possible to have a nice, boring production control department.

Perhaps some of the problems, but not too many, ring true and sound too familiar. You might be getting close to being Jake's brother or sister, but you are not there yet. Many firms will have a few of the challenges noted in this book and will be in a good position to make dramatic improvements in production control. Things might be reasonably predictable. Management is generally supportive and trying to do the right thing. Production is not in a continual state of chaos. These types of factories are fun to work in. There is work to be done, but the end can be seen and targeted. There is good stuff going on. It should be identified, reinforced, and encouraged to go farther. The other stuff needs to be addressed.

If you recognized your firm or situation in almost every chapter or story, and you started calling yourself Jake, we sincerely hope that you can change the situation and recover. Firms that had almost every problem and issue in this book had an uphill battle. Few recovered, some kept limping along on life support, but most closed the doors. When there is total decay of the complete manufacturing system, there is almost nothing you can do in production control to fix the situation. All you can do is give palliative care to the terminally ill patient.

Last thought on production control:

If production control is not flexible and does not function in a proactive fashion, the requirement for production control will soon cease to exist.

REFERENCES AND SUGGESTED READING

Occasionally, we have noted material from other sources. Here we offer those references and additional readings that you might find useful.

HISTORICAL REFERENCES

Coburn, F.G. (circa 1918), Scheduling: the coordination of effort, in *Organizing for Production and Other Papers on Management 1912–1924*, Mayer, I., Ed., Hive Publishing, 1981, pp. 149–172.

Diemer, H., *Factory Organization and Administration*, McGraw-Hill, 1910.

Emerson, H., *Twelve Principles of Efficiency*, The Engineering Magazine, 1913.

Gantt, H.L., *Work, Wages, and Profits*, The Engineering Magazine, 1910.

Gantt, H.L., *Organizing for Work*, Harcourt and Brace, 1919.

Knoeppel, C.E., *Maximum Production in Machine-Shop and Foundry*, The Engineering Magazine, 1911.

Knoeppel, C.E., Graphic production control. II. Industrial management, *The Engineering Magazine*, 56(4), 284–288, 1918.

McKay, K.N., Historical survey of production control practices, *International Journal on Production Research*, 41(3), 411–426, 2003.

O'Donnell, P.D., *Production Control*, Prentice-Hall, 1952.

Plossl, G.W. and Wight, O., *Production and Inventory Control*, Prentice-Hall, 1967.

Reinfeld, N.V., *Production Control*, Prentice-Hall, 1959.

Robb, R., *Lectures on Organization*, privately printed, 1910.

Sweet, J.E., The unexpected which often happens, *Transactions of the American Society of Mechanical Engineers*, 7, 152–163, 1885.

Younger, J., *Work Routing in Production Including Scheduling and Dispatching*, Ronald, 1930.

REFERENCES FOR RESEARCH FOCUSING ON PLANNERS AND SCHEDULERS

Crawford, S., A Field Study of Schedulers in Industry: Understanding Their Work, Practices and Performance, Ph.D. thesis, University of Nottingham, 2000.

Higgins, P.G., Job Shop Scheduling: Hybrid Intelligent Human-Computer Paradigm, Ph.D. thesis, University of Melbourne, 1999.

MacCarthy, B.L. and Wilson, J.R., Eds., *Human Performance in Planning and Scheduling*, Taylor and Francis, 2001.

McKay, K.N., Conceptual Framework for Job Shop Scheduling, M.A.Sc. dissertation, University of Waterloo, 1987.

McKay, K.N., Production Planning and Scheduling: A Model for Manufacturing Decisions Requiring Judgement, Ph.D. thesis, University of Waterloo, 1992.

McKay, K.N. and Wiers, V.C.S., Planners, schedulers and dispatchers: a description of cognitive tasks in production control, *International Journal on Cognition, Technology, and Work*, 5(2), 82–93, 2003.

Wiers, V.C.S., Human–Computer Interaction in Production Scheduling: Analysis and Design of Decision Support Systems for Production Scheduling Tasks, Ph.D. thesis, Eindhoven University of Technology, 1997.

REFERENCES ON PRODUCTION CONTROL

Bertrand, J.W.M., Wortmann, J.C., and Wijngaard, J., *Production Control — A Structural and Design Oriented Approach*, Elsevier, 1990.

Euwe, M.J., Decentralized Control Systems for Logistical Coordination, Ph.D. thesis, Eindhoven University of Technology, 1999.

Goldratt, E.M., *The Goal*, North River Press, 1984.

Goldratt, E.M., *Critical Chain*, North River Press, 1997.

McKay, K.N., The Factory From Hell — A Modelling Benchmark, in *Proceedings of the NSF Workshop on Intelligent, Dynamic Scheduling*, January 1993, Cocoa Beach, Florida, 1993, pp. 97–113.

McKay, K.N. and Buzacott, J.A., The application of computerized production control systems in job shop environments, *Computers in Industry*, 42, 79–97, 2000.

McKay, K.N. and Moore, J.B., Planning and Control Reference Case Study — Version 1.3, CAM-I IMMP Technical Report R-91-IMMP-01, Arlington, Texas, 1991, 132 p.

McKay, K.N. and Morton, T.E., Critical Chain — E. Goldratt, Book review, *IIE Transactions*, 30, 759–763, 1998.

McKay, K.N. and Wiers, V.C.S., Unifying the theory and practice of production scheduling, *Journal of Manufacturing Systems*, 18(4), 241–255, 1999.

Morton, T.E. and Pentico, D.W., *Heuristic Scheduling Systems*, Wiley, 1993.

Wortmann, J.C., Euwe, M.J., Taal, M., and Wiers, V.C.S., A review of capacity planning techniques within standard software packages, *Production Planning and Control*, 7(2), 114–125, 1996.

GENERAL REFERENCES

The following are some additional readings or books that you might find of interest. Many of them will help you understand some of the inner workings and concepts behind production control concepts, advanced planning systems, and scheduling engines. Some references are for general insights and understanding.

Babbage, C., *On the Economy of Machinery and Manufacturers*, 2nd ed., Knight, 1832.

Bauer, A., Rowden, R., Browne, J., Duggan, J., and Lyons, G., *Shop Floor Control Systems: from Design to Implementation*, Chapman & Hall, 1991.

Brooks, F.P., *The Mythical Man-Month*, Anniversary Edition, Addison Wesley, 1995.

Conway, R.L., Maxwell, W.L., and Miller, L.W., *Theory of Scheduling*, Addison Wesley, 1967.

Gershwin, S.G., *Manufacturing Systems Engineering*, via gerswhin@mit.edu, 2002.

Hopp, W.J. and Spearman, M.L., *Factory Physics*, McGraw-Hill, 1996.

Markus, L. and Tanis, C., The Enterprise Systems Experience — from adoption to success, in *Framing the Domains of IT Management: Projecting the Future Through the Past*, Zmud, R.W. and Price, M.F., Eds., Pinnaflex Educational Resources, Inc., 2000, pp. 173–207.

Nahmias, S., *Production and Operations Analysis*, 4th ed., McGraw-Hill, 2000.

Pinedo, M. and Chao, X., *Operations Scheduling with Applications in Manufacturing and Services*, McGraw-Hill, 1999.

Scherer, E., Ed., *Shop Floor Control — A Systems Perspective*, Springer-Verlag, 1998.

Stadtler, H. and Kilger, C., Eds., *Supply Chain Management and Advanced Planning: Concepts, Models Software and Case Studies*, Springer-Verlag, 2000.

Vollmann, T.E., Berry, W.L., and Whybark, D.C., *Manufacturing Planning and Control Systems*, Irwin, 1988.

INDEX